CONSUMPTION AND CLASS

Consumption and Class

Divisions and Change

Edited by

Roger Burrows
Principal Lecturer in Sociology and Social Policy
Teesside Polytechnic

and

Catherine Marsh
Lecturer in Economic and Social Studies
University of Manchester

St. Martin's Press New York

First published in the United States of America in 1992

Printed in Great Britain

ISBN 0–312–06867–0

Library of Congress Cataloging-in-Publication Data
Consumption and class: divisions and change/edited by Roger Burrows and Catherine Marsh.
p. cm.
Based on presentations at the British Sociological Association annual conference held at the University of Surrey, Apr. 1990.
Includes index.
ISBN 0–312–06867–0
1. Social classes—Great Britain—Congresses. 2. Consumers—Great Britain—Attitudes—Congresses. 3. Social mobility—Great Britain—Congresses. 4. Public health—Great Britain—Congresses.
I. Burrows, Roger, 1962– . II. Marsh, Catherine. III. British Sociological Association.
HN400.S6C665 1992
305.5′0941—dc20 91–22442
CIP

Contents

List of Tables

List of Figures

Preface

The chapters in this book are based on presentations at the British Sociological Association annual conference held at the University of Surrey in April, 1990 on the theme of 'Social Divisions and Social Change'. The conference was organised by Roger Burrows, Catherine Marsh, Sara Arber and Nigel Gilbert. Four of the chapters in the book were derived from conference panel sessions organised by Peter Saunders and Peter Taylor-Gooby. Three other volumes of conference papers are published simultaneously: *Women and Working Lives: Divisions and Change* (edited by Sara Arber and Nigel Gilbert), *Fordism and Flexibility: Divisions and Change* (edited by Nigel Gilbert, Roger Burrows and Anna Pollett) and *Families and Households: Divisions and Change* (edited by Catherine Marsh and Sara Arber).

We should like to thank all those who gave papers, the organisers of the panel sessions and those others who contributed to the success of the conference. In particular, we would like to thank the contributors to this volume, and Anne Dix and Sheila Tremlett of the British Sociological Association for all their encouragement and support.

ROGER BURROWS
CATHERINE MARSH

Notes on the Contributors

Sara Arber is a Senior Lecturer in Sociology at the University of Surrey. She is the co-author of *Doing Secondary Analysis* and the co-editor of *Women and Working Lives: Divisions and Change* and *Families and Households: Divisions and Change*. She has also published many articles, chapters and reports in the areas of sociology of health and illness, social gerontology, gender and housing.

Robert M. Blackburn works in the Department of Applied Economics at the University of Cambridge. He is the author of a number of books including (with K. Prandy and A. Stewart) *White Collar Unionism* and *Occupations and Social Stratification*.

Frances Bonner has taught Media Studies in Australia and is now a Research Student at the Open University completing a doctoral dissertation on the representation of the future in film and television.

Roger Burrows is a Principal Lecturer in the School of Health, Social and Policy Studies at Teesside Polytechnic. He is the editor of *Deciphering the Enterprise Culture* and co-editor of *Fordism and Flexibility: Divisions and Change*. He has also published numerous chapters, articles and reports on the sociology of economic life.

Joan Busfield is a Reader in Sociology at the University of Essex. She initially trained as a clinical psychologist at the Tavistock Clinic. She is the author of *Managing Madness: Changing Ideas and Practice* and other books and articles.

Michael Calnan is a Reader in the Sociology of Health Studies at the University of Kent. He is the author and co-author of numerous papers, chapters and books including *The Sociology of Health and Medicine* and *Health and Illness: the Lay Perspective*.

Sarah Cant is a Research Assistant at the University of Kent. Recent published work concentrates on the sociology of food consumption and alternative medicine. Her current research interest is in the private health care market.

Rosemary Crompton is a Senior Lecturer in Sociology at the University of Kent. She has written and edited a number of books and articles in the area of industrial sociology and class analysis. Her most recent book is *Gendered Jobs and Social Change*.

Paul du Gay is a Research Student at the Open University. He is currently investigating work-based subjectivity in the retail sector of the UK economy.

Rob Flynn is a Senior Lecturer in Sociology at the University of Salford. He is the author of *Structures of Control in Health Management* and co-author of *Structures and Processes of Urban Life*, He has also published articles in various journals and chapters in edited collections on urban and political sociology, and more recently on health services.

David Knights is a Reader in Management at the Manchester School of Management, UMIST. He has written many articles on social theory and its relationship to management and organisations. He is the co-editor of (*inter alia*) *Labour Process Theory*, *Gender and the Labour Process*, *New Technology and the Labour Process* and co-author of *Managing to Discriminate*.

Catherine Marsh is a Lecturer at the University of Manchester and previously worked at the University of Cambridge. The work for this chapter was done while she was a Nuffield Social Science Fellow. She is the author of *The Survey Method* and *Exploring Data* and a number of articles and chapters. She is the co-editor of *Families and Households: Divisions and Change*.

Glenn Morgan is a Research Fellow in the Financial Services Research Centre, Manchester School of Management, UMIST. He has written articles on various aspects of work and organisation and is the author of *Organisations in Society*.

Geoff Payne is Dean of Human Sciences at Polytechnic South West, Plymouth. His work on social mobility includes *Employment and Opportunity*, *Mobility and Change in Modern Society*, and most recently *The Social Mobility of Women*.

Mike Savage is a Lecturer in Sociology at the University of Keele. He is the author of *The Dynamics of Working Class Politics* and co-author of *Localities, Class and Gender*. He has published several articles on the contemporary British middle classes, and his co-authored book on this issue, *Property, Bureaucracy and Culture* has been published by Routledge.

Alan Warde is a Lecturer in Sociology at Lancaster University. His interests are in urban, industrial and political sociology. He was the guest editor of the special edition of the journal *Sociology* on the Sociology of Consumption and has most recently co-authored *Restructuring: Class, Gender and Place*.

Paul Watt is a Lecturer at Buckinghamshire College of Higher Education. He is the co-author of a number of articles on housing and social stratification.

1 Consumption, Class and Contemporary Sociology

Roger Burrows and Catherine Marsh

INTRODUCTION

It is fair to say that until recently most sociologists tended to treat consumption in a reductionist manner as a distributive aspect of social class. However, of late some very strong claims have been made for the conceptual and political importance of consumption *per se*, and this has resulted in various challenges to the hegemony of those sociological perspectives which prioritise labour and production (see Warde, this volume).

Three such proclamations have been especially important: first, and the major focus of the present volume, claims of a shift from *socialised* towards *privatised* modes of consumption within the sphere of welfare provision; second, claims that there has been a shift from a *Fordist* towards a *post-Fordist* regime of accumulation; and, third, claims that we are leaving the age of cultural *modernism* and entering an era of *postmodernism*.

This book is concerned with the impact these claims have had upon analyses of contemporary patterns of consumption, the social class structure and the interaction between the two within the UK. It is based on papers presented at the 1990 British Sociological Association annual conference which have been developed in reaction to comments and discussion. This introductory essay attempts to briefly map out the terrain of the debate and situate the following chapters within it.

From Socialised to Privatised Modes of Provision: Peter Saunders' Sociology of Consumption

The recent work of Peter Saunders offers not only a programmatic call for the development of a distinctive sociology of consumption (Saunders, 1986: 289–351; 1988), but emerging from this, a critique of the current state of sociology in general (Saunders, 1989; Pawson, 1990) and the analysis of social class in particular (Saunders, 1990a;

Payne, this volume). His position is one which, although having some continuities with urban sociology (Saunders, 1986), also exhibits the influence of the work of Pahl (1984) on the sociology of economic life, the 'post-Marxist' writings of Gorz (1982; 1985) and, most crucially, the ideological influence of the New Right (Saunders, 1985; 1990b; Saunders and Harris, 1989). Although the subject of much criticism (Burrows and Butler, 1989; Hamnett, 1989; Sullivan, 1989; Warde, 1990a), his various interventions have stimulated debate and many of the issues he raises are directly confronted in the current volume.

The details of Saunders' sociology of consumption have been widely disseminated (Saunders, 1986: 289–351; 1988; see Burrows and Butler (1989) and Warde (1990a) for summaries). He argues that just as class relations are determined by the (non-) ownership of the means of production, so the main division within the sphere of consumption is determined by the (non) ownership of the means to fulfil consumption requirements. Thus, for Saunders, the major division within the sphere of consumption is between those who can meet their consumption needs through personal ownership and those who cannot, and are thus reliant upon the state to provide it for them.

He claims that three different modes of consumption can be identified: a *market* mode; a *socialised* mode; and a newly emerging *privatised*[1] mode. In the nineteenth century the primary form of consumption was provided through the market and the main contradiction was between low wages and the high costs of consumption. This contradiction provided the context within which a more socialised system of collective consumption developed. This socialised mode of cash benefits and payments in kind attempted to deal with the contradiction by supplementing wages and lowering consumption costs. However, this socialised mode has given rise to a new set of contradictions – often expressed in terms of the 'crisis of the welfare state' – and this has ushered in the latest, privatised mode of consumption.

Saunders suggests that in the long run the socialised mode will be seen as a 'holding operation' between market and privatised modes. The developing privatised mode will, he argues, have deep implications for the British social structure. His central conclusion is that we are moving towards a position in which the majority of the population will be able to satisfy most of their consumption requirements through some form of market (subsidised where appropriate by the state) whilst the minority will be 'caste adrift on the waterlogged raft of what remains of the welfare state' (1986: 318). Further, this division between the privatised 'middle mass' and the 'marginalised and stigmatised minority' (1986: 318; see also Saunders, 1990b: 314–71) possesses its own specificity in that it is only contingently related to class, gender and ethnic divisions – the tripartite dimensions which have hitherto dominated analyses of social divisions within welfare (F. Williams, 1989).

This has led him to argue that our understanding of existing patterns of inequality have been 'fettered' by the dominance of theoretical frameworks which have their empirical anchors in the nineteenth century – for Saunders, a period in which class location *was* fundamental to life chances. For Saunders it is 'no longer axiomatic that class location is the fundamental basis of material life chances' (1986: 319). He claims that the 'left-wing' bias of much sociology has led to an obsession with class inequalities which has 'blinkered' the discipline to the reality of the changing social structure of Britain (Pawson, 1990; Payne, this volume). For example, according to Saunders, consumption sector divisions cannot be reduced to any production-based schemas of classification (but see Savage *et al.*, this volume). They have to be understood as 'a distinct phenomenon of the distribution of power in the modern period' (Saunders, 1986: 320).

Saunders further argues that, despite some variability across classes, members of such consumption sectors still share 'fundamental material interests in common' (1986: 321). The most important factor, he claims, is the division between privatised and socialised housing sectors, although he also argues that what has been occurring here is likely to be paralleled by the expansion of private education, health care (but see Busfield, this volume; Calnan and Cant, this volume) and pension schemes (Hamnett, 1989).

Saunders accepts that some of the shift towards privatised consumption is the result of public discontent with much socialised provision (often because of politically enforced expenditure restraint) with the consequence that people are 'pushed' towards privatised solutions. However, he also attempts to make a case for an autonomous demand for privatised consumption that is independent of this pressure (Saunders, 1990b: 58–119). He views the growth of privatised forms of consumption as part of a movement for people to increase the range of control they have over their lives. He argues that few individuals can assert control within the sphere of production, but that privatised consumption can function as an alternative outlet for this 'need' (but see Warde, this volume).

For Saunders, Britain has become a 'dual society' in which the 'middle mass' of the population has remained almost untouched by the process of restructuring whilst the marginalised minority have had to take the brunt of it (Pahl, 1988). However, he regards this division as one which cuts across traditional classes and which has to be understood on a number of different social dimensions: including region, skill level, economic sector, age and gender. Thus, for Saunders, the criteria for being thrown into the 'underclass' of the 1990s cannot be understood in traditional class terms, but has to be analysed in terms of 'fragments of the population' (1986a: 335). He suggests that, increasingly, employment, home ownership and privatised consumption are corollaries of each other, as are unemployment, non-home ownership and a reliance upon socialised consumption.

His policy proposals designed to overcome this supposed polarisation have been a source of much controversy. He argues that the solution must be seen in terms of enhancing the consumption capacity of the fifth of the population currently reliant upon the 'waning' socialised mode of consumption. This involves not a defence of socialised provision, but an extension of privatised consumption via a shift away from state provision in *kind* towards state provision in *cash* (Saunders and Harris, 1989; 1990). Such a shift, he argues, would transform social power relations away from those who currently control collective consumption – the public sector 'service class' – towards those who use it (but see Flynn, this volume). He suggests that state expenditure on provision in kind should be gradually reallocated in the form of cash to those people reliant upon socialised consumption to enhance their ability to engage in more marketised and privatised consumption. Saunders' various claims, especially those relating to privatised and marketised forms of consumption, provide one of the central themes to the present volume.

From Fordist to Post-Fordist Patterns of Consumption?

The post-Fordist hypothesis, although subject to intense criticism of late (Gilbert, Burrows and Pollert, 1991; Pollert, 1991), is still the most influential of the various theories of economic restructuring. Consumption clearly plays an important part in the model.[2] If the era of Fordism was marked by an homology between mass production, mass consumption, massified provision of public services and modernist cultural forms, then post-Fordist production is associated with post-Fordist patterns of consumption (Piore, 1986; Urry, 1990a), the creation of a post-Fordist welfare state (Geddes, 1988; Hogget, 1987;

Rustin, 1989; Stoker, 1990a; 1990b) and postmodernist cultural forms (of which more below). Following Urry (1990a: 14) we can present 'Fordist mass consumption' and 'post-Fordist differentiated consumption' as two ideal types.

Fordist mass consumption is characterised by the purchase of commodities made under conditions of mass production. This is supported by a high and growing rate of expenditure on consumer products. Individual producers tend to dominate particular industrial markets and thus the producer rather than consumer tends to be dominant. Commodities are little differentiated from each other by fashion, season or specific market segments. There is thus a relatively limited choice and what there is tends to reflect both private and public sector producer interests.

Post-Fordist consumption is characterised by the purchase of commodities produced under conditions of 'flexible' production. Consumption rather than production is dominant as consumer expenditure further increases as a proportion of national income. New forms of credit permit consumer expenditure to rise, so producing high levels of indebtedness. Almost all aspects of social life become commodified. There develops a much greater differentiation of purchasing patterns within different market segments and markets become subject to greater volatility of consumer preferences. These changes are accompanied by the growth of a consumers' movement and the increasing politicisation of consumption issues. There is a reaction by consumers against being part of a 'mass' and this leads to the need for producers to be much more consumer-driven, especially in the case of service industries and the public sector. There is the development of many more products each of which has a shorter life. There emerges new kinds of commodity which are more specialised and based on raw materials that symbolically imply non-mass forms of production.

For Urry there exists 'considerable evidence that western societies have been broadly moving from the former to the latter type' of consumption (1990a: 14).

As already indicated, this shift also affects public provision, although it is 'not at all clear what the causal connections are supposed to be between the spheres of production and those of welfare' (Rustin, 1989: 59). Two hypotheses appear to be implicit. First, consumers who are led to expect variety and choice in consumer markets will increasingly settle for nothing less in the welfare sector. However, Rustin (1989: 59) argues, there that the 'ethos and goals of consumer choice cannot be pushed very far in these spheres...before they conflict severely with the overriding values of human need' (see Busfield, this volume; Warde, this volume). Second, the connection between production and welfare might be understood in relation to post-Fordist technological innovation itself. The introduction of computerised information systems and other new technologies are likely to play a part in restructuring the management and consumption of welfare (Kelly, 1991; Uttley, 1991).

Thus, it is claimed that we not only have a shift from socialised towards more privatised modes of consumption within the sphere of welfare but that this is articulated with shifts of a more general nature from Fordist towards post-Fordist patterns of consumption. As already indicated some writers also suggest that these two shifts are further overlaid by a third change as the consumer becomes increasingly embroiled in postmodernist cultural forms (Bonner and du Gay, this volume; Featherstone, 1990; 1991; Warde, this volume).

From Modernism to Postmodernism?

The literature on the supposed transition from modernism to postmodernism (see for example Featherstone, 1988; 1991; Harvey, 1989; Urry, 1990a) is complex. Postmodernism is a somewhat loose collection of sometimes ill-defined notions but the fragmenting of ideas and lifestyles and the elaboration of symbol over substance in everyday consumption are common to several versions of the thesis. Consumption, it is argued, becomes centred on the symbolic meanings attached to objects and services much more than in previous eras.

Other aspects of postmodernism are argued to include the breaking down of the unity of previously dominant cultural forms such as classicism or modernism or the linear narrative form in books and especially in the cinema and video. In their place emerges a non-time specific, 'pick and mix' aesthetic which combines elements of previous cultures in new ways. At the level of the individual and group, postmodernist theses suggest a breaking down of the traditional class systems characteristic of earlier periods. Instead, people increasingly define themselves as members of groups which seek to establish their separate identities by distinctive symbols – language, dress, home decoration and so on – to mark them off from others. Also emphasised is the way consumption becomes short-term, that is, there is an increase fluidity in consumption patterns because symbolic meanings change rapidly as individuals and groups discard and adopt new ones. The links here with claims of an emergent post-Fordist pattern of consumption are obvious.

It is argued by some that this fragmentation of culture and consumption patterns has a 'disorganising' effect (Lash and Urry, 1987). Further, it has been the emerging 'service class' (Crompton, this volume) which has provided the most fertile social base for the growth of a postmodernist sensibility and contemporary consumer culture (Bonner and du Gay, this volume). The increasingly important role of this class in the process of economic restructuring in general, and in changing patterns of consciousness, culture and consumption in particular, are also themes examined in the present volume.

CONSUMPTION, CLASS AND THE RESTRUCTURING OF BRITAIN

Broad theories of the changing interaction between consumption and class such as those outlined above are useful, but the more precise parameters of division and change are more difficult to decipher. In this volume we concentrate on a limited number of conceptual and substantive topics in order to maintain a sharper focus: theorisations of consumption and the consumer; changing patterns of class and consumption division, those relating to health, education and housing provision in particular; the consciousness, culture and role of the middle classes in the process of change; and changing patterns of access and mobility.

Warde (Chapter 2) provides a useful conceptual introduction to the rest of the collection by offering an analytic framework to account for the relationship between production and consumption which demonstrates just how one-sided and partial contributions to the sociology of consumption have been hitherto. He develops a set of concepts for understanding consumption in all spheres that can support a sociological appreciation of production and the experience of consumption. His synthesis thus incorporates elements of all three approaches outlined above and more besides.

His framework is designed to account for the manner in which people achieve three kinds of value within the process of consumption: exchange-values, use-values and identity-values. This, he argues, can only be done by considering the sequential episodes of production/

consumption that form the chain of interconnected social activities which result in 'final consumption'. These episodes are characterised by different modes of provision. To date, the sociology of consumption has tended to concentrate only on two such modes, that of market and state provision, but a fuller account would also consider domestic and communal provision. For Warde, the history of consumption is largely concerned with the process of substitution of provision between these four modes.

Whatever mode of provision it occurs within, each episode of consumption is also subject to a number of distinct facets: the process of production or provision; the conditions of access; the manner of delivery; and the environment or experience of enjoyment. The two phases of delivery and enjoyment are especially crucial for contemporary debates about the future of welfare, especially Saunders' argument that public welfare as it is currently structured should be dismantled and replaced with market or quasi-market modes of provision. The argument implies a necessary relation between the manner of delivery and the mode of provision of an episode, although, as Warde demonstrates, the relation is clearly a contingent one. Warde makes a similar point about the enjoyment of a service. The pleasure a service provides does not directly depend on the mode of its provision. However, Warde considers that sociology lacks any clear understanding of consumption as pleasure and makes a number of points which go some way towards rectifying this.

Morgan and Knights (Chapter 3) present a study of the prime actors within the sociology of consumption: consumers. They document the development of the concept of the consumer and how this consumer might be 'protected' within one particular industry, life insurance. Thus, their concern is with the history of a particular production/consumption episode occurring within a market mode of provision. They argue that it was the producers of life insurance and their agents who, until recently, defined the meaning of being a consumer in the industry. Life insurance practitioners constructed a paternalist perspective on consumers that emphasised that the latter could not be trusted to act in their own best interests. It was considered that autonomous individuals tended to be more predisposed towards immediate as opposed to deferred gratification and that in the absence of a convincing and rational morality created by the companies, consumers would tend to forego future security for the more immediate pleasures of life. The producers thus set themselves up as the true protectors of the real interests of consumers.

Morgan and Knights consider that the market for life insurance was not a meeting place of equals, but an arena in which the companies exercised their power to define reality for consumers. However, they argue that since the 1970s these traditional definitions of the consumer and consumer protection have begun to change and it is now possible to see a range of different conceptions of the consumer and consumer protection battling for hegemony. Although Morgan and Knights do not use the argot of the restructuring thesis, the parallels with Urry's characterisation of shifts from Fordist towards post-Fordist patterns of consumption are obvious.

Whilst Morgan and Knights acknowledge that life insurance is a distinctive product, they argue that the approach they adopt has a much more general application. They conclude that the sociological analysis of the operations of various market modes of provision is an urgent undertaking. Their analysis suggests that it is inadequate to treat the market as a sphere of exchange between equals as many on the sociological New Right would have us do (Marsland, 1988: 44–69). Rather, markets must be understood as socially constituted in the context of specific social relations which link organizations, the state and consumers. Studying the way in which markets are structured and restructured would enables us to better comprehend how particular groups are advantaged or disadvantaged by their operation.[3]

Savage, Watt and Arber (Chapter 4) report further on their study of the housing and labour market in Guildford, a locality situated in the economic 'sunbelt' of the Southeast of England (Savage *et al.*, 1990a; 1990b). They directly confront some of the central issues in the recent debates concerning the relative causal efficacy of consumption sector and social class as manifested in the sphere of housing. They examine claims concerning the salient role of housing in the creation of distinct 'consumption sector cleavages' and the existence of an 'underclass'.

On the one hand, they find some evidence that council tenure is becoming increasingly confined to those in unskilled, marginal employment. In this respect, housing tenure destinations do cross-cut established class divisions. On the other hand, their results clearly contradict Saunders' contention that the tenure gap is becoming increasingly difficult to cross and that as a result the growing division between the 'middle mass' and the 'underclass' is being reproduced through tenure-based inequalities.

Their conclusion is clear: the housing market is not a contributory factor in producing social divisions. Although council tenure is increasingly becoming residualised, the cause appears to be related to the structure of employment opportunities. The unskilled are more likely to live in council tenure, while the other social classes are more likely to live in owner occupation. However, this division is entirely explicable in terms of intensifying labour market divisions, perhaps between a 'core' and 'periphery' workforce, or even as the latest manifestation of the continued division between skilled and unskilled workers within the working class, rather than in terms of the rise of 'consumption sector cleavages' in which housing tenure itself becomes an axis of social division.

Joan Busfield (Chapter 5) opens a series of three chapters on different aspects of divisions and change in health care. She extends her analysis of sectoral divisions in the consumption of health care (Busfield, 1990) by exploring the nature of consumers' relations to the private medical sector. Her conclusions are that the model of the free market developed by liberal thinkers provides a very inaccurate picture of the character of private medicine in Britain and thus gives a severely distorted picture of the real power of the consumers of private health care. Her reasons for coming to this conclusion are twofold. First, the state registration of medical practitioners, which is necessary for the protection of patients' interests, invokes a partial monopoly over healing in both the public and the private sectors and thus increases the medical profession's power as producers over consuming patients (see also Calnan and Cant, this volume). Second, private corporations play an increasingly important role in both the production and consumption of private medical care as well as mediating the relationship between producers and consumers. Such corporations restrict the choice of consumers and increase the likelihood that medical care develops in ways that enhance corporate rather than patient interests. In short, liberal writers have tended to ignore the reality of market monopolies and the constraints that both professional and corporate producers impose upon the consumers of private sector health care. She concludes that private medicine does not secure much in the way of consumer sovereignty even for those who can afford it.

Calnan and Cant (Chapter 6) set out to examine why people take out private health insurance (PHI). In particular they aim to unravel whether it is caused by a real dissatisfaction with the NHS or by changing values about health and welfare as part of a wider ideological shift. They show using survey data that respondents' satisfaction with the NHS is related to whether they subscribe to PHI and to how they pay their subscriptions. Nevertheless, PHI subscribers do not appear to base their judgements about the NHS on recent, personal experience; these judgements appear to be tied to broader ideological values. However, qualitative data designed to decipher the meanings of these quantitative relationships revealed a rather more complex picture within which almost all respondents display a strong regard for the NHS. Following Busfield (this volume), they suggest that most people 'commute' between the public and private sectors. There is thus little evidence to support the notion of a growing political divide based on different consumption sectors in the area of health. Most PHI subscribers recognize the advantages of private medicine, but at the same time exhibit continued support for the welfare state. Calnan and Cant argue that support for the NHS is dependent on the practical need for continued use of the service. However, pragmatics intervene when individuals require the speed or prefer the comfort of private provision. They conclude that there continues to be a basic consensus of support for the NHS at the level of principle. However, at the level of practice the 'choice' that PHI provides will on occasion be activated. The private sector functions well for some individuals, but it does not provide a paradigm for future developments in health care provision in the UK as a whole, nor is there much support for such a development.

Flynn (Chapter 7) examines contempoary reforms of the NHS in the light of debates on the sociology of consumption. His principal conclusion is that despite all the rhetoric of consumerism that has surrounded the changes, it is unlikely that the changes will enhance consumers' choice or enlarge their influence over health services. Rather, the balance of power within the NHS is likely to move away from medical professionals and towards health authority managers. The position of patients as consumers will remain largely unaffected. Following Busfield (this volume) he also questions the conceptual appropriateness and validity of regarding health care as a market with clearly identifiable 'producers' and 'consumers'. His analysis leads him to conclude that the proposed 'internal market' will consolidate and intensify the embryonic 'new managerialism' (Kelly, 1991) in the NHS. The people most likely to benefit from the reforms are not the patients, but members of the public sector wing of the middle class working in the NHS: researchers, accountants, financial and management consultants and so on. This group of people are members of what some writers have termed the 'service class' and they provide the focus for the next two chapters.

Crompton (Chapter 8) offers a stimulating attempt to do for the middle classes in the 1990s what Lockwood (1966) did for the working classes in the 1960s: endeavour to understand the broad structural differences which underpin variations in the social consciousness of the group. This is an important exercise because recent influential discussions of the middle classes, especially the service class, have characterised them in a starkly contradictory manner. On the one hand Goldthorpe (1982) views them as a 'conservative' force, whilst on the other, and as already noted, Lash and Urry (1987) view them as being at the forefront of the 'disorganization' of capitalism, especially in relation to their role as consumers, especially of postmodern cultural forms.

Crompton makes the simple but crucial point that as the proportion of the occupied population in higher-level professional and managerial occupations, and thus the heterogeneity of the grouping, increases, so does the diversity of social consciousness within it. She suggests that there are at least two axes which might differentiate their social consciousness: geographical mobility and the mode of occupational regulation. This generates a typology of six possible perspectives within the middle classes: uncommitted; universalists; organisationally incorporated; new locals; old locals; and organisational locals.

Although some of these locations could possibly generate patterns of social consciousness which fit with either the 'organisation' or 'disorganisation' theses, many do not and the exercise demonstrates the problems that 'binary-history' accounts of the Fordism/post-Fordism, organised/disorganised capitalism and modernism/postmodernism variety generate. The internal complexity of the middle class and the contradictory roles they are playing within the process of restructuring is a point well taken.

Bonner and du Gay (Chapter 9), however, find some evidence for certain aspects of the Lash and Urry thesis concerning the leading cultural role of the service class. They draw upon the cultural studies literature to examine the use of the title of the American TV programme *thirtysomething* as a name for a particular service class fraction, the 'new petite bourgeoisie'. They demonstrate how the characters in the series both reflect and promote the distinction of this social group. They focus upon what they term the characteristic 'investment orientation to life' of the group and how the series acts as a vehicle for its promulgation.

They perceive this class fraction as being a product of the Thatcher decade, and as such it has increasingly absorbed and disseminated the idea of competitive individualism inherent in the spread of an 'enterprise culture' (Burrows, 1991; Keat and Abercrombie, 1991). They argue that through the 'investment orientation to life', this new petite bourgeoisie may well be in the process of creating the 'perfect consumer' (Featherstone 1987). They argue that this class fraction is ideally located to function as a cultural 'transmission belt' and to haul into the 'race for consumption and competition' all those from whom it is attempting to distinguish itself. They argue that one of the defining features of the group is precisely its sense of legitimacy in educating others in 'how to live', which not only produces the need for its own goods and services, but also, in the long run, legitimates itself and the lifestyle it puts forward as a model.

The final two chapters in the collection are concerned with divisions and changes in access to higher education and social mobility. Both demonstrate the continuing salience of social class in understanding key aspects of structured inequality within Britain and point towards fertile new research agendas for some of the more traditional concerns of the discipline. These two papers and the one by Crompton remind us that although the emphasis on consumption and culture within recent sociology has been important, social classes and the divisions and changes which they invoke still remain at the core of contemporary sociological concerns.

Marsh and Blackburn (Chapter 10) offer a methodologically innovative analysis of class differences in the access to and the 'consumption' of higher education. They challenge the view of the New Right that tastes and consumption styles are distinct components of the structure of social inequality and demonstrate the pertinence of class-based social policy.

They demonstrate the effect of social policy on the pattern of changing class inequality. The combination of universal grants and expanding opportunity achieved a narrowing of class differentials; but when provision failed to keep pace with potential demand the increased competition led to a return to greater inequality. For Marsh and Blackburn the conclusion is clear: changes in inequalities are related to changes in those circumstances which affect advantage, and have little or nothing do with consumer preferences.

In the final chapter, Payne (Chapter 11) examines some of the recent claims by Peter Saunders concerning the determinants of changing patterns of social mobility more generally. He engages Saunders' position at three levels: the ideas which are the source of his perspective; the evidence he adduces to support his view of mobility; and the significance and causal explanations he attaches to this alternative evidence.

Although he finds Saunders' position severely wanting in many respects he is also critical of the various claims made in the studies of the British class structure which stimulated Saunders' original critique (Goldthorpe *et al.*, 1987; Marshall *et al.*, 1988). His conclusions are ones with which most would agree: in a period of such rapid social change as has been experienced in Britain over the last decade or so 'we would be as well to treat both our data and our present conceptualisation of social division with some circumspection.'

However, despite this circumspection with which we must approach contempoary divisions and change, it is clear that the analysis of consumption and class are and will remain central features of sociological analysis. The various contributions in this volume display the current 'state of the art' in this area and set out an exciting agenda for theoretical development, empirical research and political debate in the coming years.

Notes

1. On the various meanings of this term see Saunders and Harris (1990).
2. There is both a Marxist (Aglietta, 1979) and an institutionalist (Piore and Sabel, 1984) variant of the post-Fordist position. One of the major differences between the two versions is the differential causal efficacy assigned to consumption within the supposed 'crisis of Fordism'. In the Marxist model it is changes in the sphere of production which lead to changes in patterns of consumption, whilst in the institutional model it appears that it is the break up of mass markets (i.e. consumption) which is considered the prime force behind these changes. See Hirst and Zeitlin (1991) for a general comparison of the various positions.
3. Such a task is undertaken elsewhere in the volume in relation to the operation of different markets in the provision of health care. Busfield (Chapter 5) considers the consumption of private medicine, Calnan and Cant (Chapter 6) examine the purchase of private health insurance and Flynn (Chapter 7) discusses the operation of an internal market in the National Health Service.

2 Notes on the Relationship between Production and Consumption

Alan Warde

INTRODUCTION

Historically, sociologists in general, British sociologists in particular, have paid little attention to consumption. When not considered the mere reflection of production it has been treated as a derivative of distribution, a matter of the availability of resources rather than of who consumes what. When attention was devoted to actual consumption behaviour, it was usually as social pathology, concerned with social problems of inadequate diet, excess alcohol, and the like. Weber and Veblen were exceptions among the sociological classics in examining consumption for its own sake. But recently this has changed, with some strong claims being made for the importance of a sociology of consumption to challenge dominant materialist approaches that focus on labour and production (see Moorhouse, 1983; Offe, 1985a; Saunders, 1986; Bauman, 1988).

There is considerable disagreement about what might be the relationship between production and consumption. Accounts address two distinct, though often confused, levels at which a relationship exists between production and consumption. There is a tendency to confuse the systems of production and consumption with the roles of individuals in each system. Thus it may be, systemically, *pace* the Regulation School (e.g. Aglietta, 1979), that there is a symbiosis in a Fordist regime of accumulation between mass production and mass consumption. It would, however, be quite wrong to assume that because of that systemic relationship an individual consumer's pattern of consumption can therefore be read off from her/his role in production. Bourdieu (1984), for instance, examines the latter question, of how groups of people sharing a class position in production develop distinctive patterns of consumption. But at that level there is not so tight a link between production and consumption. There is a systemic connection between the driver of a combined harvester and the consumer of a bowl of cornflakes. But given an advanced division of labour, we cannot show anything but a contingent link between an individual's occupation and his/her taste in cereals.

Substantive analysis of consumption does not help a great deal in discriminating between competing analytic positions. Recent sociological discussions of consumption have concentrated in three, as yet largely unconnected, fields. The first is a revival in the study of consumerism, which raises issues of the formation of taste, the pursuit of status and aspects of the experience of personal gratification. The second area of inquiry arose from 'the new urban sociology' of the 1970s, the central concept of which was 'collective consumption'. This concept emerged from Castells' work (e.g. 1977) on the ways in which the state intervenes to reproduce labour power through housing provision, health care, transport, etc. The modern state in these ways furnishes its citizens with a great many use-values. This notion was taken up first, in the UK at least, in terms of 'consumption sector cleavages', concerning the social advantages to be derived from having access to private as opposed to state provision of services (see Dunleavy, 1980). This proved to be a way to address many contemporary political issues, including ones of distributive justice and the quality of service provision (see Busfield and Savage *et al.*, in this volume). In this vein came Saunders' programmatic statements about replacing urban sociology with a sociology of consumption (1986; 1988).

A third area, concerning households, is also of major significance, though it has not been developed explicitly in terms of consumption. This is partly because feminist scholars have rightly criticised the concept of consumption for too easily obscuring the role of domestic labour. Much economic analysis naively treats the household as the unit of consumption. As a result, what happens within households is usually neglected. If the household is treated as a black box, key determinants of distribution of use-values are totally lost. An understanding of power and control within households is an ineradicable element of any satisfactory general account of consumption.

Foremost among these attempts to theorise about consumption has been a reconsideration of consumerism. Featherstone (1990) has usefully distinguished three competing perspectives on the analysis of consumer culture, those concentrating on the production of what is consumed; those exploring modes of consumption; and those focussing on dreams, images and pleasure. These, however, say nothing about the other types of consumption, of services provided by the state or within the household. It is unlikely that an approach that begins from the problem of explaining consumerism will satisfactorily resolve issues of the links between the different spheres of consumption because of its initial emphasis on the purchase of goods (thus on marketing, advertising, choice, etc.). Focussing primarily on the ownership of commodities, it ignores much of the labour that is actually involved in producing those commodities and neither does it address other modes of provision.

The most serious attempt to make links between spheres of consumption has been the debate about consumption cleavages. The key issue concerned the effects of services being delivered through the market rather than by the state. However, that debate has grossly exaggerated the differences between the state and the market and has ignored other spheres of consumption (see Warde, 1990a). Though recent approaches to the issue of the relationships between producers and consumers in state and market sectors have become more sophisticated (see Saunders and Harris, 1990), there is still no analytic framework capable of encompassing consumption in all spheres.

CONCEPTUAL SYNTHESIS

The task is to develop a set of concepts for understanding consumption in all spheres that can support a sociological appreciation of production and the experience of consumption. I propose the following outline of a conceptual framework to reconcile the different senses, and different foci, of recent inquiries into consumption.

The Values of Consumption

The concept of consumption has several meanings. Perhaps the easiest way to distinguish them is to consider what is the function of consumption. There are broadly three sorts of ends or 'values' guiding consumption: exchange-values, use-values and identity-values.

When orthodox economists talk of consumption they usually mean the purchase of a product and what concerns them is its exchange-value, its price. This is consumption as the appropriation of an object, in the expectation that it might subsequently be exchanged for something else. This is the normal process of purchase in the market sector, and is engaged in by firms when they buy raw materials in the hope of transforming them into something else that can be sold at a profit. Private individuals 'consume' in the same way when they 'invest' in antiques or in house-purchase.

Use-values are, typically, achieved in the process of what is often called 'final consumption', as a good is demolished (eating ice-cream) or as a service is delivered (taking a taxi). This is the sort of consumption that Marx had in mind when he said that all production was for the sake of consumption, and when he, and others in the marxist tradition, link consumption to the reproduction of labour power. The 'pathological' tradition of sociological study of consumption was also concerned with use-values, with needs, with what individuals or households achieved as 'final consumption'. Consumption patterns in this approach are the satisfaction of needs or wants.

There is a third kind of purpose to consumption that is not captured in the economics literature, and that is to enhance one's identity. The sociological literature has some grasp of this – it is embedded in Weber's analysis of status, Veblen's concept of conspicuous consumption and Bourdieu's notion of distinction. Style, status, group identification, etc., are aspects of identity-value, where people choose to display commodities or engage in different spheres of consumption with a view to expressing their identity. Certain objects, and participation in certain activities, are coveted for their social-symbolic value, placing the consumer in a social circle.

These seem to me to be irreducible values, and to be obtainable in different degrees through involvement in different spheres of consumption. My analytic framework is concerned with the ways in which people achieve these values.

Episodes of Production/Consumption

It is necessary to identify cycles of production and consumption because previous accounts have unduly contracted, or telescoped, the processes involved, as they hurry either to get from capitalist production to identity-enhancement, or to argue political cases for or against state welfare provision.

First, frequently in the making of something that is 'finally consumed', several different cycles of production and consumption occur one after the other. This can be seen from considering the food chain as a whole. What we eat off our plates typically passes through a number of production processes (the growing, wholesaling, processing, retailing and domestic preparation) and several exchange transactions (some of which are often called consumption) before final enjoyment as a meal. Various producers are involved, mostly, as is the case under capitalist relations, with the object of maximising exchange values. Shopping for your uncooked food is the last episode of that kind, one that finishes with achievement of exchange-value by means of a purchase. However, it is necessarily followed by another episode, preparation and cooking of a meal, which furnishes the final use-value. Analytically, it is worth recognising the existence of sequential episodes of production and consumption, and to notice that episodes are not necessarily identical and may involve specifically different kinds of social relationships. For example, much of the time this final episode of production/consumption occurs within households, wherein exchange-values are irrelevant to the organisation of that cycle.

Modes of Provision

Second, production/consumption episodes are characterised or distinguished by the specific social relations involved in providing the final value. In contemporary society, empirically, these social relations fall predominantly into four categories. I shall call these modes of provision. Modes of provision are characterised by distinctive ways of producing the good which embodies the value to be obtained at the end of any episode and by the social relations governing access to the fruits of labour. We need to consider market, state, domestic and communal provision, the main contemporary modes.

Consider food again. I can buy a meal in a restaurant; I may prepare it myself or prevail on someone else in my household to cook for me; if I could mount a successful political campaign, I might get the state to provide it free or subsidised in public restaurants, as did occur during the Second World War; or a friend might make me dinner. These are, in principle, alternative ways to meet my needs. However, the social relations involved in production for the market, in the household, in the public sector and in the communal sphere are dissimilar in many important respects. Moreover, the criteria of access to goods and services provided in these different sectors are also analytically distinct: purchasing my meal, availing myself of the fruits of the labour of another household member, being in receipt of a state-provided service, or being invited to a friend's table, entail diverse relations of access. Typically, these four kinds of processes of provisioning are governed, respectively, by relations of market exchange, familial obligation, citizenship right and reciprocity. It is because services are produced under distinctive conditions and access to them is regulated accordingly, and because this subsequently has consequences for their enjoyment, that the substitution of services between modes is so important socially and politically.

To date, in debates about consumption, almost the only shift that has attracted attention is the shift from state to market (e.g. medical care, housing etc.). But in the last decade we have also seen some services move from the state to the household (as with community care policies), or out from the domestic mode (with the limited expansion of private nursery provision and of nannying services). A more formal and complete account would pay attention to all other possible shifts.

The history of consumption might be written around the process of substitution of provision between modes (cf. Gershuny, 1978; Mackenzie and Rose, 1983; Humphries and Rubery, 1984). For to the extent that social relations of production and of distribution are formative of social cohesion and conflict then substitution between modes is of enormous importance. For instance, Humphries and Rubery (1984) sketch an argument to the effect that domestic and market modes are partially interdependent and that consequently household form and labour market participation are closely related. Interested in the causes and effects of increases in women's paid work, they discuss ways in which household structure, kin networks, standards of living, trade union practices, etc. are interrelated forces arising from changes in modes of provision which affect the nature of working class solidarities.

Phases of a Production/Consumption Cycle

Modes of provision are defined by the social relations involved in the production of a value and which give access to that value. In practice, achieving 'values' entails that production occurs and that access is obtained by relevant people. These two steps are not, however, sufficient to give a complete account of an episode.

At least four phases can be distinguished within a production/consumption episode, namely: the process of production or provision; the conditions of access; the manner of delivery; and the environment or experience of enjoyment (negative as well as positive).

Any comprehensive account of a single episode must consider not just production and access, but also the nature of the delivery and the experience of the enjoyment of a service. Again contemplating meals, the nature of the delivery is an essential part of the enjoyment derived from eating. The 'service' offered by proprietors, spouses or public sector waiters is susceptible to variations in quality, variations not accounted for simply in terms of relations of production. For example, marketed meals are delivered in several different fashions – 'self' service in a works canteen, 'personal' service in a smart restaurant, or through the relatively 'impersonal' services of a take-away establishment. The manner of delivery is not determined by the mode of provision but is of considerable importance to the experience of final consumption of the product.

Equally, the social environment in which final consumption takes place, for instance the company at the table or in the room, is integral to the experience of enjoyment, but cannot be directly attributed to any other of the processes involved. Paying proper attention to the quality of the experience of consumption is one common message of some of the most recent discussions. Urry (1990b), for example, reflecting on Hirsch's (1977) notion of positional goods, distinguishes two types of tourist experience: the romantic, for instance viewing landscapes, which requires solitude, and the collective, as in the seaside holiday, which depends on the presence of crowds (see also Zukin, 1990).

The two phases, delivery and enjoyment, are of significance for contemporary political arguments about welfare. Both Left and Right critics have considered the state provision of welfare services unduly bureaucratic (see Offe, 1984) and that has become perhaps the central plank of arguments for dismantling public welfare and replacing it with market or quasi-market modes of provision (e.g. Saunders, 1986; Saunders and Harris, 1987). The implicit premise is that state provision is necessarily characterised by a bureaucratic manner of delivery of service to 'clients', whereas under market modes of delivery 'customers' get more acceptable treatment. However, it seems to me that this is not a necessary connection at all, manner of delivery does not coincide with mode of provision.

Retail sale, one means of acquiring a service, is a manner of delivery known to all modes, to the domestic and the informal as well as to state and capitalist modes. The same is true of professional or expert advice. There is no reason to imagine systematic variation in service depending on whether the professional is in private practice, state employment or is known informally. More likely it will depend on the extent of the client's knowledge. Nor is there evidence that large, privately owned enterprises respond to the complaints of an individual consumer any more sympathetically than does the state. There is no simple fit between mode of provision and manner of delivery. There are private as well as public bureaucracies; there are private professionals exercising control over their clients; and there are forms of democratic negotiation within the household as well as the state sector (see further Warde, 1990a).

A similar point can be made about the enjoyment of a service which does not directly depend on the mode of its provision. It is here, the sphere of enjoyment, that sociology has been traditionally least effective, having generally neglected to analyse anything quite so frivolous as pleasure. In 1919, Swinny, surveying the prospects of British sociology, commented on its tendency to be 'occupied only with the three D's, "Drink, Drains and Divorce"' (1919:9). Despite a newly vibrant sociology of leisure not much has altered. I therefore want to make some rather more extended remarks about the experience of final consumption, the experience of achieving use- and identity-values.

Enjoyment: Analysing the Experience of Consuming

There is already some attempt to understand aspects of consumption as pleasure (for a survey see Featherstone (1990: 13–20)). One approach has been to try and found analysis in the study of pleasure/emotion and/or the body: hence some interesting discussion of exceptional consumption – on excess, on carnivals, on consumption as a game, as play, etc. The experience of consumption is also increasingly being examined by authors who previously were involved in the urban sociology debates – for example Urry (1990a) on contemporary tourism and Zukin (1990) in her examination of Disneyland and gentrification. But there remains little guidance to understanding the experience of mundane consumption behaviour. I will make a number of suggestions about some possible approaches to analysis of the experience of consumption.

Pleasure and Satisfaction

Hirschman (1982) makes an intriguing distinction between pleasure and satisfaction (cf. Scitovsky, 1976). He argues that only 'the truly non-durable good' is a source of pleasure. Food, for instance, gives pleasure whenever one is hungry, and it is a pleasure that can, hence, constantly be recreated and re-experienced. 'Durable goods', by contrast, Hirschman considers to be prone to induce disappointment. This is because one's wants shift quickly and easily. Indeed it is a condition of modern consumerism that wants keep changing. As Hirschman summarises the condition:

> The world I am trying to understand . . . is one in which men [*sic*] think they want one thing and then upon getting it, find out to their dismay that they don't want it nearly as much as they thought or don't want it at all and that something else, of which they were hardly aware, is what they really want (1982:21).

On this basis Hirschman advances a thesis about the cyclical nature of public involvement. The private collection of durable goods, which through the era of affluence was seen as a dominant motivation underpinning 'civic and familial privatism' (see Habermas, 1976), ultimately causes disappointment as it gives only satisfaction, not pleasure. In reaction the disappointed begin to re-enter public life, joining new social movements, perhaps!

Besides being an intriguing hypothesis about contemporary change, Hirschman makes two important connections with the consumption literature.

First, he questions the quality of the experience induced by the ownership of commodities. In explanations of the social significance of owner-occupation much is made of the intrinsic value of owning one's own home, which is said to engender 'ontological security' and 'privatism'. On this basis 'ideals' emerge that 'emphasize household autonomy' and 'represent a stout defiance of collectivism' (see Saunders and Williams, 1988:87). Now I would not deny that owner-occupation is generally a way of obtaining increased exchange-values, nor that, to the extent that owner-occupied housing is of better quality than public housing, people will prefer the enhanced use-values that arise therefrom (see Saunders, 1990b). However, it does not follow that people get the sort of pleasure from home ownership that would sustain distinctive social and political attitudes. It is becoming apparent that the privatised home-owner is something of a stereotype (see Franklin, 1989; also Saunders, 1990b). Re-evaluation of the intrinsic importance of ownership of commodities deserves more attention.

Second, the distinction between 'final consumption' and reusable resources is important. I have always found it suspicious that the analysis of consumption cleavages took housing as its primary exemplar and puzzling that the principal indicator of consumption practices should be housing tenure. One of the most distinctive features of houses is that they are unusually durable. To use housing as the archetype of consumption is in this respect misleading.

Events and Services

The difference between the durable and the truly non-durable good is important in another way, as regards patterns in the consumption of services. The notion of something being 'truly non-durable' also makes sense of some of the recent literature on carnivals and other spectacles, whose key property is that you have to be there, at the time, to enjoy them. They are transient opportunities for pleasure, ones in which you must participate. Events, being ephemeral, have the attribute of being strictly unrepeatable, and hence also give opportunities for a particular sort of profit-making in the service sector (see Harvey, 1989:285). This has two consequences.

First, it may explain the increased attention being paid to packaged experiences. It is something of a miracle of consumer society that one can now sell an experience. Theme-parks, Disneyland, trips up the Himalayas, package holidays, etc., constitute the sale of formed and formalised experiences, packages of pleasure which, though not without precedent, were less prominent in the past. In such instances it is also important who else is present; many activities require the participation of the collective audience, a critical part of the enjoyment: without an audience that will laugh, listening to a comedian is pretty depressing. Many such pleasures require the participation of strangers, people with whom one has only a fleeting, anonymous relationship. Hence the disappointment of finding oneself in an inappropriate holiday resort where one feels out-of-place, etc.

Second, certain types of consumption, those constituted by the delivery of a service (for instance, a restaurant meal, a train ride, etc.), require the co-presence of the producer and the consumer. This, in the confused literature about the growth of 'the service sector', used to be considered a defining feature of a service, but clearly there are services, and whole service industries, where this is not the case (see Gershuny and Miles, 1983). However, an important range of services is delivered face-to-face, and that is usually true of non-durable personal services, where delivery and enjoyment coincide spatially and/or temporally. The nature of the interaction affects enjoyment.

The Values of Consumption

Consumers, I claimed above, have three predominant orientations towards that which they might consume: they might be seeking use-values, exchange-values, or identity-values. It is impossible to understand modern consumerism without appreciating all three types.

All may be 'satisfied' at once, in the same activity. Take, for instance, house purchase. I buy a house which I use (it keeps me warm and dry), which has an exchange value (I can hang on to it until the price is right), and which has an identity-value (of positive or negative valence for specified groups). Other products lack one or other of these values. Almost every product, whether good or service, has a use-value. Many products, however, have no exchange-value. Sometimes this arises because of overproduction of otherwise exchangable things, as with butter mountains. Domestic services, more significantly, have no exchange-value. Nor do many public services, like National Health Service care, where declining an entitlement to treatment does not leave the citizen with equivalent resources to obtain an alternative service.

It is less clear-cut what kinds of things lack identity-value. Youth sub-cultures are known to innovate to give their own distinctive 'meanings' to mundane objects, suggesting that symbolic significance may be attributed to a broad range of things. However, generally speaking, state services have little identity-value *per se* (though perhaps they are increasingly being given a negative valence as a result of government policy). Many commodities have little identity-value; students of consumerism, it seems to me, underestimate the role of purely routine consumption, the result of their studying most closely the more spectacular instances of consumption – the advertising industry, etc. Although some people may attempt to create total lifestyles as expressions of personal identity (cf. Featherstone, 1987), most, despite the intentions of advertising agencies, probably see choices between soaps or soups as not seriously prejudicial to their self-image.

Identity-Value and Consumer Behaviour

If identity-value is significant, then it is worth considering briefly what sociological processes are involved in its creation. There seem to me to be three general ways in which people concerned to enhance their identity-value may orient their action. They are to be distinguished broadly in terms of their orientation toward different reference groups, the 'Other' that the consumer is out to impress. That Other may be: members of a different status-group, members of the consumer's own status group, or the consumer him/herself. The first process implies the potential for hierarchical distribution of 'honour' between different social groups. Conspicuous consumption, as Veblen (1925) described it, was a way in which an aristocratic group marked its existence, and its privilege, to other groups. The second process is concerned more with differentiation than with hierarchy. The consumer uses identity-enhancing symbols in order to stress the membership of a group – perhaps of enthusiasts for whole foods, or as wine-lovers, etc. – but without that entailing any overt social hierarchy. Finally it might be considered that increasingly identity-value is narcissistic in purpose. You can play identity games on your own, a feature well-recognised by advertisers and documented by Lasch (1979) and Bell (1976), where your reference group in the identity-game is self. Consider advertisements for underwear, for example. Narcissism, differentiation and distinction are different forms of the enhancement of identity-value.

On the Relationship Between Use- and Identity-Value

While Baudrillard (1988) persuades me that patterns of consumption are oriented to identity-value, and that this is as true of poor as of opulent consumers, still very few people pursue identity-values that do not simultaneously furnish use-values. I would be impressed to find someone who bought the right kind of motor car to give expression to their identity but who could not, and had no intention of learning, to drive. There seems to me to be a strong utilitarian impulse in consumption behaviour, a discounting of identity-enhancing functions when issues of utility are pressing. This is of course most strongly present among people with limited resources: as Elster (1989) might put it, their opportunity-set severely constrains their desires and actions. The practices of the poor are a foil to accounts that see the contemporary world revolving around the play of signs and images.

Interestingly, modern marketing strategies are founded upon establishing a coincidence between use and identity values. Yet most of the signifiers of identity that can be derived from consumer behaviour are rather mundane: curtains, scarves, cars and bicycles, TVs, etc. These are commodities that are first and foremost useful. Baudrillard takes enjoyment as deriving from identity-value to the total exclusion of use-value: the signs have it. But the process of identity formation could be considered more material a process – *people play with the signs that they can afford.*

Phases of Episodes under Different Modes of Provision: an Illustration

There are, then, several phases in any episode, and episodes vary in nature depending upon the mode of their provision. It is therefore possible to describe typical episodes and explore the social significance of each. Here I offer a sketchy illustration concerning the differences between various transactions involving avocado pears:

(1) Buying an avocado from the greengrocer. The provision of the fruit is through retailing work, a petite bourgeoise or capitalist employment relationship governs this phase. Access is simply the function of purchasing power, a market relationship, though I might perhaps find it difficult to find a shop with avocados to sell. Delivery coincides with the work of provision and is governed by a customer relationship. The 'enjoyment' derived from this episode is solely transfer of ownership and though I am unlikely to feel enormous satisfaction from owning an avocado I may anticipate the pleasure of eating it.

(2) Preparing and eating my avocado. The work involved in this episode is domestic labour. Access is a function of being a member of the household. Delivery is a private, immediate, personal service. Enjoyment comes in the form of use-value (final consumption) which might give me pleasure, as might congenial company to share it with. I will also have contributed something to my personal reproduction – a straight-forward physical use-value.

(3) Ordering avocado in a restaurant. The work involved is preparation by a chef and service from a waiter. Access is again governed by market-exchange, perhaps involving a little knowledge too. Delivery will usually, but not always, be a customer relationship, but one which will vary in type between more or less personal service. Enjoyment may derive from the public context of eating, which can have identity-value, or sociability (network) value, as entertainment, or just functional use-value directed towards personal reproduction.

These trivial examples, breaking down production/consumption cycles into their component parts, illustrate some of the quite different processes that intercede in episodes of production and consumption.

DISCUSSION

(1) Examining consumption in this way emphasises its complexity, rendering the concept problematic, if not redundant. No longer is it possible to think of consumption in a simple, one-dimensional way. It is not just something that happens within the household contributing to the reproduction of labour power, nor can it be reduced to the distribution of assets, nor simply treated as an area of choice and taste.

(2) Work is involved in every episode of consumption. Usually this is transformative work, part of the complex division of labour in society. It is particularly significant that much of the work involved is not undertaken under employment relations – much of the labour involved is informal, voluntary or domestic (Gershuny and Miles, 1983). Hence, some versions of the 'end of work' thesis are potentially misleading in the way they counterpose work and consumption (e.g. Moorhouse, 1983; Bauman, 1988). Obviously, much of the time it is not the actual consumer who does the work required within any episode of the production/consumption cycle. Discrepancies between labour inputs and achieved values then constitute an accounting procedure for understanding some social inequalities (within households, for example). Also, because the relations of production vary between different modes of provision, the possibility arises of examining how consumption behaviour corresponds to different methods of labour exploitation.

(3) Often, many episodes are required before one gets to the stage of obtaining use- or identity-value from a production process. Much of the labour that goes into the final use-value is invisible (my examples, for instance, omitted to mention the growers of the avocados, the people who picked them, crated them, transported them, etc.). However, by disaggregating episodes it is possible to give a full account of all the labour that goes into the final product. To the extent that we change the focus of analysis from the quality of the final product to the processes of its provisioning we permit ourselves new perspectives on production/consumption cycles.

It seems to me that much recent analysis of consumption begins from the premise that maximising consumer satisfaction is an *a priori* value. Most arguments for privatisation of welfare services, for instance, take consumer satisfaction as the paramount value. This forecloses on alternative values that might be fostered. For instance, it is possible to prefer less choice as a consumer in exchange for improved conditions of work for the producers (as with the issue of shop opening hours). Equally, on egalitarian grounds, one could reasonably accept a poorer quality service in exchange for universal access. Or one might prefer the impersonality of a bureaucratic delivery rather than introduce opportunities for negotiation between producer and consumer which might lead to class inequalities in the service delivered (as has been shown in doctor-patient interactions). The more elements recognised in the chains of episodes, the less self-evident is the assumption of the priority of consumer satisfaction.

(4) The identification of different modes of provision renders arguments based on 'the state versus the market' too simple. Consumption cleavages are thus exposed as a restricted basis for examining consumption, partly because the role of domestic provisioning appears as a critical element in any individual or household pattern of consumption.

Moreover, there can be no simple answer to the question of what is the relationship between production and consumption. It varies both between and within modes of provision.

(5) An episode of consumption, I have argued, should be considered to comprise four discrete phases: provision, access, delivery and enjoyment. No complete account can afford to ignore any of these phases, yet existing approaches rarely entertain more than two of them. One of the principal problems with existing explanatory accounts is that they are partial with respect to the phases that they consider.

For example, Saunders (1986) in his critique of state welfare provision much of the time ignored issues of production and access, concentrating instead on inadequate delivery and the poor experiences of state provision. His fundamental point was that bureaucratic administration and allocation removed choice from clients and they hence obtained little satisfaction from receipt of state services. His critics, defending the welfare state, concentrated instead on production and access, pointing to exploitation in capitalist production and the inegalitarian effects of market relations, but saying little about delivery or enjoyment. As Pickvance (1989) has pointed out, authors in that debate tend to be highly selective in identifying the essential features of different modes of provision.

Another example might be Neil Smith's (1979: though compare Smith, 1987) rent-gap theory of gentrification which was strong on accounts of the logic of the production of housing but lacked any explanation of how or why particular sorts of people gained access to, or anticipated pleasurable experiences from living in, converted factories and terraced housing originally designed for labourers.

(6) An ability to separate out use-, exchange- and identity-values makes for a more integrated appreciation of what have been deemed 'consumption-side' pressures in, for example, discussions of gentrification. The same distinction allows a more systematic differentiation between things that might be consumed. That owner-occupied housing bears all three values goes some way to explaining the often confusing ways in which it has been attributed significance in debates about contemporary social change.

(7) The political implications of the approach are of some importance. Partly it demands a more rigorous analysis of the ways in which the mode of provision of particular services have altered over time. Perhaps there is still an overall tendency towards the commodification of use- and identity-values, but there are certainly counter-tendencies that deserve examination. For instance, Gershuny's (1978) thesis of the emergence of the 'self-service economy' identifies the extensive substitution of domestic for market modes of provision. It is then possible to identify other sources of political solidarity besides those based in class or sectoral location. Systematic bases for gender, generational and sub-cultural allegiances arise in the phases of episodes of the production/consumption cycle (see Warde, 1988).

(8) Another issue arising from approaching consumption in this way is that it raises questions of the link between property ownership and enjoyment. As Hirschman pointed out, there is some doubt about the quality of the experience induced by the ownership of commodities. To the extent that we are entering a cultural age where the spectacle and the event are increasingly valued above objects, and where the purchase of services account for an increasing proportion of household income, some of the consequences adduced to follow from personal ownership of goods and chattels may be of lesser importance in the twenty-first century than has been imagined previously.

(9) The conceptual scheme has been built around the analysis of products, most of which are in fact services. The account is an elaborate version of a 'provision thesis' (compare Kemeny, 1987).

The defining phases are those of provision and access, which account for the provision and distribution of the product. But whereas Kemeny objected to accounts which, by concentrating on provision, ignored consumption *per se*, this schema considers the phases of delivery and enjoyment as integral to any episode. It makes no sense to counterpose production and consumption, nor to ask whether supply or demand is the more important in understanding any particular set of practices.

The stages involved in the development of a product are ones which link the overall economic system to the experiences of individuals and ones which can be used to describe the connections between the production and consumption positions of individuals. What it indicates is a very complex system, and one that probably will be examinable only through historical analysis. While no-one would ever require a complete account of all episodes from point of conception to final consumption, because it would be hopelessly detailed, *heuristically the schema mitigates against one-sided and partial theoretical accounts of consumption.*

3 Constructing Consumers and Consumer Protection: the Case of the Life Insurance Industry in the United Kingdom

Glenn Morgan and David Knights

INTRODUCTION

Consumer protection is now a central feature of political discourse in western society. The re-emergence of the widespread belief that the free market is the best means for ensuring the public good is coupled with a recognition that an unregulated market can under certain circumstances become monopolistic and disadvantageous to the consumer. Accordingly, some sort of consumer protection is necessary to ensure that this does not occur. In this respect, politicians have been influenced by the emergence in the UK of a powerful 'consumer' lobby, associated with specialist organisations such as the Consumers Association and the National Consumer Council, as well as with certain sections of the press, radio and television.

The rise of consumer protection as a political phenomenon has not, however, been reflected in sociological research. Although sociologists have become more interested in the issue of consumption (see for example the various contributions in the present volume; and the special issue of the journal *Sociology* 24, 1, 1990), there has been little empirical research which examines specifically how institutions of consumer protection have been constructed. Nevertheless, recent discussions of consumption make it logical for sociologists to consider this issue. In particular, Saunders (1986; 1990b; Saunders and Harris, 1990) has raised the question of how various modes of distribution of goods serve the interests of consumers. Saunders argues that, in general, markets 'empower' consumers at the expense of producers (see Busfield, this volume, for discussion of this issue in relation to health). He has not, however, addressed the question of why, if this is the case, consumer protection movements, which attempt to limit market relations, have become more significant in recent years. In our view, this issue provides a potentially fruitful field for empirical research. To what extent does the market empower the consumer? What are the conditions under which consumer protection movements emerge? How does this affect the constitution of market relations?

In this chapter, we examine these issues by reference to the market for particular products – those of life insurance policies. We argue that for many years the power to define the conditions under which exchange took place was controlled primarily by the companies, in conjunction with the state. The market, far from 'empowering' consumers, was constituted in such a way as to enable the companies to dominate. During the 1970s, however, this domination began to be eroded as alternative perspectives on the interests of the consumer developed. The idea that the consumer needed a specific type of protection from the companies and their agents began to emerge in spite of the resistance of the companies. By the mid-1980s, the social relations of exchange and consumption within life insurance had changed significantly. In effect, one could argue that a new type of market for these products was emerging in which power relations between the companies, the consumers and the state were being reconstituted. Thus the chapter is concerned to establish the conditions under which social definitions of the consumer and consumer protection were produced, reproduced and changed in this particular market.

LIFE INSURANCE: SOME PRELIMINARY METHODOLOGICAL CONSIDERATIONS

Our knowledge and understanding of life insurance derives from both primary and secondary sources. We have conducted considerable historical research into the development of the industry in the UK. This has been coupled with detailed case study research conducted in a number of life insurance companies involving interviews with all levels of the workforce, including senior managers in sales and marketing. We have also had discussions with a wide number of senior executives in companies and industry associations as well as maintaining detailed records of current press interest in life insurance. Our research has involved discussions with representatives of consumer groups regarding their perceptions of the sale of life insurance products. We have also consulted magazines such as *Which?* and *Money Which?* as a source of alternative perspectives on consumers and consumer protection. Finally, our research has involved discussions with members of the regulatory bodies which now supervise the life insurance industry.

This immersion in the industry has not blinded us to its distinctive character. Contracts in life insurance involve a much more long-term relationship between the client and the company than in most other industries. We are therefore not claiming that the details of the process which we examine is 'typical' of other industries and markets. However, the questions asked, the methods employed and the mode of analysis adopted could be used as a model for sociological research on consumption in other industries. In this way, sociology would establish an understanding of how specific markets are constituted and how concepts of the consumer and consumer protection are developed. In our view, such an understanding would enable sociology to develop in two ways. At the theoretical level, it would contribute to a better understanding of the market and how it advantages and disadvantages particular groups. At the policy level, it would enable sociology to contribute to emerging debates about forms of consumer protection and market regulation.

CONSTRUCTING THE CONSUMER OF LIFE INSURANCE

Markets develop on the basis of an exchange between producers and consumers. Both of these categories are socially constructed. In this section, we wish to consider how the consumer of life insurance is constituted.

The basis upon which personal insurance has been sold is one of providing security for families and individuals against potential financial loss resulting from the death, accident or sickness of an adult 'breadwinner'. For the working class in eighteenth- and nineteenth-century Britain these problems were managed either through assistance from extended kin, poor law relief or friendly society insurance. While the prevalence of the former has been the subject of some historical debate (Macfarlane, 1979), there is little doubt that poor law relief sustained individuals only at the cost of the stigma of pauperism. Insurance was thereby an attractive alternative and indeed the industrial life assurance sector was built upon the foundation of weekly 'death policies' that were purchased in order to avoid the stigma of a 'pauper's funeral' (Gosden, 1973: 64; Knights 1988: 56–60).

This was encouraged and supported by government as 'an appropriate instrument for the realisation of the new politics of security' (Knights and Vurdubakis, 1990: 22).

Within contemporary society, of course, there are a number of other possible responses to the problem of financial security. Most advanced western societies now possess some sort of welfare state which provides this security, but since the level of provision has always been politically contested, many people in these societies have sought and are encouraged by government to supplement this collective solution by an individual response. This individual response can also take a variety of forms. On the one hand, people have tried to save their money in bank or building society accounts and to redistribute their earnings over the life-cycle by consciously putting money away. Others have tried various forms of direct investment in shares or property. Of course, a substantial number are unable to afford and others are unprepared to sacrifice current consumption to participate in any of these methods of saving and, as a result, often end up relying entirely on state provision.

Since the nineteenth century, the British government has been particularly concerned to encourage savings through life insurance and other schemes. The reasons for this have become more complex as the ideologies and institutions of the modern welfare state have developed. However, in general terms, the provision of a minimum level of security in circumstances of old-age, bereavement, unemployment and illness has been seen as crucial to social stability in modern societies. If this can be made an individual responsibility through an insurance system, it reduces both the fiscal and the political demands made on the state to provide security, whilst at the same time reinforcing capitalist relations through entwining individuals in financial discipline and market relations (see Knights (1988) and Knights and Vurdabakis (1990) for extended discussions of this). In the UK, the state did this in the area of life insurance primarily through a series of tax incentives such as Life Assurance Premium Relief (Zimmeck, 1985) and the relief of life insurance companies investment funds from certain other taxes. As a result, direct individual ownership of shares and government stock has tended to decline as it has been more advantageous to save through the medium of life insurance policies, leading to the concentration of ownership of British industry in the hands of life insurance companies (Scott, 1986).

Convincing individuals of their particular responsibility for life insurance has, however, never been easy. Potential clients have often been reluctant to plan in detail for the security of themselves and their dependents in the event of their own death even though life insurance provided tax advantages. Because of this difficulty, insurance companies in the late nineteenth century developed endowment policies where, if the customer survived a predetermined period of time (i.e. the term of the policy), then he/she received a sum of money determined according to various actuarial calculations concerning the value of the investments purchased with the premiums (Pearson, 1990; Supple, 1970; Trebilcock, 1985; Treble, 1984). Although the promise of a financial return before rather than after death was more attractive, this did not fully overcome 'consumer' resistance because the product was still based on a substantial time horizon; policies did not qualify for the various tax concessions unless the contract was for a minimum of ten years.

In addition to its long term nature, the product of life insurance is somewhat intangible and lacking in immediate satisfaction compared to more concrete consumer commodities such as cars, holidays and home entertainment. Despite a dramatic increase in the media coverage of personal financial services, consumer knowledge and awareness outside of the professional classes remains at a very low level. Part of this relates to a myth about, but also some substance in, the complexity of matters financial. Even those who have bought insurance policies remain relatively ignorant of their provisions simply because they are abstract and relate to a future unpredictable set of circumstances. Not surprisingly, consumers are always reluctant to buy something which they barely understand!

THE PRODUCERS OF LIFE INSURANCE

On the other side of the market are the companies which actually produce life insurance. For them, 'consumer resistance' is rationalised as a product of short termism where consumers are seen to prefer immediate to deferred gratification. In their view, this can only be overcome by appealing to, or constructing, a problem in regard to the moral purpose and responsibility of individuals. Through the process of selling, life insurance and associated products are shown to be the ideal solution to this problem.

The moral problem is created or aroused by stressing a future of uncertainty and potential insecurity as endemic to the human condition. Death, tragedy, accidents and illness can happen to anybody. The consequences of these are not just individual. People are embedded in networks of social obligations and responsibilities. They must therefore consider what may happen in the event of such unforeseeable events; they should, in other words, 'insure' against the future. In this view, life insurance can be said to serve a 'negative' protective function; it ensures that the family does not suffer economic loss and hardship on the death of the insured person. However, with the incorporation of a savings element into insurance, via endowment policies and investment or mutual fund plans, the purchase can be given a positive 'empowering' image, by emphasising future realiseable benefits.

Both the negative and the positive function of life insurance are seen by the companies to conflict with traditional spending patterns. In this perception, many people are seen to consume their income in a way which brings no lasting benefit. Whilst they are fit and healthy and earning 'good money', they spend it, thus leaving themselves and their families little in the way of reserves when earnings fall. If they just put a little bit of money away now into some sort of endowment policy, within a few months, they would hardly notice it was going out of their account and yet it would be building them a nest-egg for the future. Buying adequate insurance is perceived as a sign of a person fulfilling his/her moral obligations and putting aside short-term hedonistic influences. Accordingly, companies feel themselves to be fulfilling a moral purpose by providing people with insurance products. In effect, the sale of insurance is not simply an instrumental transaction between a seller and a buyer; it embodies a moral view of what society is and should be like.

It is not, therefore, surprising that many life insurance companies were founded in nineteenth-century Britain by men of strong religious sentiment (Gosden, 1973), a connection which appears to have been particularly strong in Scotland (see e.g. Magnusson, 1983). Whilst the nineteenth century saw a number of insurance company failures, those which survived into the twentieth century have drawn on their origins to present themselves as guardians of the nation's morality and its long-term survival. Even their names often are suggestive of such a moral commitment – the Prudential, the Scottish Widows, Provident Mutual Life, National Provident Institution, Friends Provident, Guardian Royal Exchange, the United Kingdom Temperance and General Provident Institution. Many of these companies were explicitly founded out of moral concern. Some of them even took on a mutual form of ownership so that the benefits from investment could be shared out amongst policyholders rather than distributed to shareholders. Mutuality as an ownership form significantly reinforced the claims of these companies and the industry in particular to be serving the interests of the policyholders – the consumers – rather than some extraneous body such as shareholders.

In relation to consumer protection, this produces an interesting paradox because consumers frequently resist what is 'best' for them; they are resistant to the purchase of insurance for the very reasons that they 'need' it. Their income is insecure, transient; they want to enjoy it while they have it. Thus consumer protection becomes turned on its head; consumers do not need protecting from insurance companies but from themselves. For insurance companies, the real consumer protection issue is one of preventing consumers allowing their short-term and selfish concerns with immediate gratification to undermine their sense of long-term moral obligation to self, family and society.

SELLING LIFE INSURANCE

The market for life insurance is completed by the actual process of selling. It is at this point that the contradictions and conflicts between the different concepts is clearest and we will therefore examine this in some detail.

In the period before the Financial Services Act 1986 two main types of distribution systems predominated – company sales representatives and intermediaries. It is important to examine the conditions under which these sellers seek to constitute a market with potential buyers.

Company Salesforces

With regard to company salesforces, there have been two main forms: industrial life agents and direct saleforces. We consider each in turn.

Amongst the earliest salesforces were those operated by the large industrial life assurance companies such as the Prudential and the Pearl, which were subject to the regulation of the Industrial Assurance Commissioner. The defining characteristic of industrial life business is that in comparison to what is known as ordinary life assurance, the premium for industrial life must be collected by an agent from the home of the policy-holder on a regular basis (usually at least once a month). On their regular rounds of customers, the agents have also sold other insurance products such as household and motor policies. Industrial life assurance has traditionally been the means whereby the less well-off have been able to purchase insurance. The agents have often become the link to a financial world which the customer knows little about. Their regular collection visits (often as frequent as once a week) results in them being able to develop close ties with customers on their particular round.

In the late nineteenth century, regulation of these salesforces was stepped up. Because of their closeness to an essentially working class clientele (which had little independent knowledge of financial matters), the potential for abuse was significant. Clients trusted the agent largely because of the close and regular interpersonal contact but this trust could be exploited for personal advantage. In addition, agents often traded other services (e.g. clothing, credit sales and money lending facilities) which they used as a leverage to sell insurance policies. Policies were frequently surrendered to pay off debts in these areas but were almost always replaced by larger ones from which the agent received commission. The regulations under the various Industrial Assurance Acts did little to protect clients against potential abuses of this kind.

From the early 1960s the direct sales representative model was developed. The essential characteristic of these salesforces was that they had to find their own customers through, for example, knocking on doors, telephoning long lists of potential prospects or using networks of existing friends and kin to secure leads.

A full consideration of selling practices in this sector of the market is beyond the scope of this discussion (see Knights and Morgan, 1990; 1991; Morgan, 1990, for more details). Nevertheless certain points are important. Firstly, direct salesforces have been predominantly paid by commission earnings; they are dependent upon selling in order to make a living. This obviously puts a great deal of pressure on them to get results. Secondly and related to this, the higher the premium, the more commission they receive. Thus it is not just in their interests to sell a product but to sell it at the maximum premium that can be secured from the client. Thirdly, the seller is initially primarily concerned to get the customer to listen to the selling gambit. Once the listener is hooked in then certain basic appeals can be made to the sense of insecurity described earlier; but if the listener refuses to even listen, no progress can be made. Thus at the initial stage, the seller will use devices (deceptions, even) to get the potential customer to listen without necessarily revealing his/her identity as a life insurance seller or the fact that he/she is employed solely to sell the products of one company. Fourthly, during the interview itself, the seller will be trying to convince the customer that the product is needed. This can be done by appealing to raw human emotions about dependency; or alternatively, the appeal can be made on the basis of greed, with the seller presenting possibly inflated estimates of what the policy will produce on maturity in comparison to the products of other companies or of other media of saving whilst rarely making clear the source of any such growth and its dependency on the precarious fluctuations of stock market investments. Fifthly, the seller will try to gain a commitment from the customer by obtaining a signature on a proposal or application form and a cheque for the first payment before leaving the interview.

Although all insurance sales practices involve an element of urgency because of the commission based nature of remuneration, direct sales force representatives tend to be under greater pressure since this is the sole source of income. For this reason, there is 'high pressure' at the point of direct contact with the customer. In order to justify this pressure, both to him/herself and to the client, the salesperson draws on the language of morality and insurance. The sense of this is as follows. Nobody 'buys' life insurance; they have to have it sold to them. If there is nobody around to sell it to the customer, then he/she does not buy it and when he/she dies/grows older etc., there are no savings or insurance to fall back on. Thus the seller is doing the customer a good turn.

Unlike the industrial life agent, the direct sales force representative has a single-stranded relationship with the client. It consists of the moment of sale; even if the sale is successful it is unlikely that the representative will see the client again for a considerable length of time (unless there is a complaint). Therefore, there are less inhibitions on the direct sales force representative from maximising his/her own advantage. In comparison, the industrial life agent collects premiums on a regular basis and has a continuous relationship with members on his/her round. He/she cannot therefore afford to be as aggressive in selling technique. The industrial life agent sells by drawing on preexisting trust relationships; the direct sales force person sells by using more sophisticated techniques and/or pressurising the client. Both, however, draw extensively on the language of morality to justify their sales and their own role in the sales process.

Intermediaries

Whereas company salesforces have been, as the name implies, directly or indirectly employed by the companies, there have been many sellers of insurance who have been independent of the companies. These people, known in general as intermediaries, earn commissions from the companies on each policy they sell. Unlike company salesforces, however, they have frequently done business with more than one company or have held other jobs besides insurance selling which have been their main source of income.

Some intermediaries have been genuine brokers who provided *independent* advice about the relative merits of a range of products from many different companies. Others, although dealing in insurance full-time, dealt with only a small number of companies. Still another group have been those who sold insurance on a part-time basis. Amongst this group were solicitors and accountants who sold to their clients as insurance needs were identified in the course of professional transactions. Building societies also sold insurance on this basis. Banks tended to straddle these categories. Although many of the major banks had, by the early 1970s, their own insurance companies – Lloyds had Black Horse Life, Barclays had Barclays Life, TSB had TSB Trust – bank managers tended to act like professional intermediaries who could offer general advice on insurance matters as the need arose and make recommendations not just from their own bank's insurance company. Many of them also had a special intermediary service partly to counter the fact that bank branch managers did not like to be seen as selling insurance which they felt was a low-status activity.

As with company salesforces, a central problem for most of these groups was that of identifying a prospect and then persuading that person to buy life insurance. For some, like building societies, accountants and lawyers, the conditions of client dependency generated a power relation that rendered the task of selling additional services such as insurance relatively unproblematic, e.g. the building society manager advising the linking of the mortgage to an insurance endowment; in such circumstances, few applicants would be likely to resist the advice for fear of jeopardising the mortgage.

However, another issue has also been important for intermediaries; this relates to the status of the advice given to clients. The notion of a broker has been long-standing in British commercial activities. In insurance, it has traditionally referred to people who acted on behalf of the client to find the best deal that was available from the offers made by the companies. However, this has been complicated by the fact that in insurance the broker or other intermediary received payment not from the client to whom advice had been given but from the company which received the business. This created a fatal ambiguity. Was the intermediary placing business with a certain company or selecting a particular contract on the basis of the client's best interests or because of the level of commission being thus gained? This ambiguity was compounded further because intermediaries and especially part-timers such as the smaller accountants and the building societies might in actual fact become the agent of only one or a small group of companies. Thus the client would be advised not from the range of companies in the marketplace but from the range with which the intermediary had agencies – a very different proposition! The client would be unlikely to know whether the intermediary's advice was being influenced by such considerations or not.

BUYING FOR LIFE: THE DURATION OF LIFE INSURANCE CONTRACTS

So far, we have concentrated on the role of the companies and their agents in constituting the market for life insurance. Our argument has been that the voluntary nature of the market for insurance contracts can only be understood in the context of the social and moral pressure used in persuading clients to buy life insurance products, the implications of which they do not always fully understand.

This argument can be strengthened by looking at the longer-term outcomes of such contracts. In particular, it is clear that many people cash in their policies before they have run their full course. For example, in the company where we have conducted a case study, the company is currently striving to make sure that it achieves 80 per cent of persistency so that eight out of ten policies sold on a ten-year or longer term basis are maintained for at least twelve months! Thus, two out of every ten policies are cancelled within their first year of operation, usually at a substantial loss to the consumer since the first year's premium tends to be taken by the company as charges for the service of setting up the contract.

In 1987, over 2,017,000 industrial life policies were surrendered early for cash and another 552,000 forfeited entirely without any grant of paid up policy or cash value. Policy forfeitures constituted 17 per cent of the year's new business amongst industrial life assurance companies in 1987. (The previous year they had been as high as 24.4 per cent.) In 1986, insurance companies paid out more for early surrenders of ordinary life policies (£3,057m) than they did for either death claims

(£1,112m) or maturities (£2,356m) or annuities (£1,347m) (Association of British Insurers, 1989).

Between one quarter and one half of all life insurance policies do not run their full course because the buyer voluntarily opts out at some point. Prima facie, early encashment which can sometimes involve a real financial loss, is evidence of a high degree of consumer dissatisfaction. The companies defend themselves from this interpretation of the statistics by pointing out three things. First, even early surrender can sometimes bring a bigger lump sum than would have been received by investing in a bank or building society. Secondly, even if this were not the case the client will have had the security of insurance during the period of operation of the contract. Finally, the client is being irrational in opting out of the policy early. In this way, the companies reconstitute potentially disconfirming evidence to reproduce their own view of themselves as embodying standards of financial self-discipline which the client has difficulty in meeting.

To summarise the argument so far, the market for life insurance products was embedded in a set of social relationships which was principally controlled by the companies, in conjunction with the state. Clients were considered as suffering from a 'moral deficit'; demands for immediate gratification displaced their moral responsibilities. The companies were justified in using manipulative selling techniques in order to ensure that consumers did what was good for them even if they failed to understand what they were consuming or, after a while, why they were consuming it at all!

NEW DEFINITIONS OF CONSUMER PROTECTION IN LIFE INSURANCE

During the 1970s, these traditional definitions of the market and the consumer in life insurance began to change. This process of change was complex and many-sided. In the following pages, we seek to spell out some of the forces generating this change and the consequences of this process.

The Rise of the Consumer Movement

'Consumerism' as a social movement has a relatively recent history in the UK (cf. the USA where the sociologist Robert Lynd crucially influenced the development of consumerism; see Grahame, 1989).

During the 1960s, the rising tide of concern with consumer issues was reflected in increased media coverage and the emergence of new organisations such as the Consumers Association. The Consumers Association appears to have taken a particular interest in life insurance and investment from early in its history, to the extent of publishing a special magazine entitled *Money Which?* (now incorporated into the Association's *Which?* magazine) as well as annual *Guides to Savings and Investment*. The Consumers Association is entirely funded from sales of its publications and membership fees. Thus its base has been predominantly amongst middle class professionals for whom investment and savings issues have a high saliency. Not surprisingly, then, the Consumers Association has investigated the sale of life insurance a number of times. It has in the main rejected the industry's concept of the consumer as being basically ignorant and short-term and therefore best saved from that ignorance by the greater wisdom of the company.[1] Instead, it has espoused a view of the consumer as requiring more information, as wanting to be better informed, as needing protection but not in the paternalistic way the industry presents this. The Consumers Association has argued that client ignorance is functional for the companies since it allows them to earn large profits and surpluses without being subjected to policyholder scrutiny. It has therefore campaigned for greater openness in life insurance selling so that consumers can compare products. It has also argued for the need to control bad selling techniques. In this, it has been part of a wider international movement in the growth of consumer organisations (see OECD, 1987).

The Development of the Financial Media

The 1970s and 1980s has seen a proliferation of discourses within the UK press and media on personal financial services. There is no doubt that these have a considerable influence on the public especially in encouraging financial self-discipline (Knights, 1988; Knights and Morgan, 1991) and consumer rationality. But senior executives in insurance companies are particularly anxious about the possible bad publicity of an exposure by one of the media consumer watchdogs. They are also concerned not to receive any negative comments from journalists in the mass circulation Sunday newspapers. The more upmarket media (e.g. quality newspapers) can, by providing comparative tables of charges and growth yields, do untold damage or good for any individual company. Even if the product itself remains difficult to understand, there are now many more specialist journalists trying to interpret it in a way that will help the non-expert make a rational decision. Companies and intermediaries are no longer the only source of information about products.

Competition in the Industry

The same period also has seen the industry becoming more competitive. On the one hand, increasing income opened up the possibility for higher levels of savings. The market as a whole was therefore growing throughout this period (Ginarlis 1988). On the other hand, new companies were entering the market as people realised its growth potential. Some new style companies (e.g. Abbey Life) with aggressive US based direct sales strategies expanded in just 20 years to a size that challenged the established giants in this 250 year old industry. Other new entrants sought business from intermediaries by paying higher commissions than the traditional companies.

Conflicts began to emerge as the older companies felt that the image of the industry was being tarnished by the use of high pressure salesforces and larger commissions. The newcomers, on the other hand, saw this as self-serving on the part of staid, conservative institutions anxious to protect their own position. Thus whereas, in the past, the industry had presented a fairly homogeneous front to the world in terms of the image of insurance, the companies and the sellers, this facade now began to crack. Companies began to point the finger of blame at each other, arguing that certain companies were bringing the industry into disrepute by their selling techniques or their commission payments. Thus, in our discussions with senior executives, each one believed that there were a 'few rotten apples'; furthermore each had a list of rogue scapegoats whom they charged with bad practices. However, the list varied depending on which rumour or set of prejudices they adhered to or in accordance with their own position in the market. In the case of complaints against their own company by customers, the executives believed that in many cases, customers were being egged on to complain by other companies. Thus grievances were, they argued, being manufactured to cause bad publicity for market competitors and did not reflect a 'real problem' with their own company.

The effect of increased competition was complex. It appears to have broken down old ties of industry loyalty. Companies are much more outspokenly critical of each other and, as a result, add fuel to the complaints of the consumer lobby.

Industry Self-Regulation

In response to the problem of pressurised selling, around this time the government imposed a cooling-off period for all life insurance sales; this provided the customer with a 'breathing space' or time after signature to reconsider whether or not to continue the policy. Recognising the danger of even further state intervention of a regulatory nature, the industry tried to develop some greater cohesiveness around the issue of voluntary reform. First, a number of companies joined together to fund the Insurance Ombudsman Bureau which began in March, 1981 to provide a conciliation and settlement service for personal policyholders insured with members of the Bureau. The Reports of the Ombudsman are issued annually and indicate a growing number of complaints in the area of life insurance. Second, an attempt was made to re-establish a maximum commission agreement to prevent both a commission war between companies and to eliminate the temptation for intermediaries to give advice based primarily on commission rather than the best interests of the client. However, significant numbers of companies stayed out of these industry agreements arguing that they constituted a cartel arrangement for maintaining their dominance of the intermediary market. New entrants, it was argued, could only secure business by offering higher commissions since they could not compete with the large well established companies in terms of security, service and stability. Because of these problems, the maximum commissions agreements broke down twice during the late 1970s and early 1980s.

A third strategy was the establishment of a code of conduct which in relation to insurance brokers was given statutory backing. Under the Insurance Brokers (Registration) Act 1977 the use of the description 'insurance broker' was restricted to intermediaries that registered with the Broker's Council and accepted a minimum level of regulation. The fatal flaw of the Act was that individuals could avoid all its restrictions and codes of conduct simply by renaming themselves as financial consultants or advisers. But the British Insurance Association also produced various codes of conduct for company salesforces and intermediaries. In addition a proliferation of quasi-professional bodies established themselves to represent the interests of, and encourage certain standards among, life insurance sales personnel. Apart from the Broker's Council, which failed to capture more than a significant minority of the industry, all these codes of conduct were voluntary and lacked either widespread commitment or detailed monitoring.

By the early 1980s then, regulation within life insurance consisted of a hotch-potch of governmental and self-regulatory procedures of a wide range of institutions, companies and individuals. The result of these attempts to deal with the points of tension was counter-productive in the sense that discursive space for alternative conceptions of the consumer and consumer protection was opened up. In contrast to the past, the industry was now recognising that some form of regulation was necessary but it was unable to agree as a body on its content. Organisations such as the Consumers Association could therefore draw on this and argue that since self-regulation was not working, there should be a more direct form of state intervention.

The State and Regulation of Life Insurance

It is an interesting paradox to note that it was the Conservative government of Margaret Thatcher which was known for its committment to dismantling state intervention that in fact become involved in setting a new regulatory framework for the life insurance industry in the shape of the Financial Services Act 1986.

As the Conservative government sought to encourage wider individual savings, investment and share ownership, it became clear that the existing financial institutions needed changing. One aspect of this process was the attempt to ensure that the financial scandals of the 1970s and early 1980s which had hit the City of London were not repeated (see Moran, 1986; Clarke, 1986; Levi, 1987; Bosworth-Davies, 1988). The government asked Professor Gower, a well-known authority on Consumer Law from London University, to examine the question of Investor Protection. Following the Gower Report and a White Paper on Financial Services, the Financial Services Act was passed in 1986.

Gower decided that all investment services needed to be considered together. To the surprise of some in the insurance industry, he therefore included life insurance and associated products in his analysis. In relation to this area, the Gower Report brought together the emerging alternative definitions of consumers and consumer protection. It rejected the argument of the companies that the matter could be resolved without state intervention but continued to support the view that the system should be essentially self-regulatory and financed by the industry not the taxpayer. Gower focussed on the problems of high-pressure selling and commission-based advice and sought to develop a framework within which these would be strictly controlled. He argued that investment advisers must have a statutory duty of giving best advice to the consumer. This necessitated a clarification of the relationship between agents, companies and consumers. Gower argued that the consumer needed to be clear whether the agent was employed by one company to sell their particular products or whether the agent was in fact independent of all companies and advising the client on products from all relevant companies. Similarly, the consumer needed to be confident that the adviser was not being swayed by commission levels, but was rather making an 'objective' assessment of the client's needs.

The Financial Services Act which developed out of the discussions over the Gower Report essentially maintained these principles. There was to be an over-arching authority – The Securities and Investment Board – for ensuring the industry was following these rules, but because of the complexities involved, there would be more specialist bodies run by industry practitioners and known as self-regulatory organisations (SROs) which would ensure detailed compliance with the Act. Nobody could offer advice on life assurance unless they were registered with an appropriate SRO. Failure to meet the standards of regulation would involve expulsion from SRO membership and thereby effective closure of the business.

It is still early days in terms of assessing how the new regulatory regime is carrying out its task though our research indicates that the insurance companies and distributors are having to make substantial changes in their selling practices (Morgan and Knights, 1989; Knights and Morgan, 1990). In terms of the concerns of this chapter, what is occurring is a reconstitution of markets and a redefinition of consumer protection. No longer are the companies able to speak with one voice about what the consumer 'really' needs. There are now many voices, both within the industry itself and outside in terms of consumer organisations, the financial press, the state and individual consumers themselves.

Thus old relationships of exchange and consumption in life insurance have been undermined during the 1970s and 1980s. The old consensus has crumbled and is hardly likely to re-emerge especially given the breaking down of barriers to competition which have accompanied the new regulatory regime. In this context, consumer protection has become an issue for debate in life insurance.

CONCLUSIONS

In this chapter, we have attempted to document the development of the concept of the consumer and consumer protection within one particular industry – that of life insurance. In doing so, our argument has been that, in the main, it was the life insurance companies and their agents which until recently defined the meaning of being a consumer in the industry. Life insurance practitioners have continually constructed a paternalist view of consumers that emphasises how clients cannot be trusted to act in their own best interests in financial matters. Left to their own devices, it was argued, individuals will follow their baser 'instincts' for immediate, in contrast to deferred, gratification. In the absence of a persuasive yet rational morality generated by life insurance companies and their agents, consumers would always choose to spend rather than save and be prepared to sacrifice the future security of themselves and their families for the present pleasures of life. In short, insurance companies set themselves up as the true guardians of consumers' 'real' interests. The market for life insurance was not a meeting place of equals but a set of social relationships in which the companies exercised their power to define reality for consumers. The presumed morality of life insurance as representing the true interests of the consumer despite the latter's resistance could be utilised to argue that the end (the security of insurance and savings) was sufficiently important to justify the occasional use of dubious selling practices and techniques.

From the 1970s, however, traditional definitions of the consumer and consumer protection have begun to fall apart and it is now possible to see various notions of consumer protection struggling for hegemony in the industry. The companies themselves continue to assert that consumers need life insurance more than they need protecting from the companies. Therefore regulation and disclosure should be kept to a minimum, otherwise the whole industry may be damaged. This perspective is now seriously challenged from a variety of other positions which argue that the consumer is sovereign and must receive adequate information about different policies and commission rates in order to make an informed rational decision. This argument in turn has a variety of proponents. On the one hand are those who subscribe to an individualistic view of market relations and reject any paternalistic role in market decisions whether it be that of the companies or of the state. This view is distinctive from the view of the emerging consumer lobby which asserts that the companies will always be tempted to exert their power over the consumer unfavourably unless there are countervailing consumer organisations capable of fighting back. In this view, collective organisation of consumers is a necessary supplement to individual awareness. Finally, there is the distinctive perspective on consumer protection which is emerging from the institutions of self-regulation which are seeking to bridge the gap between the various arguments. Thus the regulatory bodies simultaneously develop their own perspectives on consumer protection *and* provide the site in which the debates over the appropriate definition of consumer protection take place.

In sum, we have sought to show how the concepts of consumer and consumer protection have been constructed in one particular industry. Whilst acknowledging that life insurance is a distinctive product, the approach adopted in this research has a more general application. It is not sufficient for sociologists to treat the market as a sphere of exchange between equals. Markets are socially constituted in the context of specific social relations which link organisations, the state and consumers. More detailed attention to the way in which markets are constituted would enable us to understand how particular groups are advantaged or disadvantaged by market processes. The rise of ideas about consumer protection is one response to these processes. In the life insurance industry, this response has been significant in reconstructing the market. It would be of value to examine similar processes in other industries. Considerations of this sort potentially give sociology a leverage in public policy debates as well as contributing to a better understanding of the dynamics of modern society. It seems then for both of these reasons that more detailed consideration of the social constitution of markets, consumers and consumer protection is a worthwhile objective.

Notes

The authors wish to acknowledge the financial support of the TSB plc for the research project on which this chapter is based. We also would like to thank our colleagues on the project, Professor David Cooper and Christopher Grey, for their contribution. Finally, thanks are due to Cathie Marsh for providing detailed editorial comments on the original version of the chapter.

1. See for example *Money Which?*, December, 1977; June, 1980; June, 1981; *Which?*, September, 1987; October, 1988; September, 1989; January, 1990 for just a sample of the critical studies of life insurance investment products.

4 Social Class, Consumption Divisions and Housing Mobility

Mike Savage, Paul Watt and Sara Arber

INTRODUCTION

The relationship between the labour market and housing market has emerged in the last decade as an area of considerable research interest (e.g. Thorns, 1982; Hamnett, 1984; Allen and Hamnett, 1990). Although this subject seems initially esoteric and highly specialised, it has important implications for understanding contemporary patterns of social stratification. This paper will examine the relationship between social class position and housing tenure through an analysis of the housing and occupational destinations of 1150 adult children of existing council tenants in Guildford, Surrey. Our aim is to examine the extent to which an individual's housing tenure can be explained in terms of his/her labour market position, and in particular the degree to which social class divisions can be regarded as the primary forces affecting housing tenure destinations.

We proceed by firstly explaining why the study of the relationship between labour and housing markets is important in clarifying the nature of social stratification. Here we argue that concepts of consumption sector cleavages, and the 'underclass', are premised on a particular theorisation of the housing market as being at least partially independent of the labour market. Then we proceed to consider some of the existing research in this area, and note that a number of methodological problems have bedevilled much of it. We then present our research findings, which indicate that labour market divisions remain of prime importance in explaining housing tenure, but that the types of labour market divisions which are significant seem to have changed in the recent past.

THE RELATIONSHIP BETWEEN LABOUR AND HOUSING MARKETS

Conceptual Issues

One of the prime areas of sociological debate in recent years has been that concerning the degree to which the nature of social stratification in contemporary Britain has fundamentally changed. Some writers have argued that the former centrality of class divisions in British society have been replaced by a more complex and fragmented pattern of inequality and division. The growth of an 'underclass' (Dahrendorf, 1987; Pahl 1984), the development of consumption sector cleavages (Dunleavy, 1979; Saunders, 1986), and more generally the rise of 'New Times' (Marxism Today, 1990) is said to herald a more pluralistic politics. On the other hand, other writers have argued that despite the apparent transformation of the social and political landscape in the past decade the underlying patterns of division and inequality remain remarkably intact. Goldthorpe *et al.* (1987) argue that patterns of relative social mobility have been static, Heath *et al.* (1985) suggest that class alignments in politics have been little changed, while Gallie (1988) argues that the considerable movement into and out of unemployment and casual work makes it difficult to identify a distinct underclass. Similarly patterns of racial inequality (Sivananden, 1990) and gender division (McDowell, 1989) remain remarkably persistent.

What is striking about this debate is the way in which the independence of housing-market from labour market processes is often a key starting point for those arguing that class based stratification is of declining significance. By showing that divisions in housing affect people's life chances and that these housing divisions are *not* the simple product of labour market divisions, the conceptual ground has been established which allows the significance of class to be questioned. This is evident in two main substantive debates: one concerning the significance of 'consumption sector cleavages', the other concerning the 'underclass'.

The concept of 'consumption sector cleavage' has arisen largely through the work of Dunleavy (1979), and especially Saunders (1984; 1986; 1990b). Here the argument runs that divisions arising out of the consumption of goods and services – especially, though not exclusively in housing – are becoming more salient in modern Britain. Owner-occupiers are able to make capital gains from owning property (because of house price inflation) while council tenants cannot and are forced to look to the state to subsidise their rents. Hence, these divisions increasingly affect political allegiances – with the Conservative Party being supported by home owners and the Labour Party by council tenants. Clearly, for such an argument, it is important to show that these housing divisions are not the simple reflex, or by-product, of social class. For if they are, then it is not clear that housing tenure divisions are anything more than an accentuation of previously constituted social class divisions.

The second, more specific issue is the debate on the existence of an 'underclass'. This idea, developed in the British context by Dahrendorf (1987), Pahl (1984), and Saunders (1990a; 1990b), argues that class divisions between a 'working' and 'middle' class are being replaced by a rift between a 'middle mass' and an 'underclass' (see the discussion in Gallie, 1988). A crucial point that several writers explicitly state is that the formation of the 'underclass' should be seen not simply as the product of labour-market processes (e.g. long-term unemployment), but also housing-market ones. Both Pahl (1984), and Saunders (1990b) argue that one of the underclass's characteristics is its association with council tenure, though Saunders emphasises that only a minority of council tenants can be regarded as part of the underclass. Related to this is Saunders's argument that the underclass experiences 'multiple deprivations, a culmination of social pathologies and disadvantages' (1990b: 316), and hence 'the position of a stratum such as the underclass is structured by both its labour market situation and its housing situation' (1990b: 323). Hence proponents of the underclass thesis also claim that housing-market processes operate at least partially independently of labour-market ones, and the difficulties of moving out of council tenure help form it as a distinct group.

It is hence clear that the relationship between housing and labour markets is central to an understanding of social stratification. If it is argued that housing divisions are at least partially independent of those in the labour market, then the way is open to arguing that there is a process of stratification which has its very roots in consumption processes, and that class based inequality is of declining social significance, a position argued forcibly by Saunders (1984, 1990b). The creation of an 'underclass' is one example of the way in which divisions created partly by housing market processes cross-cut conventional, social class divisions.

Methodological Issues

Yet despite the theoretical significance of this debate, there are a series of methodological defects in most research in this area. The most common way of examining the relationship between labour and housing markets is by comparison of aggregate statistics, often in an areal context. One particularly well-used statistic is the ratio of owner-occupied house prices to average earnings (e.g. Saunders 1990b: 144–5). More elaborate is the attempt to use local statistics to see how owner-occupied house prices correlate with the state of the local labour market (e.g. Thorns, 1982; Hamnett, 1984; Munro and MacLellan, 1987).

The research here is inconclusive. It would appear that the ratio of house prices to average earnings does tend to return – over time – to a balance of about 2:7 suggesting that the labour market is, at the very least, a constraint on the housing market. The area statistics do not appear to offer any consistent pattern: Thorns (1982) argued that house prices rose fastest in buoyant local labour markets, but this has been shown to be wrong by Munro and MacLellan (1987) in Glasgow – a depressed labour market but booming housing market in the 1980s. Hamnett (1989) also shows that house prices are linked to regional housing markets, hence indicating a degree of autonomy from any particular sub-regional local labour market.

But in all this work there are serious problems, largely concerned with the 'ecological fallacy'. We don't know, from aggregate statistics, just which particular households are moving into what sorts of housing, and with what sorts of costs and gains. Thus, in the Glasgow case, even though there may be a buoyant owner-occupied housing market, we don't know who the people buying this housing, and helping to generate house price inflation, actually are; even in a depressed local economy there will be large numbers of well-off households! We cannot probe the role of inheritance in affecting entry to owner occupation. Nor can we examine factors such as household size, and the number of household earners in facilitating housing destinations.

We would therefore argue that individual household surveys are vital tools to probe the relationship between housing and labour markets. We need evidence of the determinants of individuals' and households' housing careers in order to examine the issues thoroughly. There is some work in this area, but most of it is fragmentary and problematic. Early studies such as Payne and Payne (1977) and Ineichen (1981) used problematic samples (see Savage *et al.*, 1990a for discussion). Forrest and Murie (1987) have interviewed a number of 'affluent homeowners' to see what processes had allowed them to gain entry to privileged housing situations. They found that labour market factors – especially the role of employer's 'perks' – were of major significance. Yet they only interviewed eighteen households, and lacked a group of 'non-affluent homeowners' to compare their findings with.

Saunders (1990b) has recently broken new ground with a larger survey of 450 households in three English towns (Burnley, Slough and Derby), in which housing and work careers are more fully charted. He shows that most homeowners do make capital gains from owner-occupied housing – whatever social class they are drawn from – though he fails to examine repair and maintenance costs in his calculations. This sort of work clearly points the way forward, yet it reveals two problems, evident also in most of the accounts mentioned earlier.

Firstly, the study of the relationship between labour and housing markets is pre-occupied with owner-occupiers. Most research in this area has analysed the degree of house price inflation and capital gains as the key index of housing market divisions. Indeed the housing market is regarded as being synonymous with the owner occupied housing market, which problematises some research in this area. Munro and McLellan (1987), most notably ignore the dominant tenure – council housing – in Glasgow and focus on the experience of owner-occupation alone. In this paper however our focus will be on access to owner-occupation by the adult children of council tenants (see Sullivan, 1989). If Saunders is right in arguing that most owner-occupiers of all social classes are making capital gains from their housing, then this question of initial access to owner-occupation becomes the key issue. If the labour market continues to play a vital role in enabling people to become owner-occupiers then labour-market processes will continue to be the prime movers in social stratification more generally. Similarly, it bears on the underclass issue, since the underclass is partly defined by Pahl and Saunders through its exclusion from owner-occupation.

Secondly, there is inadequate consideration of how labour-market processes relate to social class. In recent years there has been an elaborate debate on how the concept of class can be operationalised in empirical research (Marshall *et al.*, 1988; Duke and Edgell, 1987; Arber *et al.*, 1986), and this shows that it is inadequate to conflate labour-market divisions with social-class divisions. In particular, while every employed individual has a labour-market position, it has been argued that social class can best be seen as related to a household's economic position. It is thus important to consider how different ways of classifying people to social-class positions might affect patterns of association with housing tenure.

Our research therefore attempted to rectify both these problems by examining the housing tenure destinations of the adult children of council tenants. Firstly we examined whether they tended to move into the same tenure as their parents. Secondly we considered how the use of different measures of social class appears to affect the patterns of association between the social class and housing tenure destinations of the children of council tenants. This research provides a fresh look at the debate: if social class appeared to be the main determinant of housing destinations, then our findings would support the idea that housing divisions are largely a by-product of social-class ones. Otherwise, there might be more support for the 'underclass' idea, since council tenure may be inherited inter-generationally, and hence become an axis of social division in its own right.

THE GUILDFORD BOROUGH COUNCIL SURVEY

A representative sample of 1,022 council tenants in the Guildford Borough Council area, Surrey were interviewed. This included the town of Guildford and surrounding villages and small towns. Guildford is not an inner-urban area where one might expect to find a residualised 'underclass'. Nonetheless, as we explain elsewhere (Savage *et al.*, 1990a), the high costs of owner-occupied housing in the area make it a good test, since one might expect that relatively large numbers of council tenants would be excluded from owner-occupation because of the high housing costs (see e.g. Barlow and Savage, 1986 on housing tensions in nearby Berkshire).

A one in six sample of council tenants were interviewed with a response rate of 83.4 per cent in summer 1988 (see Cormell *et al.*, 1989 for more details). Three different sampling fractions were used, for example, to over-represent tenants living on council estates in more rural areas. In this paper the figures have been weighted to provide a representative probability sample of tenants across the Guildford Borough Council area. For the 58 per cent of tenants who were married or living with a partner, equal numbers of men and women were interviewed.

The analysis in this paper is primarily based on the 54 per cent of tenants where one or more children have left home – this represents 1,267 adult children. Since the unit of analysis is adult children who have left home, and generally more than one child of a council tenant has left home, this results in a clustered sample. We collected information on the housing tenure of tenants' children both currently, and in their first accommodation after they left the parental home. We also had information on the current occupations of these children, and, if the children were married women, the occupation of their partners. In a small number of cases, existing council tenants have moved into council tenure relatively recently – after their children left home. Since we need to hold constant the fact that all the children in our sample have been brought up in council tenure, these have been left out of all our analyses – 117 children (9.2 per cent of the total) were omitted, leaving 1150 cases for analysis.

It was also important to consider the circumstances of those adult children still living in the parental home. It might have been the case that those in particularly weak labour-market positions were simply unable to form an independent household themselves. Towards the end of the paper, therefore, we complement our findings by looking at those adult children still living in the parental home.

Social-class was measured using a collapsed version of OPCS Socio-Economic Groups (SEGs) in order to provide similar measures of class to those used in the Nuffield class schema. Goldthorpe *et al.* (1987) have a seven-class schema which is broken down into three classes for many of his analyses: the 'service class' of professionals, managers and administrators; the 'intermediate class' of junior white collar, supervisory, and self-employed workers, and the 'working class'. Heath (1981) argues that although Goldthorpe's seven class schema is useful, it is necessary to distinguish the unskilled working class (which includes the semi-skilled) from the skilled working class, since the former are clearly disadvantaged *vis-à-vis* the latter. Heath's point is important since the significance of the division between the skilled and unskilled working class is particularly important for us in order to probe the 'underclass' issue – the underclass is specified as unskilled workers for the purposes of our analysis.

Three different ways of measuring the units of social-class were examined. Firstly, the 'conventional' approach, associated with Goldthorpe (1983), where the class of all members of a household is based on the occupation of the male head of household. Women's social class is only used when they do not live with a man. Secondly, the 'dominance' approach, where the social class of all household members is determined by the occupation of the partner in the highest social class (Erikson, 1984). Thirdly an 'individualistic' approach, where all individuals are given their own class position on the basis of their own current or most recent occupation. We also experimented with 'household' measurements of class, where the occupations of both partners were combined into a composite class. However, as well as being unwieldy these measures were not especially powerful, and we do not discuss them here.[1]

Before proceeding we need to add a further rider. We are restricted by only having information on the current labour-market position of adult children. Since housing tenure will be critically affected by earlier forms of employment, it is not possible to demonstrate that labour-market position causes mobility into housing tenures. All we can do is point to patterns of association. In order to establish causal relationships, research into the housing and work histories of people would need to be carried out. It should be emphasised that the causal claims we make are conjectures.

PATTERNS OF HOUSING MOBILITY

One of the most striking findings was the remarkably high rate of mobility out of council tenure evident in our survey (see Savage *et al.*, 1990a for further discussion). Table 4.1 shows that only a quarter of the children of council tenants were themselves council tenants. The majority of children of existing council tenants have moved into owner-occupation, a fact which shows that there was little clear social closure taking place around access to owner-occupation; indeed the proportion who were owner-occupiers was very little different from the Guildford average.

Perhaps the housing destinations in our sample are temporary ones, and people will move to other tenures as they grow older? One way of assessing this issue is to consider tenure mobility between their first accommodation on leaving home and their present accommodation. In Table 4.2 we have simplified the tenure categories into four.

Table 4.2 indicates that owner-occupation and council tenure are the two distinct destination tenures, while private renting is mainly a 'transitional' tenure in which individuals live when they leave home (see also Jones, 1987). There is virtually no movement away from owner-occupation and two thirds of people who move initially into

Table 4.1 Housing tenure of children of Guildford BC council tenants who have left their parental home, 1988, and population of Guilford, 1981 (%)

Tenure	*1988 survey*	*1981 census*
Owner-occupation	61.5	60.0
Council tenure	24.2	24.4
Private rented – furnished	4.2	4.8
Private rented – unfurnished	3.7	6.1
Tied accommodation	3.7	4.7
Housing association	1.4	
Mobile home	0.7	
Other	0.5	
	100.0	100.0
Number in survey	**1,006**	

Source: 1988 GBC survey and 1981 census
Notes: 'Don't knows' excluded.
This table is similar to Table 5 in Savage *et al.* 1990a, but has been slightly differently calculated. See Savage *et al.*, 1990c for further details.

Table 4.2 Mobility between first tenure after leaving parental home and current tenure of children of council tenants (%)

			First Tenure		
Current tenure	*Owners*	*Council*	*Private*	*Others*	*All*
Owners	95	28	57	43	61
Council	2	68	20	22	24
Private	1	3	18	5	8
Other	1	1	5	30	7
All	31	19	36	15	100
Number of individuals	**314**	**194**	**372**	**150**	**1030**

Source: 1988 GBC survey
Note: Private means private rented, both furnished and unfurnished, whilst all other tenures are grouped as 'other'.

council tenure have remained within it. The 'Right To Buy' legislation of 1980 probably explains a significant proportion of the 28 per cent who have moved into owner-occupation; a comparison with Robson's examination of housing mobility patterns in the 1950s (1975), shows that the proportion of people moving from council tenure to owner-occupation has increased substantially.

Table 4.2 indicates that the children of council tenants tended to end up in either council tenure or (especially) owner-occupation. The other tenures were important as points of entry into the housing market, but were less significant as long-term 'housing destinations'. For this reason many of our subsequent analyses will focus on the specific issue of how labour-market position affected the prospects of being in owner-occupation rather than council tenure, and we will say little about mobility into other tenures.

The overall picture is clear: despite high owner-occupied housing costs, the children of council tenants as a whole were not an underclass who are prevented from moving into other forms of tenure by their tenure background. Saunders (1990b) does not of course make such a grand claim. He points out that only a minority of council tenants might be considered as part of the underclass, though he argues that the proportion is increasing. We therefore need to consider the social characteristics of the adult children concerned to see how they affect their housing tenure destinations. We turn to this in the next section.

SOCIAL-CLASS MEASURES AND HOUSING TENURE DESTINATIONS

We have discussed our three ways of operationalising social-class above. Table 4.3 shows that the use of different class measures is not a trivial matter, since the apparent size of social-classes vary considerably according to the procedure used. If the unit of class analysis is the individual, then over half the sample are working class (skilled and unskilled manual workers). On the other hand if the children are assigned to class on the basis of the occupationally dominant member of the household, then only 38 per cent are working class. What is more interesting is that there are significant differences according to whether a 'conventional' or 'dominance' approach is adopted. If a 'conventional' approach is used then the sample contained a high proportion of working class people, largely because of the relatively large numbers of men in skilled manual work. On the other hand, if the 'dominance' approach is used, the sample appeared significantly more middle-class, because of the relatively large numbers of women in the intermediate class.

Table 4.3 Different measures of social class of children of council tenants who have left parental home (row %)

Class measure	*Service*	[*Socio-Economic Group*] *Intermediate*	*Skilled*	*Unskilled*	*Number of individuals*
Adult sons					
Individual	17.7	25.0	38.7	18.5	**490**
Conventional	17.7	25.0	38.7	18.5	**490**
Adult daughters					
Individual	13.7	39.6	3.4	43.3	**487**
Conventional	16.8	29.1	33.4	20.7	**487**
Dominance	23.0	39.0	20.5	17.6	**434**
All children					
Individual	15.8	31.9	22.2	30.1	**927**
Conventional	17.3	27.0	36.1	19.6	**978**

Source: 1988 GBC survey.
Notes: The 'dominance' measure can only be calculated for daughters, since only information on the occupation of the husband's of women respondents was collected.
Social-class measures used are explained on pages 58–9.
Service class: SEGs 1, 2, 3, 4; intermediate class: SEGs 5, 6, 8, 12; skilled working class: SEG 9; unskilled working class: SEGs 7, 10, 11, 14.

How do these class measures correlate with housing tenure destinations? Table 4.4 is complex, but shows that whatever measure of class is used there was a very strong association with housing tenure destinations. The first column allocates every individual to their own class position based on their own occupation. Of individuals in service-class occupations, 85 per cent were in owner-occupation, compared with only 42 per cent of individuals with unskilled manual working-class occupations.

The main difference between class measures is that an 'individualistic' measure finds more people from unskilled manual occupations in owner-occupation than other measures. These are probably women in unskilled jobs whose husbands may be in higher class jobs. A measure based on the occupationally dominant partner shows the highest proportion of the unskilled in council tenure. But, for the higher classes there is relatively little differences in the proportions in owner-occupation, whatever measure of class is used.[2]

Table 4.4 Children in social classes in owner occupation and council tenure, by alternative definitions of social class (column %)

Social classes	*Method of classifying people to classes* Individuals	Conventional	Dominance
Service			
In owner-occupation	85	88	87
In council tenure	7	5	6
Number of individuals	**145**	**167**	**112**
Intermediate			
In owner-occupation	74	71	75
In council tenure	10	13	15
Number of individuals	**287**	**256**	**185**
Skilled manual			
In owner-occupation	64	65	57
In council tenure	21	24	38
Number of individuals	**199**	**345**	**99**
Unskilled manual			
In owner-occupation	42	29	24
In council tenure	44	51	63
Number of individuals	**273**	**196**	**86**

Source: 1988 GBC survey
Notes: Percentages do not add up to 100 since balances are in other tenures. See pages 58–9 for discussion of class measures.

Table 4.4 indicates that a majority of all classes except the unskilled lived in owner-occupation, however class is measured. This is not surprising amongst the service class and intermediate classes, but it is noteworthy that almost two-thirds of skilled manual workers also lived in owner-occupation. There is support here for Pahl's and Saunders's views about the growth of an owner-occupied 'middle mass' which includes substantial parts of the working class. It is only amongst semi-skilled and unskilled manual workers that more people lived in council renting than in owner-occupation.

Ultimately then, it seems that in terms of explaining housing tenure destinations measures of class based on the occupationally dominant partner reveals slightly stronger associations between tenure and class than one based on the male head of house alone. Another way of probing the significance of household composition for access to owner-occupation is to look at the housing tenure of single people (including divorced, separated and widowed). By comparing it with the housing tenure of married couples in the same social-classes, it becomes possible to see if there are any systematic differences. The difficulty with this comparison is of course that single people tend to be younger. However, this problem is not overwhelming since we are concentrating on the final tenures of owner-occupation and council tenure rather than the transitional tenures.

Analysis of the 148 children who are not married shows that service-class individuals are extremely likely to be in owner-occupation (82 per cent of the sample, a proportion little different from other service class households). However, for non-married children in other classes, the proportion who are owner-occupiers is considerably less than for married couples (50 per cent for the intermediate class; 41 per cent for the skilled manual workers; 18 per cent for the unskilled). Further analysis also shows that single service-class and intermediate-class women are more likely to be owner-occupiers than equivalent men. Ninety per cent of single service class women are owner-occupiers.

What this appears to show is that the importance of household composition in facilitating entry into owner-occupation varies by class. For the service class, level of income is sufficient to ensure owner-occupation regardless of the class of partner, or whether they have a partner. The single can still afford to move into owner-occupation. For intermediate or skilled manual classes, there are good chances of becoming an owner-occupier, but it helps if they are married. Married members of these classes are considerably more likely to be owner-occupiers than non-married members. But male unskilled workers are unlikely to earn enough to enter owner-occupation, even if their wives are in a reasonably high class.

To summarise this section we would emphasise two different points. On the one hand it is clear that labour-market position is the key factor distinguishing those households who move into owner-occupation from those who do not, yet it is also true that most households in most social-class positions – except unskilled manual workers – move into owner-occupation. The choice of emphasis depends on whether we are more impressed by relative or absolute patterns of mobility, and there are remarkable parallels with debates concerning the extent of social mobility in modern Britain. Those writers arguing that there is high social mobility (Payne, 1987a; this volume; Saunders, 1990a) focus on absolute rates of mobility between social-classes, whilst those who are more impressed by inequality of opportunity (Goldthorpe *et al.*, 1987) focus on relative rates of mobility. It is partly a matter of choice as to whether the high numbers of absolute numbers moving into owner-occupation is more significant than the relative disadvantages of the unskilled workers moving into owner-occupation compared with the other classes.

As regards measures of class, it seems clear that those based on the occupationally dominant partner provide a somewhat more powerful predictor of housing tenure. We would however argue that the relative significance of class measures varies itself by class. For the service class and the unskilled manual working class, an individual measure of class is as powerful as a household one, and it is amongst the intermediate and skilled manual working class that the employment of both partners is likely to be of crucial importance in affecting housing tenure.

CHANGES OVER TIME

One crucial theoretical question, however, is whether the relationship between labour-market position and housing tenure is becoming closer over time. Saunders (1986; 1990b) argues that it is becoming less close as more people gain access to owner-occupation, and as privatised consumption is allowing consumption location to be a more important axis of social stratification. Change over time is also important for allowing us to consider the 'underclass' issue. If this group is becoming more significant in the 1990s, then it is to be expected that the association between unskilled manual work and council tenure will have increased.The relationship of class and housing tenure over time is examined using the class of the occupationally dominant partner for three age groups in our sample. We decided to use this measure rather than one based on male head of house since we have argued that it is a more powerful correlate of housing destinations, and because it is more theoretically meaningful.

Table 4.5 Children living in owner-occupation and council tenure, by social class and age group (%)

Social class	*Under 31*	*Age group* *31–40*	*Over 40*
Service			
In owner occupation	55	93	96
In council tenure	21	3	1
Number of individuals	**19**	**51**	**41**
Intermediate			
In owner occupation	51	83	87
In council tenure	38	12	10
Number of individuals	**57**	**59**	**69**
Skilled manual			
In owner occupation	47	61	63
In council tenure	38	39	37
Number of individuals	**31**	**42**	**25**
Unskilled manual			
In owner occupation	13	24	44
In council tenure	64	70	56
Number of individuals	**42**	**19**	**23**

Source: 1988 GBC survey
Notes: Social class defined by the occupational class of the partner in the highest social class where respondent living with a husband.
Percentages do not add up to 100 since the balances are in other tenures.
For definitions of classes, see pages 58–9.

Table 4.5 is difficult to interpret because age effects, cohort effects and time effects are mixed together. It is striking that around one half of members of the service class, intermediate class, and skilled manual working class were owner-occupiers by the time they were 30 years old. The big division for this age group was hence between the unskilled working class and other classes. For the 31–40 age group there was a more gradual gradient. The vast majority of the service class are owner-occupiers, and the intermediate and skilled manual classes lagged behind somewhat. Once again the unskilled manual workers stand out as being especially unlikely to be in owner-occupation.

For the oldest age group there were similar proportions of the service class, intermediate and skilled manual classes in owner-occupation, but a significant number of the unskilled manual workers over the age of 40 were in owner occupation compared with those in their thirties. The skilled manual workers were also closer to the unskilled manual workers than to the service class. For children of council tenants aged over 40, housing tenure was related strongly to class divisions. The service class were far more likely to be in owner-occupation rather than council tenure compared to other social classes, and there were relatively small differences between skilled and unskilled manual workers.

The problem is that it is not clear whether the changes between age groups reflect the age of the children or the time of entry to the housing market. The relative similarity in the housing tenure destinations of service class, intermediate class and skilled manual workers in the youngest age group might reflect the fact that earnings for skilled manual workers peak in their twenties, whilst the service class peak much later. But equally, it might be consistent with changes in the basis of housing provision in line with Hamnett's (1984) arguments about socio-tenurial polarisation, where it is argued that council tenure is increasingly becoming a 'residualised' form of housing. Certainly the crucial point is that the main axis of polarisation for younger children is not between the service class and other social classes, or the manual working class and other classes, *but between the unskilled working class and the rest*. This is compatible with the idea that the unskilled working class's housing tenure is becoming increasingly differentiated from other social classes as they become confined to council tenure.

ADULT CHILDREN IN THE PARENTAL HOME

Our analysis so far has examined the social-class and housing tenure of those children who grew up in council housing and have left the parental home. It might be objected that this omits the crucial question of the numbers and social-class of those adult children who still live in the adult home. There was indeed considerable concern about the extent to which high housing costs for owner-occupied and private rented housing, combined with a scarcity of council accommodation was causing a problem of 'hidden homelessness' in Guildford, and through much of the Southeast (GBC, 1987). It might also be the group of children still in the parental home who have an especially weak labour-market position. Table 4.6 tests these ideas by comparing the ages and social-class of children living in the parental home with those who have left it.

Table 4.6 Children of council tenants in social classes, broken down by age group, and residence in the parental home (%)

	Age group			
(*a*) *Living in parental home*	*20–25*	*26–30*	*31–4-*	*41+*
Service class	14	–	7	6
Intermediate	24	38	41	33
Skilled manual	20	30	22	33
Unskilled manual	43	32	30	27
Number of individuals	**74**	**37**	**27**	**18**
(*b*) *Not living in parental home*				
Service class	9	13	18	18
Intermediate	32	28	32	33
Skilled manual	19	25	24	21
Unskilled manual	40	34	26	29
Number of individuals	**104**	**127**	**359**	**311**
(a) as % of total	42	23	7	5

Source: 1988 GBC survey.
Notes: Social class for those living in parental home based on an individualistic measure in order to allow comparability with those not living in parental home.

Table 4.6 indicates that a high proportion of children in their twenties continue to live with their parents: 42 per cent of those aged between 20 and 25, and 23 per cent of those between 26 and 30. There is, however, remarkably little relationship between whether a child is at home or not, and their social-class position. The only slight exception to this is that there are fewer service class children living in the parental home for the age groups of 25 plus. There is no evidence of a concentration of unskilled manual workers amongst those living at home, and it seems that older children staying at home are more likely to do so for individual, familial or personal reasons, than because of labour-market constraints. Hence, we must conclude that the high percentage of adult children of council tenants in owner-occupation is not because those unable to gain access to owner-occupation are still living in the parental home.

CONCLUSIONS

Our findings are in one sense consistent with the arguments developed by Pahl and Saunders. Most children who are not unskilled workers moved into owner-occupation, and hence council tenure does appear to be becoming increasingly confined to those in unskilled, marginal employment (see also Hamnett, 1984). Most of those gainfully employed, even though they have been brought up in council housing and hence have probably not been able to use financial support from their parents or from inheritance windfalls, have become owner-occupiers, even given the high cost of housing in the Guildford area. In this respect housing tenure destinations do cross-cut established class divisions.

Yet in another sense our findings go against the ideas developed by Saunders. Saunders argues that housing tenure is an increasingly important social division, and that 'the tenure gap is...becoming increasingly difficult to cross' (1990b: 336), and that as a result, the growing division between the 'middle mass' and the 'underclass' 'is reproduced through tenure based inequalities' (1990b: 369). Yet it is clear from our survey that tenure is not an axis of social closure in the way Saunders suggests. The children of our sample of council tenants have moved into owner-occupation in very high numbers. The only evidence one might use to suggest that tenure is itself an axis of division, is to point to the significant numbers of young service class and intermediate class who are in council tenure (see Table 4.5), but even here, no doubt many will move into owner-occupation at a later stage.

Saunders' argument is actually contradictory. At times he speaks as a political advocate of owner-occupation, at other times as a social scientist commenting on the social impact of owner-occupation. In his former guise he is keen to argue that owner-occupation is not an axis of social closure, and that anyone can move into owner-occupation and hence gain the benefits it is supposed to convey (e.g. Saunders, 1990b: Chap. 3). In his latter guise, however, he argues that tenure is a growing social cleavage, and that council tenants and owner-occupiers are becoming increasingly divided. In arguing the former case, high degrees of housing mobility are grist to Saunders' mill, but in proposing the latter, high degrees of housing immobility would need to be demonstrated in order to show that tenure itself was an axis of social closure. Saunders cannot have his cake and eat it!

Our survey shows firmly that housing tenure destinations appear to be largely the product of the labour market, and social-class position.

We fully endorse Forrest and Murie's claim that 'divisions in consumption are significant, and notably in housing, but the analytical starting point must be labour-market and economic restructuring' (1986: 49). It is very difficult to see how the housing market is a contributory factor in producing social divisions.

As a result, whilst we agree that council tenure is increasingly becoming residualised, the causes of this appear to be related to the structure of employment opportunities. The unskilled are likely to live in council tenure, while the other social classes are more likely to live in owner-occupation. Rather than testifying to the rise of 'consumption sector cleavages' however, in which housing tenure itself becomes an axis of social division, our findings could quite easily be explained in terms of intensifying labour-market divisions – say between a core and peripheral workforce, or even just the latest manifestation of the continued division between skilled and unskilled workers within the British working class.

Notes

Thanks to Guildford Borough Council for allowing us to use the results of the survey they commissioned, and to Simon Duncan, Chris Hamnett and Cathie Marsh for comments on earlier drafts. This chaper is a much shortened version of Savage *et al.* (1990c), copies of which are available on request from Mike Savage.

1. Further details of this are reported in Savage *et al.* (1990c).
2. This argument is elaborated in Savage *et al.* (1990c).

5 Medicine and Markets: Power, Choice and the Consumption of Private Medical Care

Joan Busfield

INTRODUCTION

The recent sociological attention to consumption is undoubtedly a reflection of the continuing power and pervasiveness of the Tory ideology of the market and the emphasis given to the 'consumer society'. It is in the context of this political concern with consumption that writers like Peter Saunders (1986; see also Dunleavy, 1979; Dunleavy and Husbands, 1985), who is himself critical of what he sees as the biases of other sociologists, have developed the argument that divisions associated with consumption have replaced divisions generated by production as the key dimensions of stratification within present-day society. A more detailed examination shows that, in this country at least, the consumption of medical care does not fit this analysis at all well. This is because, put simply, most people consume – or more neutrally use – both private and public medical care (Busfield, 1990).[1] Consequently, it is not possible to identify any clear sectoral divide between public and private consumers, even though there is a marked division between the private and public sectors in the production of medical care – a division that is the usual basis of the distinction between private and state medicine (however, the interpenetration of these two sectors is now greater than formerly (Busfield, 1990: 82–3)). Instead there is a continuum of consumers ranging from those who rely exclusively on state services to those who never do so (a point about which we can only be certain at death). Most people consume both private and public medicine.

However, although a detailed analysis of the consumption of medical care provides little support for Saunders' claims about sectoral divisions in consumption, a number of interesting and important questions remain about the consumption of medical care. These are questions that the current focus on consumption, for all its ideological and political gloss, encourages us to examine – and which, indeed need to be examined if that ideology is to be challenged. A major issue concerns what is commonly called consumer sovereignty, that is, the domination and power of consumers in the market (see also Morgan and Knights, this volume).[2] What are the powers of individuals when they use private medicine? Do individuals as consumers of private medicine have more power and more choice than they do as consumers of state medicine? Are the powers of individuals when they obtain private medicine sufficient to counterbalance the powers of producers? Are their rights adequately protected in law? We cannot and should not expect absolute, fixed answers to such questions. Consumers' power in both the private and public sectors depends on the precise nature of the arrangements governing private and public provision. It is important, therefore, to examine the organisation and character of private medicine in specific historical contexts. This paper analyses private medicine in Britain at the beginning of the 1990s.

Underlying the questions listed above are ideal–typical models of the private and public provision of goods and services constructed by liberal theorists. These models, which stand in an oppositional relation, not only structure the questions themselves, but also generate a standard set of answers, serving as an ideological prism through which the reality of private and state provision are interpreted and assessed. They suggest that individuals as consumers of privately produced goods and services have more power and are generally favoured over individuals as consumers of publicly produced goods (see Hayek, 1944; Friedman, 1962; Harris and Seldon, 1977; 1979). On the one hand there is the model of the free market constructed by libertarian thinkers (see Hindess, 1987a). This model assumes that the consumer's advantages in terms of power, control, choice, price and so forth, are maximised in the private market. On the other hand there is the free marketeers' model of state provision in which the consumer of state services is seen as powerless and dependent, lacking in choice, and the recipient of care that could be supplied more cheaply and efficiently in the private sector. However, the politically constructed model of the free market does not fit the reality of private medicine in Britain at all satisfactorily and the continuing assumption of its salience and validity distorts the assessments which are frequently made both of private and of state medicine and of the powers of consumers within them. Liberal thinkers deal not with the reality of private and public medicine but with idealised and mystifying constructions. We need, however, to examine the models in more detail.

THE LIBERAL MODELS

Markets

The characteristics of the free-market model, so beloved of liberal thinkers, are well known and have been made familiar in the post-war period through the writings of authors such as Freidrich Hayek (1944), Milton Friedman (1962) and Ralph Harris and Arthur Seldon (1977). The model assumes that producers are free to supply goods on the market and that the price they obtain is a function both of the level of supply of the goods in question and the demand for them. In a free market, if the demand for a particular good increases so does its price, since demand outstrips supply. However, as prices increase, more suppliers come into the market, production is raised, and with increases in supply, prices begin to fall. It is this competitive market, in which supply can and does increase to meet demand, that helps to keep prices down and is held to ensure that the market provides the most effective and efficient means of meeting consumer preferences – preferences which are themselves assumed to reflect individual needs. As a result, as long as there is free competition, producers' pursuit of self-interest, which is recognised to be an important feature of the market, does not conflict with, but actually furthers, the public good. Harris and Seldon outline the way the interests of producers and consumers, which potentially stand in conflict, are reconciled:

> both buyers and sellers must gain from trading on price and other terms which they freely choose to accept. The prevalence of competition reconciles what might otherwise be the opposing interests of suppliers (in high prices) and consumers (in low prices) by creating a common interest in doing business at the ruling market price. The competitive process is not, in the jargon, a 'zero-sum game' in which some gain only at the expense of others. It is a social mechanism that converts potentially conflicting interests into 'mutual gains from trade' (Harris and Seldon, 1977:5).

Consequently the pursuit of profit and the possibilities of consumer exploitation are counterbalanced by the power of consumers – power that comes from the fact that it is their preferences which generate the demand suppliers seek to satisfy. It is consumers who are free to choose the goods or services they want at the quality and price they choose: competition prevents the abuse of the powerful producer.

State Provision

The model of state provision derived from liberal principles can also be readily characterised. Here the absence of a market is assumed to mean that the price at which goods are supplied is no longer subject to the discipline of the market; as a result, production is less efficient and more costly and suppliers have little incentive to provide the range of choice the free market offers. Individual consumers are, therefore, faced with goods and services that are less efficiently produced and are denied much in the way of choice over what they consume. Consequently consumers in the state sector are held to be relatively passive and powerless, unable to ensure their wants and preferences, or indeed their needs, are met. The state determines what goods and services should be supplied and inefficiencies arise because the supply of goods is not determined by demand and because there is no pressure to supply at the cheapest price for a given quality. It is the state, not the consumers, who are sovereign. The state is assumed to be insensitive to needs, bureaucratic and inefficient. It is all powerful, varyingly characterised as the autocratic, paternal father or the all powerful 'nanny' to the dependent child. Friedman tendentiously contrasts the 'voluntary cooperation' of the market place with the 'use of coercion' under the central direction of 'the modern totalitarian state' (1962:13). Harris and Seldon see state welfare services as 'taxing away so much of the income of most families that they are reduced to dependence on state services, whether satisfied with them or not' (1979:74). Saunders comments 'the state is in a position to restrict consumer power and maximise the power of producers. The reason for this is that it enjoys unparalleled powers of monopoly and physical coercion' (Saunders and Harris, 1990: 63). The major problem for consumers is that they 'lack the ability or the right to "exit" from the relationship' (ibid). According to such authors the proper role of the state is to provide the necessary conditions for market activity, beyond that its role must be kept to a minimum.

Social scientists have frequently noted that the ideal–typical market model does not correspond at all precisely to the reality of the medical provision in either the private or public sectors (see Le Grand and Robinson, 1984: Chap. 2) and that there are major market imperfections. Nonetheless the power and influence of liberal theorising is such that, notwithstanding the known departures from the model, it is continually assumed that, at least on matters concerning the power and choice of individual consumers, if not on the question of access, private medicine is superior to state medicine. The actual way in which medicine is organised in the private sector is ignored and the validity and salience of the ideal–typical model is presupposed. Yet careful examination shows little sign of the liberal theorists much vaunted consumer sovereignty in the private sector; power and choice are limited, arguably even more limited than in the public sector. This can be seen by an examination of the nature and character of private medicine in two areas: professional power and corporate power (issues of access, equity and social justice require separate consideration).

PROFESSIONAL POWER AND THE MARKET IN MEDICINE

If we accept, for the moment, that the market in private medicine consists of a set of individual producers, then the first and most widely noted point of departure from the market model is that the main producers of medical care – the official or orthodox healers – have a partial monopoly over healing. Entry into the medical market is regulated and only individuals with specific qualifications who become registered practitioners are free to offer certain medical services and to hold certain appointments. This regulation is integral to the notion of medicine as a profession – a body of persons with specialist skills and expertise not shared by others – and is supported by both state and profession (Friedson, 1970). At present the state gives powers to the profession to set the necessary standards for entry and may also directly limit the number of new entrants by imposing quotas on medical schools. It also gives the profession a considerable degree of clinical autonomy.

Registered practitioners' monopoly over the market in healing is by no means complete. There are a range of unorthodox healers offering services in the market and 'the law does not forbid in general terms the practice of medicine or surgery by unqualified persons' (*Halsbury's Laws of England*, 1980, Vol. 30: 10). However, in order to protect and strengthen their activity, these groups of alternative practitioners also often try to regulate those who practise in their name, so that though they compete with orthodox practitioners they may secure a partial monopoly over their own type of healing. Moreover, the competition they provide is limited since, as I have indicated, official practitioners have secured important monopoly powers such as those over prescribing certain drugs, holding certain hospital appointments, providing certain certificates, and so forth (Carr-Saunders and Wilson, 1933). The access of non-orthodox practitioners to National Health Service provision is particularly limited; however, even in the private sector qualified practitioners have very significant monopoly powers. Indeed the very idea of a profession derives much of its meaning in opposition to that of 'trade' or 'business' – the very trade the free-market model presumes.

The profession's main justification for its partial monopoly is that a completely free market in medicine does not and cannot ensure that consumers receive the best services at the lowest price. Three reasons are given. First, that medicine requires a high level of expertise and those without this essential expertise should not be free to provide services if standards of medical care are to be maintained. Second, since the relation between treatment and prognosis is often difficult to establish, consumers are usually in a poor position to assess the quality of medical care they receive. Consequently consumer choice is of little value since it does not provide an effective mechanism for ensuring high standards of service. In an unregulated market, far from being sovereign, consumers are readily exploited. Third, an unfettered trade in medicine provides direct incentives for healers to exploit patients in pursuit of profit. In contrast, professional regulation and training help to ensure the altruistic motivations and high ethical and clinical standards which are considered the *sine qua non* of proper professional practice (see Johnson, 1972:13). From this point of view, self-interest and the search for profit, which are at the core of the free market and of activities categorised as trades, are antithetical to the maintenance of high standards and diminish rather than enhance consumer power.

In fact, the medical profession's frequent opposition to a free trade in healing is qualified and does not extend to competition between professionals. The profession has been a strong defender of private medicine – that is, of the existence of a competitive market amongst medical professionals – as long as it is restricted to properly qualified practitioners. Its opposition has not, therefore, been to market principles *per se* but to unrestricted access to the healing market. However, in the face of the latest (1990) reforms of the NHS quite a high proportion of doctors in Britain are emerging as strong defenders of state medicine.[3]

Critics of the medical profession, including a range of sociological writers, have emphasised the power doctors exercise over patients and have seen medicine's opposition to a free trade in healing as much more to do with the profession's attempt to secure and enhance its own power, status and material interests than with the protection of patients' interests (Friedson, 1970; Parkin, 1979). Professional regulation has been considered an exclusionary tactic that allows doctors to keep their prices and incomes high rather than exposing them to the rigours of the market. And, in their criticism of the profession's exclusionary tactics, and their emphasis on the patient's dependence on practitioners, these critics have seemed to ally themselves with defenders of the free market (see Illich, 1977). According to market ideology such protective practices are undesirable, and although no frontal challenge has been made to them by the government in the way that solicitors' monopoly over conveyancing has now been formally removed, certain medical monopolies are being chipped away. For example, the government has increased the rights of pharmacists to give medical advice and has accepted in part the case for 'nurse practitioners' with limited powers of prescribing (*Promoting Better Health*, 1987:37, 41–2).

However, the polarisation implicit here between professional monopolies and free markets, the one ensuring medical power and status, the other consumer sovereignty and the realisation of patients' interests is false. We can accept that practitioners' claims about the dangers of patient exploitation in an unregulated market are valid, even if the solution is not to give unfettered powers to the profession itself. Medical power can be limited by other means than by free competition.[4] On the one hand, as we shall see, the corporate production of medical care may limit professional power, although historically this has not happened to any great extent. On the other hand, the state can play an important role in controlling medical power. In Britain such controls have been uneven, but have been particularly extensive in the area of price, with doctors generally earning less in the NHS than in the private sector, usually by virtue of a shift away from fee-for-service medicine.[5] Direct control over other matters, such as the nature and standards of medical work, has been more limited, though there are examples of the state encouraging particular types of medical work (as in recent incentives for preventive medicine (see Flynn, this volume).[6] In addition there are important mechanisms of local accountability, such as that through the Community Health Councils which provide a collective public voice for NHS consumers. The powers of such bodies may not be very extensive, but there is no equivalent representative body in the private sector.[7] To imply that just because the NHS does not always control professional powers effectively the private sector necessarily does better is surely mistaken (Saunders and Harris, 1990: 64).[8]

The medical profession's case for regulation of the market in healing is strong. The precise boundaries can be contested as can the freedom that should be given to the profession to control its own activities. So too can the profession's success in maintaining high clinical standards. However, examination of the issue of the profession's monopoly powers does not provide an argument for increasing competition by allowing healers who are neither qualified nor registered to practice. Rather it highlights the irrelevance of the market model to the organisation of medical care in the private as well as the public sector. There neither is nor should be a free market in medicine.

CORPORATE POWER

The ideal–typical market model assumes a set of individual producers standing in a direct relation to a set of individual consumers. It largely ignores the complexity and diversity of the processes of production and consumption (Warde, 1990a; 1990b; this volume) (including production and consumption within the home). In so doing it fails to examine the differing types of producers and the differing types of consumers in existing markets. In particular it ignores the role of private corporations in both production and consumption, as well as in mediating the relations between producers and consumers. These three corporate activities are now examined in turn.

Corporate Production

When the market model is applied to medicine it tends to be assumed that individual doctors are the producers, so that even though professional practitioners have a partial monopoly, the existence of a large number of individual practitioners still generates a fair degree of competition. However the reality is more complex. One complexity derives from the fact that doctors themselves may not own the physical plant and equipment necessary to their practice. This is especially true of hospital medicine, where ownership in the private sector is in the hands of either charitable bodies or commercial groups. Consequently, doctors' relation to patients is mediated via these corporations, whose potential powers are considerable. In Britain at present a relatively small number of corporations control quite a high percentage of the market, so that competition is reduced and the corporations' powers are considerable. In theory, of course, private patients seek treatment from individual doctors and the hospital merely provides the location and equipment that enable treatment to be carried out. However, patients also consume hospital facilities and are affected by the hospital's relation to the immediate producers of health care, the medical practitioners. They are also affected by the degree of competition in the hospital market.

During the 1980s the private hospital market became increasingly dominated by commercial companies seeking to profit from an expanding market and the once pre-eminent charitable groups declined in significance. In 1979 commercial companies had 28.5 per cent of the private market; by 1989 they had 56 per cent (Independent Hospitals Association, 1989:5). Interestingly the share of American companies, who played an important part in the expansion of the commercial sector at the end of the 1970s, has declined.[9] The commercial sector is currently dominated by three companies. The key British company is BUPA Hospitals, a commercial wing of the British United Provident Association (BUPA) which was set up in 1978.[10] In July, 1989 it purchased ten hospitals from the Hospital Corporation of America, giving a total of 27 hospitals and around 1,500 beds, and making it the largest private hospital owner in Britain with about 14 per cent of the market measured both by hospitals and beds (Independent Hospitals Association, 1989). Since BUPA is also the major company in the medical insurance market, the Office of Fair Trading was worried at the impact of this vertical integration on BUPA's buying power (Guardian, 12.11.89.) and the purchase was referred to the Monopolies and Mergers Commission. However in March, 1990 the Commission cleared the takeover.

The other major British company is Nuffield Hospitals, an earlier progeny of BUPA. It was originally set up as a charitable trust in 1957 on BUPA's initiative with the explicit objective of ensuring the survival of private hospitals and nursing homes threatened with closure. It began to build new hospitals almost immediately and at the end of 1989 its market share was close to that of BUPA Hospitals (it had more hospitals but fewer beds). For much of its life it was given some financial support by the parent company in the form of preferential loans and covenants and there was some cross-board membership (Monopolies and Mergers Commission, 1990: 28–9). However, with the establishment of BUPA Hospitals quite fierce competition developed between the two hospital groups and the close supportive relation with BUPA disappeared. The third major owner is AMI Healthcare. This is largely owned by American Medical International who have been looking for a buyer for its two-thirds holding. Together these three companies had nearly two-fifths of the hospital market in Britain in 1989 (Independent Hospitals Association, 1989). This percentage does not indicate a very high degree of market concentration. Nonetheless it represents a significant departure from the ideal–typical model of individual practitioners freely competing with one another. It gives a small number of hospital corporations considerable power to shape the market in private health care, thereby reducing consumer sovereignty, most obviously by definite restrictions on the type of care they offer – namely, cold, elective surgery, whose timing can be chosen but which is generally low cost and easier to provide (Nicholl *et al.*, 1989). Private sector medical provision is far less comprehensive than state provision, offering only a limited choice of services to the consumer.

There is a further point. Given the capital intensive nature of hospital provision, private hospitals, though typically smaller than state hospitals, are generally rather thinly distributed (with the exception of the major conurbations, particularly London) (Griffith and Rayner, 1985). Consequently there is often only one possible private hospital available to a patient, since even in the private sector most people use hospitals within 15–20 miles of their homes (Monopolies and Mergers Commission, 1990:15). The majority have, therefore, little choice over which private hospital to use, and in that respect have no more choice of hospital than those using state hospitals (in whose vicinity private hospitals are often found). The famed 'right of exit', supposedly a major feature of the market, may in practice be non-existent.

Nor is there much evidence that private hospital corporations exercise much power and control via corporate patronage (Johnson, 1972) over the professionals working within them to the benefit of patients. Such power could be used to keep medical fees down and enhance the quality of services. In practice, however, doctors, by retaining their formal independence and avoiding employee status, have not been subservient to the corporations, who have been very dependent on them for the success of their ventures and have often included them as board members. Consequently the corporate production of hospital care has not historically served to constrain professional power, yet it limits the power and choice of consumers.[11]

Corporate Consumption

In the market model individual consumers with wants and preferences choose between a range of goods and services on sale at particular prices. Individual choice is central to the model and to claims as to its superiority; the market is assumed to enhance individual choice as well as the efficiency of suppliers, and to keep prices down to the benefit of individual consumers. However, a key feature of the present market in private medicine is that just over half of those insured for hospital treatment (who account for something like four-fifths of private consumers of health care (Nicholl *et al.* 1989:241)) are covered by a company scheme and not as a result of individually purchased insurance.[12] The rest are covered either through individual policies or group schemes in which some organisation, such as a company or a trade union, secures special rates for group members – a collective discount. In group schemes, however, it is the individual who chooses to become a subscriber; in company schemes it is the company that chooses the insurance for its employees, and it is the company not the individual who is the consumer. What we have is not individual but corporate consumption.

A major part of the post-war expansion in private medical insurance has occurred through the development and marketing of company schemes. In 1977 individual subscribers constituted some 43 per cent of all subscribers and company purchase subscribers another 40 per cent; by 1983 individual purchasers had fallen to 28 per cent and company schemes had increased to around 50 per cent (Grant, 1985: Table 39). The high proportion of company schemes is a significant departure from the market model, since it means the consumption of private hospital care is not a matter of individual choice, nor can we attribute the individual any simple 'right to exit'. The company chooses the insurance company and the precise policy in terms of comprehensiveness of coverage, the band of hospitals to be used and so forth. In so doing they are taking away choice rather than adding to it, denying individuals choice over employment benefits (see Calnan and Cant, this volume). Companies provide employees with medical insurance for a range of reasons. These may include assumptions about employee preferences, but they also include the company's economic interests (control over the timing of medical treatment may be more important to them than to individual employees) as well as the status and prestige that may accrue to the company when its employees – or at least those towards the top of its occupational hierarchy – are known to have private insurance.

Corporate Insurance: Mediation and Monopoly

Corporations also play a further important role in the private medical sector, for the relation between producers and consumers is often mediated via an insurance company. This is especially common in the case of hospital medicine because of its expense, and means that the relation between producers and consumers is not as direct as the market model presumes. Again it might seem initially that this mediation is of relatively little importance for the power of either consumers or producers – insurance companies simply providing the means whereby individuals can afford private hospital care. Viewed in this light insurance companies merely facilitate the link between producers and consumers, allowing individuals to translate their preferences into actual demand. Consequently the modification to the market model appears minimal, and the fact that insurance companies have typically accepted the paradigmatic fee-for-service basis of private medicine supports this view.

However, insurance companies do not merely facilitate demand, they channel it in particular directions. This they do by the way in which they write insurance policies. For example, it has long been recognised that in the United States, where there is no ready access to publicly funded primary care, the insurance companies direct individuals towards hospital care, since standard insurance policies typically provide coverage for in-patient not primary care (Bodenheimer *et al.*, 1977). Of course, it could be argued that the way policies are written is itself a function of consumer demand; that the demand for coverage for hospital care is greater than for primary care because of the far higher and more episodic costs of the former. However, whilst this argument has some force, the interests of the companies also play a part and the profitability and financial viability of different policies are crucial, as can be seen from the exclusion of cover for chronic illnesses. Indeed the major providential schemes in the United States, Blue Cross and Blue Shield, had their origins in protecting hospitals' and doctors' income and did not have their impetus from consumers (Starr, 1982: 295–8). Consequently the companies are not simply passive facilitators. Instead they are active agents with their own interests which shape the relation between producers and consumers. This is seen most visibly in recent attempts by some companies to control the high costs of private medicine. This has led them to play a more interventionist role, by, for instance, banding hospitals and requiring higher premiums for the more expensive hospitals and by setting limits on the level of medical fees covered, thereby directly structuring consumer demand. Indeed their power as holders of the purse strings over both corporate producers and consumers is considerable. Interestingly they have not, until recently, tended to exert much control over professionals, typically accepting the high medical costs occasioned by fee-for-service medicine.

The medical insurance market in Britain is more concentrated than the private hospital market and is dominated by three major providential associations who had over 80 per cent of the business in 1989.[13] BUPA is by far the largest of the three, with about 60 per cent of the market (Guardian, 23.12.89.). The other two are Private Patients Plan and Western Provident Association. Overall their hold on the market declined a little during the 1980s. Commercial groups, especially American ones, have played an increasing role since the end of the 1970s and had about 10 per cent of the market in 1989, the rest being held by small providential associations.

More significant, however, are the increasing ties between the corporate producers of health care and the insurance companies. I noted earlier (p.79) that BUPA Hospitals' takeover of the Hospital Corporation of America in 1989 was referred to the Monopolies and Mergers Commission. The major concern was that close ties between insurance companies and hospital corporations could prevent free competition in the hospital market. The fact that the takeover was allowed despite strong opposition (Monopolies and Mergers Commission, 1990) does not eliminate such worries or diminish the market concentration it represents. The domination of the insurance market by three companies and the links between BUPA Insurance and BUPA Hospitals introduces, therefore, considerable distortions in the market for private medical care.

Overall, therefore, the activities of private corporations represent important departures from the assumptions of the ideal–typical market model. Corporate production strengthens the power of producers and diminishes the choice of consumers. Corporate consumption means that the consumption of private medical care is in many cases not a matter of individual choice, preference and decision making at all. Finally corporate insurance, though it increases consumers' access to private medicine, largely for elective surgery whose timing they can choose, diminishes their power to influence the character of the care they receive. In the light of these observations it is hard to see the private market in medicine as the means of enhancing individuals' power and choice as consumers to any great extent. Indeed comparisons suggest that they are no greater than those of consumers of state medicine. Let us turn, therefore, to the issue of the individual consumers' protection in the private market. Are they better protected than consumers in the state sector?

CONSUMER PROTECTION

Saunders and Harris (1990) have suggested that the consumers of privately produced goods and services do have greater safeguards than consumers of state services. However, in the case of private medicine the evidence does not support such claims. Certainly there are a range of legal rights designed to protect consumers who can seek redress through the courts if the care they receive is inadequate. Nonetheless, the protections provided for consumers of private medicine are considerably more limited than it initially appears and actually more limited than those of the users of state medicine.

As we have seen, medical expertise and the uncertain link between treatment and prognosis (few treatments have been fully evaluated (Cochrane, 1972)) means it is frequently difficult for consumers to assess the standards of medical services. Consequently they are often in a poor position to determine whether the care they receive is adequate, thereby undermining an important premise of the theory of consumer sovereignty via the exercise of consumer choice. This is one justification for professional regulation and training. Even so, incompetencies and malpractices can still occur and mechanisms allowing consumers some redress are vital. However, the obvious market mechanism of returning a faulty good or having the work redone is not usually feasible for medical treatment and the options open to private consumers, beyond a complaint to the General Medical Council that the doctor is not fit to be registered, are limited. The formally prescribed remedy is via the law. However, at present there are major problems with the law as a means of individual redress or as a general mechanism for maintaining medical standards.

In Britain medical services are governed by the common law as well as by statutory regulations and are subject to the law of contract, which governs market relations between producers and consumers, as well as the law of tort (civil wrong-doing), and actions founded on the law of contract do not preclude actions in tort (Dugdale and Stanton, 1989:90). Medical services are, for instance, subject to the Supply of Goods and Services Act of 1982, whose sections governing services represent a codification of common law. The legislation lays down three basic obligations on the suppliers of services with respect to quality of workmanship, the time for performance of services and the determination of price. It indicates that where there is a contract for the supply of a service there is an implied term that the supplier will carry out the service with reasonable care and skill. However, in practice the law of contract is rarely used in medical cases. Almost all court cases dealing specifically with failures or inadequacies in services are founded in medical negligence.

The tort of negligence occurs when there is a failure of the duty of care which a person owes to his or her 'neighbour'.[14] It covers cases in which 'a practitioner's failure to show care or skill in treatment results in the patient's suffering consequential death, injury or pain' (Dugdale and Stanton, 1989:90). It has also been applied to situations where a patient was not informed of the risks involved in a course of treatment 'if it can be proved that the patient suffered damage as a result' (ibid). A duty of care exists quite independently of the cash nexus and does not require that there should have been any payment for the service. An action founded on negligence can, therefore, be pursued whether the service was provided within the framework of private or state medicine. In this respect, therefore, consumers of private medicine have no advantage over consumers of state medicine. Indeed health authorities are vicariously liable for the negligence of those performing services on their behalf and both in theory and typically in practice consumers of state medicine can make a claim of negligence against the authority as well as the individual practitioner. However a major limitation of any such legal action, whether in relation to private or state medicine, is that the victim must demonstrate that the practitioner has shown lack of care or skill, and that identifiable and measurable damages have been caused by the practitioner's actions. The fact that medical cases are almost always dealt with via the law of tort means that the law really only provides a means of seeking redress against, and consequently controlling, relatively gross incompetence not rather poor performance. Routinised lack of care and skill is not affected by such remedies. It also means that the individual contractual relationship between producer and consumer, so central to free market ideology, is actually of rather little relevance in protecting the consumer of private medicine under the law.

The law is further limited as a means of consumer protection in that access to it is typically restricted because of the expense of taking legal action. Any case against a doctor working privately has to go through the civil courts. Consequently those with limited resources are doubly disadvantaged (the costs of medical litigation are generally far higher than those of buying private medicine). Not only is it increasingly difficult to secure legal aid because of the government's failure to raise the limits of eligibility for aid in line with inflation, but the criteria for eligibility for civil cases are more severe than for criminal cases.

There are further problems with the use of the law as a means of trying to control medical activity and secure the maintenance of adequate standards. One is that it puts up medical costs. In the United States, where litigation in cases of medical negligence is common, insurance for doctors is very expensive and this cost is passed on to patients. Another is that doctors' fears of litigation lead them to practise a type of 'defensive' medicine that is not in patients' interests. Indeed, it encourages the tendency to unnecessary treatment that is a feature of fee-for-service medicine.

While the limited protection afforded by law is as accessible to the consumer of state as of private medicine, in Britain the consumer of state medicine has the additional mechanism of institutionalised complaints procedures within the NHS. These are better developed in relation to primary than hospital care and arise through the contract made between the practitioner and the NHS. For example, although general practitioners working for the NHS have the formal status of independent contractors not employees, their NHS contracts specify certain obligations on them and, within the framework of a formal complaints procedure, they are subject to various penalties for breach of that contract. The contract is quite detailed and potential breaches include failure to visit a patient at home in an emergency, failure to make a thorough diagnostic assessment and the providing of inappropriate treatment. It also extends to actions taken by ancillary staff such as practice receptionists for whom the doctor is responsible, although matters such as brusqueness and rudeness of staff and practitioners are excluded. In addition all Family Health Service Authorities (formerly Family Practitioner Committees) now have to have informal complaints procedures. District Health Authorities also have complaints procedures covering complaints against NHS hospital doctors.

Complaints procedures are far from perfect. Nevertheless their existence is important not only because they avoid the costs of a court hearing and cover a broader range of failures and incompetencies than legal actions, but also because the objective of any hearing is not to secure damages, but some recognition that a mistake has been made. This is important since many complainants are more concerned that mistakes be acknowledged than that they should receive financial compensation. The absence of institutionalised complaints procedures in the private sector means that expensive litigation is usually the only alternative for private consumers and their protection is correspondingly limited.

CONCLUSION

The model of the free market developed by liberal thinkers provides a very inaccurate picture of the character of private medicine in Britain and, consequently, of the power and choice of the consumer. On the one hand, state requirements for the registration of medical practitioners and the restriction of certain activities to qualified practitioners, which are widely recognised to be necessary for the protection of patients' interests, give those registered a partial monopoly over healing in the private as well as public sector and increases their power as producers over patients. On the other hand, private corporations play an important role in the production and consumption of private medical care, as well as in mediating the relationship between producers and consumers. Such corporations restrict the choice of consumers and increase the possibilities that medical care develops in ways that enhance corporate rather than patients' interests. In both respects, therefore, private medicine does not correspond to the market model at all well and there is little sign of consumer sovereignty.

Liberal thinkers have been highly critical of state provision, claiming that it deprives consumers of choice and power and forces them into passivity. Such critics have offered us a distorted picture of the position of consumers of state services, and an idealised portrayal of private medicine. They have ignored the tendencies in the private sector towards market monopolies and the constraints, both professional and corporate, producers impose on the consumer. State medicine undoubtedly has its deficiencies, although it has the major virtue of enhancing access to medical care. Private medicine does not secure much in the way of consumer sovereignty even for those who can afford it.

Notes

1. I have used the terms consumption and consumers despite their ideological connotations in order to engage with ongoing sociological debate about production and consumption. The use of the term medical care rather than health care indicates a focus on medical intervention rather than the long-term care of those with chronic complaints.
2. The term power is used here in its Weberian sense of ability to realise one's will even against the resistance of others.
3. Arguably the balance of self-interest has changed.
4. Indeed it would be hard to find a proponent of the view that there should be entirely unregulated competition between healers.
5. Fee-for-service medicine typically generates high incomes for medical practitioners as it does, for example, in the United States.
6. Special payment for contraceptive services is an earlier example.
7. Saunders would argue that there is no need for such bodies in the private sector because consumers are more powerful – a view that the argument here questions.
8. Saunders' refers to Green's (1985) writings to back up his claim.
9. Compagnie Générale de Santé of France and Paracelsus-Kliniken of Germany now have significant investments (Guardian, 23.7.90).
10. BUPA Hospitals, unlike BUPA Insurance, is liable for corporation tax.
11. Health Maintenance Organisations provide one example of the possibility of greater corporate control of professionals (Starr, 1982: 428–30).
12. Around 57 per cent of BUPA's insurance is via company schemes (Financial Times, 29.1.90.). Of course, subscribers' dependents, who have insurance taken out for them, do not make an individual choice to have private medical care.
13. In recent years providential companies have increasingly acted in very similar ways to the commercial groups.
14. In this respect it has strongly social origins.

6 Principles and Practice: the Case of Private Health Insurance

Michael Calnan and Sarah Cant

INTRODUCTION

Much of the debate on 'consumption sector cleavages' has focused on housing tenure (Savage *et al.*, this volume; Warde, this volume), although, as Hamnett (1989) points out, many of the claims made in relation to housing are thought to be indicative of wider shifts in other areas of provision. This chapter aims to extend this analysis into the field of health care. More specifically, the objective is, drawing on evidence from a study examining decisions to subscribe to private health insurance, to empirically examine the explanatory power of Saunders' sociology of consumption. If social divisions can be made on the basis of public/private divisions in consumption patterns then, at the least, it might be expected that subscribers to private health insurance would be distinctly different in terms of social, political and cultural values than non-subscribers. More specifically, it might be expected that subscribers would be antagonistic towards collective provision of health care and the values that are tied to it.

Over the last two decades there has been a continued growth of the private medical sector, principally in the areas of long term care and the provision of acute services. There are now over 200 private acute hospitals, providing some 10,000 beds and between 1979 and 1984, the number of pay bed authorisations increased by 26 per cent (Griffith *et al.*, 1987). Another area where there has been a significant growth is in the proportion of the population covered by private health insurance. In 1964, the number of persons per 1,000 in the population of the United Kingdom who were insured under the three major provident schemes (BUPA, PPP, WPA) was 25.0. By 1984, this figure had risen to 77.6 (Laing, 1985). More recent evidence from the *General Household Survey* (OPCS, 1989) showed that in 1987 the percentage of the population covered by private health insurance was 9 per cent and the percentage who were policy holders was 5 per cent. However, for some groups, the percentage is a lot higher. For example, the percentage of people in professional occupations in 1987 who were aged 45 to 64 who were covered by private health insurance (OPCS, 1989) was 34 per cent and, given the marked regional variation in coverage, this figure is probably higher for those amongst this group who live in or around the London area. These figures also show that the majority were in company-run schemes (54 per cent) and the remainder in individual (24 per cent) or group schemes (18 per cent) and, over the last decade, there has been a shift from the majority of subscribers being in personal schemes to the majority being in employer run insurance schemes.

There is some debate about whether private medical insurance can be viewed as a consumption good given that the social relations of consumption in medicine and health are so highly complex and problematic (Flynn, this volume). In addition, there is the question whether private medical insurance is led by consumer demand or whether enrolment into schemes is primarily initiated by employers. There are some (Higgins, 1988) who have suggested that the development of occupational health insurance schemes could be seen as the emergence of an embryonic occupational health service. This has been encouraged by the government through tax concessions and might be seen as an attempt to shift the burden of the responsibility for occupational welfare from the state to the employer. Employers, however, may have other motives for providing insurance schemes and one of the most common suggests that it is viewed as a form of investment capital to minimise the disruption caused by illness to productivity (Laing, 1985). Alternatively, it might be argued that it is a form of wage-substituting policy pursued by trade unions, and encouraged by employers during periods of wage containment. Clearly, then, employers do play an important part in contributing to the decision to use private medical insurance, although even in employer run schemes, the role of the consumer may still be significant. For example, as the data from the *General Household Survey 1987*, show, only a third of medical insurance policies are paid entirely by the employer, and even in some of these schemes, the employee has to pay for cover to be extended to their families (OPCS, 1989). In addition, if private medical insurance is used as a 'perk' to attract workers (Higgins, 1986), it must be perceived by the consumer as being of value. Thus, the focus of the study described here is primarily on the part played by the consumer.

What of the possible explanations for the apparent increase in consumer demand for private medical insurance and private medical care (Laing, 1985)? One of the most common is the claim that there has been an increase in dissatisfaction with the National Health Service (Taylor-Gooby, 1986) such as the perceived problem of waiting time for operations. There are, at least, three possible explanations for this apparent increase in dissatisfaction. One is associated with the provision of services in that this dissatisfaction may be a response to the relative deterioration in the National Health Service generated by constraints on public expenditure and concessions to the private sector. Alternatively, the dissatisfaction may be not so much a reflection of perceptions of a deterioration in the quality of the service available but a product of the vehemence with which the view that the NHS is collapsing has been expressed in public debates over the last few years. For example, as Day and Klein (1989) point out, throughout the history of the NHS, the medical profession has regularly pointed to the shortcomings of the service as a way of drumming up support for extra funding. However, according to Day and Klein (1989), the public debate in the 1980s was specifically characterised by the ferocity of the confrontation between the profession and the government.

The third explanation suggests this dissatisfaction may be associated with the broader social changes in the social relations of consumption which were outlined earlier. For Saunders (1984) the increase in disposable incomes amongst middle-class and working-class households has created the conditions which have led to a widespread desire for personal control in the sphere of consumption. Thus, the dissatisfaction may not just be a reflection of the quality of the service provided but the changing expectation of the consumer which involves a demand for a wider range of choice and for higher standards of service. Certainly there is evidence of changing expectations about health from the *General Household Survey, 1987* data (OPCS, 1989) which showed between 1972 and 1987 a substantial increase in the proportion of people reporting a long-standing illness. This may reflect a change over time in people's expectations of health as well as in the prevalence or duration of chronic sickness. In addition, as Horne (1986) shows, the perceived attractions of the private sector are usually articulated in terms of choice and control such as choice of consultant or pre-arranged admission.

The change in expectations of the consumer may also be tied to more broadly based changes in the nature and role of state welfare in recent times. Since the end of the Second World War, there has been a general political consensus that the state had a major responsibility to provide certain essentials for living. Amongst these was the provision of an accessible universal health-care system. However, the growing strains on state budgets has, over the last ten years, seen the emergence of another ideology based on the value of self-reliance and individual responsibility. The growth in private health insurance may be a manifestation of these beliefs in that it may be seen as a means of enhancing an individual's control over his/her health and its management. As Weale has suggested:

> The Welfare arrangements on which there was consensus in the 1950's are not the amendments we have today. Ideology tracks welfare as much as welfare provision tracks ideology (Weale, 1986).

The value of these and other explanations were examined in a recent study which focused on decisions to subscribe to private health insurance and decisions to use it. The data presented in this chapter focus on why some people subscribe to private health insurance schemes and others do not, within a segment of the population which is financially capable of enrolling in a scheme.

METHODS

There may be a number of different ways of exploring this particular question, although the approach used in this study was to place the question in the broader context of an investigation into how people evaluate the adequacy of health care. A conceptual framework (Calnan, 1988a) was developed which provided the basis of the approach although the exploratory work in this study suggested it needed to be modified and extended.

This type of question has been traditionally examined through surveys although doubts have been expressed about the value of this methodology at the conceptual level (Calnan, 1988a) particularly in the 'managerial bias' adopted by the studies and at the empirical level about the reliability of the questions. Recent evidence has suggested a more fruitful approach to this question may be through the use of qualitative methods such as tape-recorded interviews (Calnan, 1988b). Thus, the emphasis in this study was to examine lay evaluation of health care through the use of qualitative methods although quantitative data were collected to provide background information about the profile of the subscriber to private health insurance (PHI).

The small proportion of the adult population who are covered by private medical insurance, the variety of schemes that these policy holders are involved with and the fact that the majority of policy holders are confined to a certain social group in the population meant that a two-stage sampling method had to be used with the first identifying the groups for investigation in the main or second part of the study.

The first sampling frame consisted of sampling people who have a high likelihood of having private medical insurance, that is men aged between 35 and 55 in relatively high-income groups. Thus, a sample of 3,060 men aged between 35 and 55 was selected from the age–sex registers of general practices based in relatively affluent areas of Kent. The accuracy of these age–sex registers is difficult to estimate and the error rate appears to vary between 10 per cent and 25 per cent (Bowling and Jacobson, 1989). Self-completed questionnaires were sent to each person in the sample. 1688 (55 per cent) sent back a completed questionnaire. (Of these 26 had to be excluded from the analysis because they did not allow the nature of (non-) subscription to be identified.) However in one practice (N = 923) the response rate was particularly low (47 per cent) and this response rate could be explained, at least in part, by the inaccuracy of the age-sex register. Included in the questionnaire were details about whether the person was currently subscribing to private health insurance, their use of private health insurance, their socio-political beliefs about the health service; their satisfaction with and patterns of use of the health services; their health status, socio-demographic characteristics, and a question asking if the respondent would take part in the second stage.

The second stage of the study involved tape-recorded interviews with small samples of men who:

(i) have personally chosen to take out private health insurance;
(ii) have been co-opted into employer run schemes;
(iii) have not subscribed to a scheme.

Twenty interviews were carried out with each of the three groups, with the third group being matched to the first two in terms of socio-demographic characteristics. Since there is evidence emerging to suggest that women may be less likely to subscribe but more likely to use private health insurance, interviews have also been carried out with small samples of women in each of the three groups. The qualitative interviews covered a range of research questions but the data presented here will only focus on decisions to subscribe to private health insurance.

FINDINGS

The focus in this chapter is on examining decisions to take out private health insurance. As was suggested in the introduction, one explanation for the increase in subscription to private health insurance which is common in political rhetoric is that people are becoming increasingly dissatisfied with the NHS. However, there is some doubt about whether this is based on people's first hand experience of use of the health service or is more likely to be tied to people's ideological beliefs about health and welfare (Taylor-Gooby, 1987).

It was suggested earlier that surveys examining satisfaction with health services and other social services have some theoretical and methodological limitations and such an approach needs to be complemented by a qualitative approach. However, before the qualitative data are discussed, it might be useful to briefly examine some of the characteristics of subscribers to private health insurance, particularly their attitudes to the National Health Service.

Table 6.1 shows the statistical relationships between current subscription to private health insurance and levels of satisfaction with the health service or certain parts of it. Those who reported current subscription to private health insurance were divided into three groups according to the source of payment. It was felt that this classification is a better measure of the extent to which the respondent is committed to a scheme than using a classification which merely identifies the type of scheme the respondent subscribes to. The 'current' non subscribers were divided up into those who had 'never' subscribed and those whose subscription had 'lapsed'.

The table shows some support for the proposition in that there appeared to be generally a lower level of satisfaction with the NHS amongst subscribers compared with non-subscribers. However, there were also differences between the different groups of subscribers with those in employer run schemes being more satisfied than the other two groups. The group who paid for their insurance jointly with their employers showed the lowest level of satisfaction. However, it was also apparent that the lapsed subscribers' views were closer to those of current subscribers than those who never subscribed.

Table 6.1 Satisfaction with NHS and private health insurance

	Non-subscriber to private health insurance		*Subscriber to private health insurance*			*Total*
	Never	*Lapsed*	*Employer pays*	*Joint payment*	*Individual pays*	
N =	**1047**	**135**	**169**	**130**	**181**	**1,662**
	%	%	%	%	%	%
How satisfied would you say you are with the way in which the NHS runs nowadays?						
Very satisfied	12	7	7	2	4	10
Quite satisfied	43	43	31	25	23	38
Neither	23	27	28	28	35	26
Quite dissatisfied	15	13	24	25	24	17
Very dissatisfied	5	9	7	19	11	7
How satisfied or dissatisfied are you with the way in which each of these parts of the NHS runs howadays?						
(i) Attending hospitals as as out patient:						
Very satisfied	14	9	8	3	4	11
Quite satisified	32	30	20	16	17	28
Neither	14	17	12	17	13	14
Quite dissatisfied	15	22	28	28	28	20
Very dissatisfied	8	10	17	20	14	11
Don't know	12	12	12	15	20	13
(ii) Local doctors/GPs:						
Very satisfied	43	37	31	30	35	39
Quite satisified	43	45	52	45	44	45
Neither	8	4	9	12	11	8
Quite dissatisfied	4	10	5	111	7	5
Very dissatisfied	1	2	2	2	2	2
Don't know	< 1	1	–	–	–	–
Say whether you think the NHS is, on the whole, satisfactory or in need of improvement in the following areas?						
(i) Hospital waiting list for non-emergency operations:						
In need of improvement	56	60	54	62	61	51
In need of some improvement	34	33	36	30	31	36
Satisfactory	5	4	7	5	6	5
Very good	1	–	–	1	1	1

Table 6.1 continued

	Never	*Lapsed*	*Employer pays*	*Joint payment*	*Individual pays*	
N=	**1047**	**135**	**169**	**130**	**181**	**1,662**
	%	%	%	%	%	%
(ii) Quality of medical treatment in hospital:						
In need of improvement	3	3	2	7	6	4
In need of some improvement	21	24	19	27	27	22
Satisfactory	47	46	51	51	54	48
Very good	25	22	23	13	12	22

Note: In tables 6.1–6.6 missing answers are excluded from the percentages which explains why not all reported percentages add up to 100.

Results from the *British Social Attitudes Survey* (Jowell *et al*., 1988) and from this study show the major area of public dissatisfaction was with hospital outpatient services and waiting lists for non-urgent operations which are areas covered by private health care. In contrast, general practitioner services and the quality of medical treatment in hospitals were areas where there was a high level of satisfaction. These contrasting areas were included in the analysis.

Once again, a greater level of dissatisfaction was found amongst those with private health insurance and this was evident for outpatient services, for waiting lists, for non-urgent operations and for general practitioner care.

What is the source of this dissatisfaction? Is it based on experience of use of the NHS or is it tied to broader socio-political values? According to evidence presented in Table 6.2, this dissatisfaction does not appear to be tied to their recent experience of use of NHS hospital outpatient or inpatient services as subscribers have tended, over the previous 12 months, to make less use of these services than non-subscribers. This is not surprising given that as Table 6.3 shows, their perceived health is on the whole better than non-subscribers perceived health status. This supports evidence found in previous studies (Higgins, 1988) and probably can be explained quite simply because subscribers tend to be the more affluent members of the population.

The dissatisfaction amongst subscribers to private health insurance may, then, be linked to broader socio-political values. As Table 6.4 shows, subscribers, particularly those in schemes where the employer pays all the subscription, were more likely to support the Conservative

Table 6.2 Use of health services and private health insurance

Use of health services over the last twelve months	*Non-subscriber to private health insurance*		*Subscriber to private health insurance*			*Total*
	Never	*Lapsed*	*Employer pays*	*Joint payment*	*Individual pays*	
N =	**1,047**	**135**	**169**	**130**	**181**	**1,662**
	%	%	%	%	%	%
GP visits						
None	33	31	31	29	30	32
Once	24	24	26	30	25	25
Twice	17	17	20	15	24	18
Three times	8	9	7	4	8	7
Four times	6	6	9	10	2	9
Five times +	8	10	6	10	8	9
Don't know	1	2	–	1	–	1
Outpatient in an NHS hospital						
None	71	65	84	86	78	74
Once	11	16	6	6	8	10
Twice	5	4	3	2	4	5
Three times	4	6	2	2	1	3
Four times +	5	5	1	3	4	4
Outpatients in private hospital						
None	92	90	76	79	76	87
Once	2	3	14	10	8	5
Twice	1	1	5	4	4	2
Three times	<1	2	1	2	1	1
Four times +	1	1	2	2	2	1
Admission NHS hospital						
None	88	87	95	97	93	90
Once	6	7	1	2	1	5
Twice	1	2	1	1	1	1
Three times +	1	–	–	–	–	1
Don't know	–	–	–	–	–	–
Admission private hospital						
None	96	96	91	94	90	95
Once	1	1	5	5	3	2
Twice +	–	–	1	–	1	<1

party than non-subscribers. Also, when their beliefs about the NHS and private medicine were examined, some differences emerged between the groups.

Table 6.3 Health status and private health insurance

	Non-subscriber to private health insurance		*Subscriber to private health insurance*			*Total*
	Never	*Lapsed*	*Employer pays*	*Joint payment*	*Individual pays*	
N =	**1,047**	**135**	**169**	**130**	**181**	**1,662**
	%	%	%	%	%	%
Perceived health status						
Good	71	75	82	77	75	74
Fairly good	23	20	17	19	23	22
Not good	5	5	2	4	2	5
Long standing illness						
Yes	25	24	24	27	24	25
No	73	73	74	73	72	73
Not sure	2	2	1	–	3	2

Table 6.4 Political affiliation and private health insurance

If there was a general election tomorrow which political party do you think you would be most likely to support?	*Non-subscriber to private health insurance*		*Subscriber to private health insurance*			*Total*
	Never	*Lapsed*	*Employer pays*	*Joint payment*	*Individual pays*	
N =	**1,047**	**135**	**169**	**130**	**181**	**1,662**
	%	%	%	%	%	%
Conservative	42	55	75	60	60	50
Labour	20	13	8	10	9	17
SLDP	9	10	3	8	11	8
SDP	4	4	5	5	2	4
Other	5	4	2	2	6	4
Would not vote	10	4	3	9	6	8

In the survey, respondents were asked whether, on a five point scale, they agreed or disagreed with a series of statements about the National Health Service and about Private Health Care. There were two sets of statements. The first focused on general beliefs about health care and examined dimensions such as 'egalitarianism', 'individualism versus collective responsibility', 'consumer versus provider defined need' and 'free market economy versus state intervention'. The second set of statements focuses on specific beliefs about the qualities of private health care as against NHS care.

Table 6.5 (on following page) shows the relationship between these general beliefs and subscription to private health insurance. On almost all the belief items, there were differences between the subscribers and non-subscribers and the general picture which emerged suggested that subscribers supported a mixed economy of health care more than non-subscribers and provided more support for the values of individual responsibility and consumer sovereignty than non-subscribers.

Table 6.6 (on page 101) shows the relationship between subscription to private health insurance and specific beliefs about the value of private versus NHS care. These belief items covered issues such as the quality of nursing and medical care, hospital facilities, over-treatment and under-utilisation and private health insurance as a status symbol. Once again there were consistent differences between the subscribers and non-subscribers with, as might be expected, subscribers being more likely to see the benefits of private health care compared with non-subscribers. However, the major differences appeared between the groups in terms of the negative aspects of private medicine. The danger of over-treatment and under-utilisation were much more likely to be identified by non-subscribers than subscribers.

In summary, the evidence suggests that non-subscribers are different to subscribers in terms of their socio-political beliefs and in their beliefs about the specific advantages and disadvantages of private medicine. The picture, however, is not a simple one and the intention is to turn to the qualitative data to unravel the link between beliefs about health care and subscription to private health insurance.

QUALITATIVE DATA

The analysis of the quantitative data thus established a relationship between expressed dissatisfaction with the NHS and subscription to private health insurance, but suggests that this dissatisfaction is less related to actual use and experience of the health service and more related to socio-political beliefs about health and welfare. However, such data tells us little about why the statistical relationship exists. The aim of the qualitative analysis, therefore, is to explain the possible relationship between socio-political values, pragmatic reasoning and action. Subscribers may express dissatisfaction and align themselves to

Table 6.5 Socio-political beliefs and private health insurance

Percentage who agree 'strongly' or 'a little' with the following statements	*Non-subscriber to private health insurance*		*Subscriber to private health insurance*			*Total*
	Never	*Lapsed*	*Employer pays*	*Joint payment*	*Individual pays*	
N =	**1,047**	**135**	**169**	**130**	**181**	**1,662**
	%	%	%	%	%	%
The NHS should only be available to those on low incomes	11	10	11	5	10	10
The increasing provision of private health care creates further division between rich and poor	76	76	65	62	58	71
Having to pay encourages patients to be more responsible about their health	46	43	60	58	63	51
Government-funded health care encourages patients' dependence on the state	29	31	33	32	40	32
Government should raise taxes to increase spending on the NHS	58	52	45	56	43	55
Government should make private health insurance tax deductable	49	63	70	69	82	58
Private health care is undermining the NHS	46	58	24	33	22	43
Health care should be treated like any other commodity where you shop around to get the best buy	32	48	54	55	51	39

Table 6.6 Beliefs about private versus NHS care and private health insurance

Percentage who agree 'strongly' or 'a little' with the following statements	*Non-subscriber to private health insurance*		*Subscriber to private health insurance*			*Total*
	Never	*Lapsed*	*Employer pays*	*Joint payment*	*Individual pays*	
N =	**1,047**	**135**	**169**	**130**	**181**	**1,662**
	%	%	%	%	%	%
Nursing care is better under private than under NHS	42	45	53	68	52	46
Doctors spend more time with their patients in private health care	60	60	67	64	66	62
Facilities in private hospitals are far superior to those in NHS	57	55	62	66	64	60
Having to pay for treatment would discourage going to the doctor when you need to	76	76	62	61	64	72
Patients are given more treatment than they actually need in private care	37	37	19	20	22	32
Doctors will look after your health better when there is money involved	51	39	41	46	39	48
Having private health insurance is a status symbol	53	46	26	27	21	44

certain political values; but does this accurately convey the logic of the reasoning that is used? The analysis is based on 60 interviews (20 from each of the groups).

Generally, the evidence from the qualitative analysis appeared to support that from the quantitative analysis. Subscribers were more likely to express dissatisfaction with the NHS, although this was directed at certain aspects of the service, particularly waiting lists, rather than the idea of the NHS *per se*. None of the respondents identified differences in the quality of treatment in the NHS but were concerned about receiving 'speedy' treatment. When asked why they used private medicine replies included the following:

> You can't go when you want to go. If you can go where you want and when you want, nobody would be bothered about buying health care.

> For convenience I took out the lowest grade because of economics, I only wanted to be able to time it, not the luxury of it. It's just bed and fed.

> Peace of mind; I mean I'm not running down the NHS, I have had a good service from them, it's just the time . . . doesn't mean privatise further, emphatically not.

> Just in case something major comes up and there's waiting . . . a guy came round and told us about the long waiting for hips and what have you.

> The attraction is the time you go in, being able to tie it in with the life you lead.

> Timing, and it wasn't too expensive but I would like to see a very, very good NHS.

> . . . was getting older and you tend to get more ailments so I thought as I am the bread-winner and the wife can't work (she has MS), I thought I had better get covered . . . with the NHS there's sometimes a long waiting list.

It appeared also that many subscribers' judgements were likely to be based on hearsay rather than actual experience:

> I've heard it's a lot better . . . the meals are absolutely splendid, you have no limited time for visiting, as you have in the NHS hospital.

Differences between the types of subscribers were less evident although individual subscribers tended to emphasise the benefits of private medicine for saving time:

No problems with using the NHS, but I am self-employed and if I need to have something done, I need to do it when I can fit it in, not have to wait and then be called at an inconvenient moment.

It's speed . . . the comfort of instant treatment, which is very important if you are in business.

There was also evidence that subscribers were more likely to be self-employed and clearly they were concerned about the time and money lost through unplanned hospitalisation:

I am self-employed and time is money . . . and you get superior treatment and more personal attention.

Self-employed – no qualms about using NHS, but need convenience.

Non-subscribers were characterised by their lack of criticism and their use of justifications to explain why they evaluated the service in this way.

At the moment the NHS covers all my needs and in the main it covers them very well. I have affection for it anyway.

I think a lot of people that knock the medical service are just bellyaching for the sake of bellyaching, to be honest, it's political.

Comfort, privacy and individualised care were referred to particularly by individual subscribers, as the advantages of private medicine:

. . . Saw the attractions of private after we took it out, when my wife was in hospital; the children could visit at any time, watch cartoons on the telly.

To feel you are an individual and to get attention.

I go privately because I can afford to do so, the service I get is better in that they treat you as an intelligent, human being and spend more time with you. I don't blame NHS for the short-fall but private gives me a top-up, a means of being able to circumvent the short-falls. I want attention but I am not dissatisfied with the NHS.

You are treated like a person, I don't know whether it's because they get a fat salary.

The whole ambience is nicer, quieter.

And there was one example of the importance of status:

By using private health, you meet a better class of person. In the NHS there's no telling who you are going to be sitting next to – for some people that's a bad thing.

However, once again they suggested that the medical care was no different from a technical point of view.

Non-subscribers, as was found in the quantitative data, readily expressed the problems and disadvantages with private medicine, however, they also imagined there would be advantages too:

I suppose it must be like a first-class hotel, you should get better food and more attentive nursing.

Dissatisfaction with the private sector was also examined, and the responses supported the quantitative data in that non-subscribers expressed more criticism, particularly in response to the question: 'What do you think of the public-private mix?'

The company and individual subscriber did recognise problems with private provision.

They take the easy part of the medical field, the bits where the profit is perhaps higher . . . it's not comprehensive enough (company subscriber).

It's expensive and there are certain conditions they are not interested in. It's alright if you have got a minor complaint, if you are in and out of hospital pretty quickly, but a long-term illness, you fall back on the NHS.' (company subscriber)

The criticisms were directed at expense and non-comprehensiveness of the service, rather than excess treatment. One company subscriber did dislike the individualised treatment in the private sector:

I feel more tense because it's private, exactly because you are not one of the crowd.

Individual subscribers complained most frequently about cost:

It's very expensive, you are limited by how much you pay.

or

It's hellishly expensive, at the end of the day you get what you pay for, which means it's out of the reach of some individuals and you are not covered for everything, but you know the NHS is there . . .

Non-subscribers talked of the expense and profit-making side of the private sector ('It's expensive, it must be a money-spinner'), but in addition talked of poorer facilities and unnecessary treatment:

> People have unnecessary cosmetic treatment to get their monies worth . . .

> You get unnecessary operations, doctors will increasingly put business each others way.

> Private gives you greater comfort but not as good medical facilities.

In response to the question, 'What is the impact of the private sector in the NHS?', differences were again evident. The non-subscribers saw most problems with the public/private mix of health delivery:

> Private sector is damaging the NHS, it takes resources away, particularly staff trained at state expense; they should pay the state back, working in both is a disgrace. Further privatisation will mean the NHS will become a safety net for the old and poor.

and further privatisation was viewed with caution:

> Further privatisation will weaken the NHS and lead to a downgrading of the service.

Company and individual subscribers were difficult to divide in terms of the degree of support for a mixed economy of health care. The private sector was seen to give choice, to reduce waiting lists, and to provide competition. However, the issue of staff working in both sectors and the possible negative implications for the NHS were identified:

> The private system is a parasite in that it poaches staff, resources and equipment . . . You release more places but still NHS doctors can't be in two places at once. It's swings and roundabouts.

In summary, the qualitative data suggests that dissatisfaction with the NHS is more strongly voiced by subscribers than the non-subscribers and that this is in part based on hearsay. Certainly if these data are taken at face value, it might be argued that the consensus supporting the NHS is beginning to break up. However, if these beliefs are placed in the broader context of the respondents socio-political beliefs about the health service, a different picture emerges.

The following analysis examines how and why respondents decided to take out private health insurance. It shows a stark contradiction between principle and practice and illustrates how individuals can hold a number of apparently conflicting values at the same time.

Principle and Practice

If we start from the premise that values are logically associated with behaviour, and if we can assume that the holding of insurance should be related to socio-economic and political values held by the respondents, it might follow that clear differences should emerge between individual subscribers and the comparison group of non-subscribers. These differences also may emerge, but to a lesser degree, between individual and company subscribers. What values would subscribers to private health insurance be expected to hold? Certainly a recognition of the benefits of private medicine, the support for a competitive mixed economy, stress upon self-responsibility, and agreement, at least in some degree, with the thinking of the New Right. The evidence from the quantitative analysis showed that subscribers did hold some of these values, but what of the evidence from the qualitative data?

Individual Subscribers

A strong degree of coherence between principle and practice might be expected amongst those respondents who have bought private health insurance as an individual decision and in some cases this was evident. For example one respondent saw the private sector giving better treatment and less waiting. The problems that besiege the NHS mean, in his view, that it should be abolished and that the health sector would move towards US style medicine:

> I think it will improve it because it will become more of a competition for one company to get more customers than another company.

Having said that, his actual behaviour appeared to contradict his beliefs because he preferred to use the NHS unless the waiting time was very long for a major operation:

> In a sense you feel that you are paying for your national health treatment anyway so although you are paying privately as well you feel you want to get some sort of service from the NHS.

Thus, he would use the NHS because he was still paying National Insurance contributions. In an ideal world he would want to opt out of this altogether. There were only four examples of subscribers who were in principle pro private, three of them were individual subscribers and one a company subscriber.

'Would you like to see a completely private system?'

> Well since I am paying so much into private already, I would, if I was financially better off. . . but if I had got a decent NHS, I wouldn't need to, it comes back to that again.

Thus NHS principles were still expressed and the idea of a wholly private sector seemed to hinge on financial considerations. Another subscriber recognised the advantages of a free market:

> I think the NHS will eventually be abolished.
> *Will that be a good thing?*
> Yes, we will be like America, with competition and that will improve health.

And finally:

> If I could go, I would go for a completely private system. I just feel strongly that way. . . but still have an NHS for those that can't afford it so I wouldn't opt out of National Insurance.

The remainder of the respondents articulated clear arguments against the principle of private medicine and voiced pro-NHS sentiments. Their ideal system would be an effectively functioning NHS:

> PHI is a necessary evil; well, ideally I am all for having an NHS that works, that I don't have to pay through the nose for and an NHS that I could use. . . But given the amount of waiting and so on, I think it's a necessary evil. I would like in an ideal world to be on NH.

They recognised that the NHS has problems but also argued that the present system of health care, the mixed economy, provides a structure with choice. If choice exists you 'play the game' and this 'playing the game' may involve rejecting the choice which you 'ideally/ideologically' prefer.

> . . . if it's available on the NHS, one ought to use it, but if you're paying for the thing [private] you might as well use it; once you've got it you might as well use it really. Get your money back.

Thus, the context is one that enables the 'use' of the private sector because of concern about waiting lists in particular. As one respondent said, 'if there's a ladder, climb it.' Thus, the structure of health care determines to some extent how the respondents behave. Individuals opt out because of the choices offered to them and the belief that the NHS is being run down. In a sense this may suggest increased demand is state-induced. In addition, those respondents who do support private in principle want a continued NHS in practice for others.

Thus 'use' of the private sector appears then to be a response to problems in the NHS and to gain returns on insurance, but in principle, NHS would be preferred. For example one respondent saw problems of waiting and was self-employed and needed convenient admission dates. He preferred the idea of a state run system and like the majority would be prepared to pay more NI [National Insurance] contributions to that end. In practice he would like to use NHS first before resorting to the private sector, but with the system as it stands, he recognised that private patients had clear advantages:

> I wouldn't want it, not on me conscience, perhaps that's the wrong word, but I think it's wrong where you can still pay your money and jump the queue; but at the same time if there is any queue-jumping to be done, I want to be at the front of the queue, as opposed to be at the back. Terrible aren't I, but I am afraid that is the way the world is!

Similarly another recognised that the NHS can't meet everyone's needs but also stressed the importance of a conducive environment:

> Now one would argue, a political argument that private is wrong. I won't join that debate. I will just say it exists therefore take advantage.

Again, he stressed the importance of not losing the NHS and believed he should continue to pay National Insurance.

> It's my right and duty as someone who earns more than the average, to pay my contribution, for those who can't afford to pay.

> Perhaps someone would say. 'Well, this is a good thing, privatise medicine'. But all I would say is 'God forbid that day comes when we have to privatise the totality of medicine'. I am only in it because it [the NHS] has certain things wrong with it, but at least I continue to contribute my bit of income to it.

It could be that the NHS is a very special service – there is a moral connection, a consensual loyalty. This is an important issue that will be examined in more detail, in another forthcoming publication, by looking at the degree of coherence between beliefs about privatisation of medicine and privatisation in other areas, but suffice it to say, the contradiction in principle and practice may be partly attributable to the especially high regard the NHS commands.

> I was around almost from when the NHS started; I always regarded it as, not one of, but *the* most major social reform that had ever come about, and you know, although we are not talking politically, I talk as someone who has never in his life voted socialist. I am not a socialist in voting terms but there are parts of me that say what came in for the NHS was the greatest thing ever and unfortunately there has been an erosion of that over the years and it has forced more and more people to go into private medicine.

Thus the take-up of PHI was partly the result of the choices that existed and partly because of the practical consideration of self-employment:

> I've no qualms about using NHS but I am self employed and need convenience.

Company Subscribers

Senior managers, are presumably, in a financial position to afford PHI through an individual subscription, and certainly some did hold individual insurance before the introduction of the company scheme. However a number of our sample did not have cover prior to joining the company scheme. A number of reasons were cited and it was clear that many respondents were politically and morally against private medicine. Nonetheless, they joined the scheme. A very small number from one of the companies used in the pilot study actually rejected the company insurance.

So why accept? One explanation is that the insurance is a company 'gift' offered as part of the wage negotiation or even just an added 'perk'. Subscription to insurance is, at least according to these accounts, employer-induced. The contradictions are clearly voiced in the following accounts:

> Didn't take it out before for the reason of principle, we didn't think it was a good thing to do . . . It seemed to us that if all the middle-class people could afford to leave the NHS, that would remove some of the pressure to keep it going and keep it good.

It was a company perk. I am basically against the private system, I just ignore it – I would never use it . . . But its all very well me saying that; if it was an emergency and the well being of my family, I don't know, I am principled but also a realist.

or

I don't really agree with private medical schemes . . . well they are divisive. I think they separate society and I don't see why people because they have money or their companies have money should have advantage over other people. I think it takes resources away from NHS.

If now you were to fall ill, would you ask to use your PHI or see if the NHS had a waiting list first?
I think I would probably make use of the PHI.

or

I must admit it is selfish in a way because I wasn't keen on it in the first place, from the principle point of view but you know we did it [took company insurance] to protect the children's interests, you put your principles to one side...

Had you thought about it before the company provided the scheme?

No; I mean if they hadn't provided the scheme, I doubt if I would have done anything about it, to be honest.

I had different conversations with people at work; you know, what shall we do with our principles on this one! Well there is another chap, who was in exactly the same boat, not keen on the idea, on the simple premise that if you have got a health service provided for on a national basis, through taxation, then it ought to provide for all eventualities . . . you shouldn't have to pay to go outside that . . . I think I would probably go [private] just to get my money's worth.

Thus, while some saw the subscription to private health insurance as posing a problem for them in terms of their principles, once they had decided to join the scheme, they followed a more pragmatic line of reasoning about its actual use. 'Getting one's money's worth' was one approach adopted. The employment-induced aspect is more clearly illustrated by the following:

I mean, taking it out, it was given, that's the difficulty, if it exists and someone gives it to you, you will probably say 'oh, I will take it'.

or

The company discount scheme put the seed in my head.

or

I wanted to object because I don't agree with it, but it was offered to me.

One respondent did not articulate the same incongruity between principle and practice, he recognised problems with the NHS and saw benefits of private medicine (although would not want to see further privatisation). However, the notion that PHI is to a degree an 'enforced gift' was expressed in his answer to the question: *If the company said you can choose, you can have group discount or an increase in your retirement pension, what would you choose?*

A pension increase.

There appears then to be a hierarchy of desired goods; PHI has recognised advantages but it is not always a priority and often it is accepted because it is offered. A follow-on question to develop this theme was to ask whether respondents would take out insurance individually if company subscription lapsed. Certainly this was not a straightforward decision. Respondents would either drop the insurance or evaluate the extra expense of continuing. In this analysis, no respondents argued they would definitely maintain their cover. The one respondent who received company insurance without any personal contribution, argued he would almost definitely let his subscription lapse:

If I had the choice, I would prefer to spend the money how I want to spend it.

Would you take it out yourself?

I don't think so, no – I can't really see why I should want to take it out because it is rather like insurance really you know, you can't take it out as soon as someone is ill, you have really got to take it out at a time before it. They are not going to accept you as a member of a scheme if, as soon as you sign the dotted line, you say, oh I want to go into hospital.

However respondents who were on discount schemes and so had decided to pay already said they would look at the difference in price:

> I do not see myself stopping insuring myself in the foreseeable future, but it would depend on what the new individual premiums were and then review it from that.

In addition to evaluating cost, one respondent said he would take account of health needs and standards of treatment:

> I wouldn't have joined prior to the company scheme and I wouldn't look for it in a new job. . . I think we'd sort of stop and look at what is happening so far. . . so far we've not needed to use it [PHI] and have had good treatment on the NHS.

Thus, continued subscription will be determined by factors such as extra cost and the degree to which this will sway underlying principles. A number of company subscribers whilst recognising the value of the insurance said they would have preferred a wage or pension increase. This was especially the case when the insurance had been given as part of a wage negotiation.

We asked all respondents why they thought companies offered insurance. It was seen as a perk.

> It's just a perk.

> Incentive to attract workers.

Because they are a caring company:

> They are very good caring company.

or want to appear caring:

> It's now a standard perk and it makes you think the company cares about you.

To get their workers back to work and enhance productivity.

> Get their people treated more quickly.

or

> I think it's a fringe benefit, a perk, but I think it is also because they are putting it in for certain categories of people whom they want to schedule. They don't want their top sales people to go sick at the start of an important campaign.

or

> So they can slot me into the Chaucer [local hospital], get me mended and back out again onto the front line.

Finally it was seen as a response to competitor pressure and part of the wage deals process:

> Keeps workers happy and keeps wage costs down, a way of having a pay rise, and means they will get their workers back working quicker.

Non-subscribers

It might be expected that the comparison group should contain people who do not see problems with the NHS and so do not feel the need to exercise their right of choice; are not provided with private health insurance by their employers; have very strong principles against private health insurance; would not be accepted by insurance companies because of their health problems or are healthy and do not perceive the need for insurance or prefer to spend their money in different ways. Do we see these principles clearly expressed?

Certainly, in this group, principles and practice were most clearly matched. Pro-NHS sentiment and non-use of the private sector was prevalent:

> I rebel against private. NHS is good enough and I pay enough NI for it and I should help pay for those who can't afford it. Everyone should get the same standard of service.

> Because of principle, if you are a socialist, then private medicine is a sort of total anathema.

> No, in my heart of hearts, I believe in the NHS and nobody should need to entertain purchasing private health.

> I'm a firm believer in the NHS.

> Don't want to; by taking out private health insurance, you are running down the NHS . . . we'll end up like up America with people ill and unable to afford insurance . . . people opt out of the NHS because they are forced to with waiting, it shouldn't happen.

There was one exception where one respondent preferred to pay privately because of waiting lists and his poor health status (a history of heart disease) meant insurance contributions were very expensive.

The non-subscriber also gives us some insight into how principle and practice can become separated. As the following extract shows, principles can be modified when individual's circumstances intervene:

> I disagree with the principle of private medicine. It damages the NHS and their staff are trained at the expense of NHS – they work both sectors which is a disgrace – but my views are more likely to go towards private as I get older and the possibility of me needing care becomes statistically greater.
> *So principles go in certain circumstances?*
> Sure, I haven't let them get in the way of practicalities, if my principles get inconvenient, I have got others!

> I'm totally against the idea of private medicine in principle but when it comes down to practice and making sure my family is okay, then I will pay . . . so now I am contemplating a scheme that I don't want to.

> My political principles say it is bad . . . but being self-employed I think about it and I could afford it . . . At the moment principles outweigh it, I've looked at it for twenty years and still haven't taken it out.

There were six examples which worked the other way – that is non-subscribers who would like to have private health insurance but pragmatic factors got in the way.

> *What stops you joining?*
> Probably three things: the first one, probably, is that it would cost me a lot of money; the second is that I don't believe it is a full system, they will work on certain areas and not on others; the third thing is that I am not sure what I feel about it politically, how it undermines the system. I was one of the very odd people who likes the idea of private beds in hospitals because the money goes to help pay for National Health patients and the consultants who are in the same building.

In this case, principles and the issues of cost are important. Practical considerations proved more influential for others.

> It's going to cost a fortune and doesn't cover you for everything.

Others did not see the need:

> I am healthy and young

or

> I don't see the need, people that do base their decision on conjecture, the impression that treatment is better and quicker – if you can believe what

you see on TV adverts and that sort of thing. If I was wealthy maybe I would take it out as an added insurance.

I am happy with the service. . . I am not against private medicine but I am healthy and satisfied.

This idea of a basic attachment to the NHS is further examined through two other questions. All the respondents were asked whether they would pay more for the NHS; or alternatively, would they welcome the choice to opt-out of National Insurance contributions and move to an entirely private scheme. In a sense this latter question was included to ascertain whether attachment to the NHS was at least in part because of statutory financial commitment. In response to paying more, all the non-subscribers answered 'yes' and one welcomed minimal charges for certain services on top, which he saw as ensuring individual responsibility for health. Only one of the company subscribers did not want to contribute additional amounts of money, as he did not see the logic in paying 'lots more just because you are earning more.' The remainder accepted the idea of increased expenditure, as the following extract illustrates:

I would just as soon pay more tax and get an NHS that provided everything that we are likely to need within reason. It would be preferable to charge the money and pay insurance to the NHS. If you earn more you should pay more for it.

Finally, the individual subscribers again said they would be willing to contribute more:

Absolutely, no equivocation on that whatsoever, I would be quite happy to pay more to achieve, first of all, two things: one to achieve social justice for everyone and secondly to improve the quality of health medicine.

Don't privatise further, I would rather see people who can afford it pay more towards NHS.

The commitment to paying more sometimes carried the condition that there would be an assurance that the money went to the health service.

I don't know where the taxes go, I would love it if they took it from guns and put it into health. If they said they can't do that and said will you pay £1 per week more and this will go specifically to the health service, I would say yes (individual subscriber).

> If the money went to the health service (Non-subscriber).

Alternatively, one individual subscriber suggested extra payment should be at point of service.

> Rather than increase taxes, those who can afford it should pay something when they go; it would perhaps stop people wasting the doctor's time.

No one said they would not pay extra.

A similar picture was conveyed in response to opting out. Only five respondents would welcome this choice, the remainder saw clear disadvantages:

> No because I believe if you start on that particular activity, then all that happens is a worsening of the service provided for other people. If I don't pay my NI, then there would be a lot like me all over the country who would do the same and if the reduction of that investment in the NHS meant the service would reduce which may tempt more people to move out . . . I should continue to contribute . . . No. I think I should pay towards the NHS. No, no, no . . .

The majority, then, did not want to opt-out of National Insurance contributions even if they were subscribers to private health insurance. There was a recognition that they still used the NHS as a commitment to ensuring that the NHS remained for those on lower incomes:

> No because I still go to the NHS.

> No, I'll pay National Health and avail myself of the services of that system, I'm in support of the NHS and will pay for it and would like to see it improve.

and ideologically:

> I'm against it [opting-out], I want to see the private sector run down, not expanded. I think it is important that everybody in this country gets the same level of health not just those that can afford it (company subscriber).

or

> No, I think it is totally wrong. I would fight tooth and nail for the taxes that support the NHS . . . I don't mind if people have extra but they should not be allowed to get out of taxes. Taxes are a part of belonging to a community. You can't unbelong to a community just because you have extra money and buy yourself luxuries.

> I don't like paying twice, but, if I stopped paying, the National Health would become even more deflated, so I pay it.

> It would be nice to opt-out, but then the standard would drop in the NHS – it was our choice to pay the extra...and I wouldn't want a system like America.

A strongly voiced fear was a development of an America-style system:

> No I don't want a system like America. I've lived there and doctors are purely financially money motivated (company subscriber).

Interestingly this illustrates that respondents are committed to the NHS on ideological grounds, but also because of practical reasoning, i.e. they need the NHS, particularly for primary care and emergencies. This is apparent in other studies (Busfield, this volume) which show that respondents are aware of the limitations of private health insurance and so recognise they need the NHS to supplement the cover, and recognise that material/financial considerations mean that they have an interest in maintaining the NHS since high use of their private facilities inflate private health insurance premiums.

Five of the respondents (3 individual subscribers, 1 company subscribers, 1 non-subscribers) would like to be able to opt out, if opting out was financially favourable:

> If I could opt-out completely, then I would because I feel I could get a pretty good policy with the money I pay into the NHS, although I would sooner the government sink all the cash into the NHS, so you didn't have to contemplate it.

> Yes I would be mildly pleased if there was a tax concession; if that came about an awful lot more people would go for it and that would leave more for the people that can't afford it.

So again the more favourable alternative was to commit more resources to the NHS.

> I'd opt-out of it, didn't cost me anymore...but I would pay more for the NHS, as long as it's not as outstanding as this poll tax.

> I'd like to opt-out or pay more tax and then I wouldn't have to pay into a private scheme.

DISCUSSION

The focus in this chapter was to examine why people take out private health insurance and in particular whether it is dissatisfaction with the NHS and/or changing values about health and welfare which have a major influence on the decision making process. Both the quantitative analysis and the qualitative analysis suggested a relationship between subscription and level of satisfaction. Levels of satisfaction were shown, through the quantitative data, to be related to mode of payment, with subscribers who paid jointly with their employer being the most dissatisfied. The quantitative analysis also suggested that subscribers to private health insurance did not seem to base their judgements about the health service on recent, personal experience as Saunders and Harris (1989) might argue, but these judgements appear to be tied to broader ideological values (Taylor-Gooby, 1986). However, one limitation of the quantitative analysis was that it could not account for why the relationship between satisfaction and mode of payment exists nor show how different aspects of individuals' beliefs are related to each other. The qualitative analysis identified this most clearly by showing how dissatisfaction with aspects of the NHS is not necessarily matched with broad principles about health care as a whole. The respondents' accounts suggest a strong regard for the NHS; one which would like to see a continued service relieved of its present problems. The response to the question of opting out and paying more National Insurance supported this.

What are the implications for theories of consumption? Busfield (1990; this volume) argues that private medical care does not fit the analysis that divisions of consumption have replaced divisions of production, mainly on the grounds that most people are both private and public consumers or as Day and Klein (1989) state, they 'commute' between the public and private sectors. Evidence from our study supports Busfield's standpoint in that consumption of private health insurance does not provide a new basis for social divisions and stratification. Our data, particularly the qualitative data, suggests that beliefs and values in relation to health care appeared to be more consistent across subscribers and non-subscribers than actual behaviour and thus there is little evidence to support the notion of a growing political divide based on consumption style differences – at least in the area of health care.

Our data certainly suggest that those respondents who are pro-private are in a minority. The majority recognise the advantages of private medicine but at the same time exhibit continued support for the welfare state. Several authors have found similar 'ambivalent' attitudes in their research but have put forward different explanations. For Taylor-Gooby (1987), support for both public and private sectors is explained by self-interest. People derive their rather narrow and individualistic perceptions of interests according to Taylor-Gooby (1987), from capitalist ideology. Under capitalism, goods and services become private property, so that what are really social relations become experienced as exchange relations. Attention is focused on to the exchange of things as 'values'. Individual purchase of a good is continually legitimated as the normal way to conduct a social relation, and self-interest is to do with the capacity to command goods. Thus, there is an in-built prejudice in favour of private provision because it is a market relation. At the same time, the principle of maximising command over goods produces an interest in favour of the use of state collective services, where those offer a good deal. Thus, there is support for the state service because it is beneficial but the public assert the legitimacy of the market since this is the basis of consumption in our society. Exit from state use and support of the private sector depends on the balance of state and private provision. The lack of subsidies to the private sector, however, limits enrolment and yet the nature of capitalism ensures support for market principles and privatisation. Therefore, self interest ensures support for both the state and the market and a belief that the private sector offers better facilities is not in opposition to support for state services.

Saunders and Harris (1989), in contrast, interpret ambivalence in a different way. Their empirical findings also show that the majority of their sample are 'ambivalent' although there was evidence of a group of resolute anti-statists. This, for Saunders, is the direct consequence of a state which depends on contributions and as such the public are coerced clients of state systems of health. It is impossible to avoid the state sector and as such we are 'trapped consumers'. Thus ambivalence is not surprising. Individuals have to pay taxes and want a good service but cannot afford to pay twice and thus it is logical for them to support state financed welfare and show preparedness to pay extra for such facilities. Thus, people are pragmatists and so support the state but this should not be translated as a popular support. The reason for ambivalence is the lack of choice offered by the state, not the choice offered by the market as Taylor-Gooby would argue. Thus these writers approach the issue of ambivalence from opposite ends.

A further and more materialist explanation of ambivalence emerges from Busfield's (1990) work. She argues that, as has been described previously, support for both sectors emerges because individuals consume both. Limitations of insurance, i.e. the typical caseload of elective surgery and omission of primary and chronic care, means that the insured necessarily have to use the NHS which of course means strong public support for the service. This too incorporates the notion of self-interest recognising the material gains from adherence to the NHS.

Our understanding of ambivalence is somewhat different. The majority of our respondents have a strong commitment to the NHS in principle and yet some take out private health insurance. The purchase of private health insurance is not because of a commitment to the market nor is the support for the NHS because of the lack of choice. Rather, the very fact that the market provides an alternative (and in 50 per cent of the cases this is a 'given' alternative by companies) which offers some benefits, means that there is support for the private sector. However, although support for the state is dependent on the practical need for continued use of the NHS (Busfield, 1990), we have shown that pragmatic considerations also intervene when individuals require the speed or prefer the comfort of private provision. Saunders (1984) argues that respondents do not want to pay twice because they cannot afford it and are constrained to opt for the state sector. We would argue that they did not want to pay twice because the general principle held is pro-NHS.

The NHS is held in high regard even by those who choose to purchase private health insurance. Decisions to take out private health insurance, judging from the analysis of the qualitative data, seem to be influenced by a number of different types of influence. Two of these influences appear to be related to the supply side, such as where the employer gives private health insurance as a 'gift' and where the movement towards a mixed economy of health care provides a setting which people 'use' because it is there, not because they desire the system as it stands. The other three influences are related more to the 'demand' side. One of these is associated with the 'social relations' of care in that one of the perceived advantages of private health care is that the patient is treated as an individual. In addition, for some, private health insurance might also be seen as a status symbol. The second one is associated with resource or financial judgements such as the loss of time and money associated with waiting lists or, on the other hand, the escalating premiums and increased cost of private health insurance. The third influence is associated with the individual's perceived risk or need; a deterioration in health status, for example, may lead to a consideration of the advantages and disadvantages of private medicine, or an awareness that certain circumstances such as age make the individual or family more 'vulnerable' to ill-health.

What of the implications for policy? Saunders and Harris (1989) argue that despite the evidence that consumer experience of state health care systems is fairly positive, there is a strong potential demand for private alternatives. We found little evidence to support such claims in that there appeared to be a basic consensus of support for the National Health Service which existed at the level of principle. Thus, the private sector may be fulfilling an important function for some individuals at the moment but in terms of the development of a policy for the population as a whole, there is strong political support for the expansion of the National Health Service.

Acknowledgements

Thanks to J. Gabe and L. Opit for their help with setting up the sudy and to the ESRC for funding it.

7 Managed Markets: Consumers and Producers in the National Health Service

Rob Flynn

INTRODUCTION

Increasing attention is being given to the significance of consumption, in an attempt to gain a better empirical understanding of contemporary social changes (Warde, 1990b; this volume). In seeking to understand consumption fully, it is necessary to analyse the experiences and views of consumers, and the social context of the use of goods and services, and not simply confine our interest to producers and the production process. There is also a normative argument that the beliefs and preferences of clients and consumers have been neglected in both theory and practice, and that this should be remedied. According to Saunders (1986: 347):

> The sphere of consumption is as important and crucial as it is precisely because it is here that the potential exists for extending people's control over their own lives. In general, this potential does not exist in the sphere of production.

This theoretical interest in consumption is a reflection of the fact that generally in Britain there has been growing concern with consumers' attitudes, more questioning of modes of provision in the public sector, and intensive scrutiny of the effectiveness and efficiency of welfare state activities. Undoubtedly the political success of New Right doctrines and policies has been (partly) based on these themes; they have been effected through a variety of privatisation measures, and have led to a fundamental reappraisal of the appropriate functions and boundaries of the state. In the fields of education, housing, personal social services, social security and transport, government policies in the 1980s and early 1990s have sought to reduce the burden of public expenditure, diminish the influence exercised by public employees and state bureaucrats/professionals, and have encouraged individuals' and households' self-reliance rather than dependence on the state.

Consumerism, of course, is not simply synonymous with New Right philosophy. Critiques of paternalistic welfare agencies, and support for voluntary and cooperative forms of mutual aid are part of New Left platforms as well. The recently revived stress on the virtues of individualism, autonomy and freedom of choice coincides with long-standing and widespread (if ambivalent) values in popular consciousness (Pahl and Wallace, 1988; Papadakis and Taylor-Gooby, 1987a; Taylor-Gooby, 1985). Market or quasi-market mechanisms are being championed as the most effective means for articulating people's demands, and for making producers and providers more responsive to consumer preferences. This trend may be applauded by anti-collectivists, and accepted by citizens supportive of the welfare state but dissatisfied with increasingly underfunded and inadequate public services.

There are, then, strong pressures facilitating the resurgence of interest in markets and consumers. Proposals for major reforms in the British National Health Service (NHS) were made in 1989, and provide an important and interesting example of the attempt to apply market principles to a key, and perhaps the core, institution of the welfare state, and therefore merit analysis. This chapter first considers some of the factors leading to the plans for a reorganisation of the NHS delivery system. It then outlines the main proposals of the White Paper *Working for Patients* (Department of Health, 1989, CM 555; hereafter referred to as the White Paper). The likely impact of a managed market is then discussed broadly in relation to the position of different groups – patients (and potential patients), doctors in general practice and hospitals, and health authority managers.

The principal argument of this chapter is that the planned reforms will not enhance consumers' choice nor enlarge their influence over health services. If fully implemented, the White Paper may indeed shift the balance of power away from medical professionals, but it will not necessarily improve the position of patients as consumers. The most likely outcome will be that health authority *managers* will extend their span of control and, in determining the content of contracts and prices offered by providers, managerially-defined criteria of efficiency and effectiveness will challenge medical definitions of need and clinical quality of care, and function as substitutes for consumer demand. The discussion will also raise questions about the appropriateness and validity of the market (producer/consumer) model in health care, and suggest that while a consumption approach to health services research may be useful, the concept of consumer sovereignty in health is unworkable.

It will be evident that this chapter is concerned solely with the NHS in England, and predominantly with the acute hospitals and primary care (General Practitioner) sectors. Moreover, it is acknowledged that by focusing on doctors, managers and patients, it does not examine the position of the many other staff groups working within it who can reasonably be described as producers – administrative and ancillary workers, nursing and paramedical staff. This reflects constraints of space but also a fundamental conceptual difficulty in analysing health and health services.

CONSUMPTION IN HEALTH AS A PROBLEMATIC CONCEPT

The very concept of consumption is sociologically problematic, and as Warde (this volume) suggests, we need to analyse its constituent interrelated elements in terms of different modes of provision, each having different social relations of production, criteria for access, and methods of delivery. However, a complete and systematic account of consumption processes and phases may be impractical. Moreover, there are many ambiguities and difficulties when applying consumption categories, and even in identifying consumers and producers. This is especially true in the sphere of health and health care.

Who *are* the producers and consumers of health, and health care? Individuals produce their own health (or not) in relationship to numerous environmental and socio-economic factors. They may define and categorise states of health/illness in different ways; resort to self-medication and various forms of lay and professional diagnoses and therapies; and may ignore advice, misuse medicines or fail to comply with the treatment prescribed. Drugs and treatments may not be effective, and may even be harmful. Health care is not a discrete, homogeneous product, although in various forms it can be a commodity bought and sold for profit. Doctors, nurses and paramedical staff may be conventionally regarded as the primary producers/providers of health care *services* to patients, but care is also given by households informally.

Nevertheless, because of the special characteristics of health care (life-chances literally may be at risk) patients are dependent on professional expertise. They may or may not be passive clients/ recipients, but because of the intrinsic uncertainties surrounding health and medical interventions, patients are not easily able to shop around, compare prices and quality, or penalise suppliers for poor service or faulty goods by refusing to purchase their service or product. Thus the term consumer can only be applied to patients in a very loose way, and for some analysts it is wholly inadequate and inappropriate (Stacey, 1976).

The social relations of production and consumption in medicine and health are evidently highly complex and problematic. Neo-Marxists argue it is a mistake to focus on the interpersonal aspects of doctor–patient relationships and issues of institutional autonomy and professional dominance; health, illness and medicine must be understood within specific modes of (capitalist) production and class exploitation (Navarro, 1986). Whether medicine is ultimately functional for capital accumulation and ideological control or not, it is obvious, however, that its institutional structure and practice are extremely diverse and variable, and unlikely to be exclusively explained in terms of class struggle and bourgeois hegemony. As in other welfare state services, production and consumption in health have become increasingly blurred, and subject to a variety of competing and contradictory influences (Offe, 1985b; Turner, 1987).

Categories of ownership, possession, disposal and use cannot be straightforwardly applied to health services, especially in predominantly nationalised and non-profit systems. On the supply side, there are divisions between clinical specialties and types of treatment, hospital size and function, staffing mix and resource provision, as well as important divisions between acute, community and primary care, and public health measures. In the NHS, medical professionals may formally be independent contractors, but their ownership and control of facilities is ambiguous and largely contingent upon the NHS collective infrastructure.

There is also much differentiation among consumers reflecting (and limiting) their access to, demand for, and use of services. Thus there are well-known variations in morbidity and mortality rates between social classes and regions. There are also differences in General Practitioner consultation rates and patterns of treatment, and referrals to hospital. Variations in the incidence and severity of disease also reflect age and gender composition, and therefore the need (demand) for services (Morgan *et al.*, 1985; Richman, 1987; Townsend *et al.*, 1988; Wilkin *et al.*, 1987). Consumers of health are thus probably more heterogeneous than their analogues in other markets for goods and services.

Even in the private medical sector, the competitive market model has little validity, and the notion of consumer sovereignty is inappropriate (Calnan and Cant, this volume; Busfield, this volume). Indeed, Busfield has further shown that private medical subscribers are consumers of both private *and* state medicine, and she has rejected the argument that medical care constitutes a distinctive basis for political interests founded on consumption sectoral divisions (Busfield, 1990). Consequently, concepts of ownership, control and use (and consumer demand) derived from a commodity/property exchange relationship are difficult to operationalise in health services, especially in a system founded on citizenship rights to obtain comprehensive care free at the point of consumption.

Having outlined the conceptual difficulties (which are discussed again later), it is nevertheless the case that a major objective of recent government policy is precisely to introduce or expand the capacity of patients to function as real consumers. Providers in the NHS – General Practitioners, consultants, hospitals, and District Health Authorities – will be required to behave like commercial firms competing for customers within a nationalised tax-financed public system, alongside a small but significant private (for-profit and non-profit) health sector. Elements in the social relations of production in the NHS are to be changed in order to approximate to a market system, but as yet the effects on the social relations of consumption in health are unknown. The context of, and reasons for, these changes are known, however, and can now be considered.

THE CRISIS OF THE NHS

Since its inception, there has always been government anxiety about the rising level of NHS expenditure, and there have been numerous attempts to improve efficiency, as well as two major structural reorganisations in 1974 and 1982. Despite increases in total funding, signs of a crisis emerged in 1987. It became widely acknowledged that health authorities were underfunded – that is, the money allocated to them by central government was inadequate to cover the actual costs caused by increases in patients treated, above-average inflation in NHS salaries, drugs and equipment, and new developments in treatment and medical technology (Maynard and Bosanquet, 1986; NAHA, 1987,

1988a, 1988b; Robinson and Judge, 1987; Social Services Committee, 1988a, 1988b).

This crisis led to a variety of cost-saving and retrenchment measures as health authorities tried to balance their cash-limited budgets, and from 1987 to 1990 there was unprecedented media and parliamentary debate about the consequences of hospital bed and ward closures and other reductions in patient services. In the wake of considerable public disquiet, complaints about hospital waiting lists and cuts, and protests by medical, nursing and other NHS staff groups, an internal review of the NHS was carried out by the Prime Minister, health ministers and their advisors.

Initial expectations about the wholesale privatisation of the NHS, or a shift away from a collectively-financed, tax-based system to a more restricted insurance-funded system proved premature. Probably as a result of widespread public anxiety and political criticism, the White Paper steered away from a radical change in the method of financing the NHS, and instead proposed important changes in the provision and delivery of primary care and hospital sectors. Although it did not specify the precise nature of the problems facing the NHS, the White Paper observed merely that there was a need for reform in the organisation and delivery of health care. Two objectives were explicitly mentioned – to obtain better choice for patients, and greater satisfaction and rewards for employees (Department of Health, 1989, CM 555: 3–4). Near the end of the document three central aims were given: to extend patient choice; to delegate responsibility; and to secure the best value for money (ibid. 102).

There is thus a clear commitment to embracing the principles of a market in the *supply* of services, and to extending the influence of patients as consumers of those services. Before describing the planned reforms in detail, we must consider why these principles and objectives have acquired such saliency. Obviously these proposals are linked to a much larger programme of rolling back the state and reviving private enterprise in all its forms. New Right philosophies regard market mechanisms as the most efficient method of allocating resources and of maximising individual freedom and choice. State intervention and public provision, it is argued, lead to allocational inefficiencies and are unresponsive to consumer preferences; bureaucracies and state employees may pursue their own interests rather than meeting real demands. The NHS is thus regarded as a public monopoly which artificially restricts supply (because of professional medical dominance), restricts and/or ignores customer choice, and is slow to innovate (Bosanquet, 1983; Green, 1988; King, 1987; Letwin and Redwood, 1988).

Such criticisms are not simply theoretical or ideological assertions, however: for many members of the public they appear to be accurate or plausible explanations for a declining service. Long waiting lists for hospital tests and treatment, complaints about the standard of service offered by consultants and General Practitioners, and concern about the implicit and explicit rationing of resources between different care-groups and medical conditions, are real sources of disappointment and grievance among many actual and potential patients in the NHS. This dissatisfaction coexists with apparently strong public support for the welfare state and the NHS *as well* as substantial support for a private sector in health (and education). Taylor-Gooby (1985) has shown that there are seemingly contradictory or ambivalent attitudes about state intervention in welfare, and has suggested that support for the private sector reflects consumers' experience and perceptions of public provision.

In surveys of public opinion, the most frequent complaints about the NHS have concerned the length of waiting lists, insufficient doctors and nurses, lack of communication and bureaucratic inflexibility (Papadakis and Taylor-Gooby, 1987a). There is also some evidence to suggest that in health, consumers are more interested in 'voice' and 'choice' rather than control of services (Papadakis and Taylor-Gooby, 1987b; Busfield, this volume; Calnan and Cant, this volume). National studies of social attitudes have revealed very strong support for the principle of a state universal health scheme, but simultaneously rising levels of dissatisfaction with the NHS. For example, according to Bosanquet (1988), 39 per cent of those surveyed in 1987 were generally dissatisfied with the NHS, compared with 25 per cent in 1983. Health receives the most support as a first priority for increased government spending, and while there is confidence in the overall quality of NHS medical and nursing care, there is also significant discontent about waiting lists, inadequate staffing levels, and day-to-day organisation of hospital services (Bosanquet, 1988).

In the face of this evidence, it has been argued that most consumers are primarily concerned with improving the availability, accessibility and standard of health services, rather than whether they are *delivered* by public or private sector bodies. Taylor-Gooby (1989) advances this view, and also claims that pressures to exit from the NHS to the private sector do not reflect a desire for increased control, but instead a wish to control the *level* of provision. Saunders and Harris (1987) dispute this interpretation, and argue that most NHS consumers are coerced clients, unwillingly dependent on the state and preferring private health insurance and private medical treatment if tax and other arrangements permitted. The ambivalent attitudes reported in many studies are a result of constrained choices, and so Saunders and Harris advocate a switch in policy towards greater consumer choice. Irrespective of normative arguments about the data, it is nevertheless reasonable to conclude that:

> Perhaps the Conservatives are merely articulating the disquiet voiced across the political spectrum over the decline of the welfare state, be it a legitimation crisis, or the failure to achieve greater equality, or a stifling paternalism, or gross inefficiency (Papadakis and Taylor-Gooby, 1987a: 51).

It is against this background then, that the 1989 White Paper must be analysed: government determination to apply market disciplines to the production and delivery of health services, and dissatisfied customers demanding increased provision and improved quality within the NHS.

THE PROPOSED INTERNAL MARKET

What are the White Paper plans, and how significant are they in the history of the NHS? Taking the latter point first, some expert commentators have claimed that the White Paper marks the beginning of a completely new era, the transformation of the original 1948 NHS model, and that its far-reaching proposals will lead to unprecedented change and dynamic instability (Day and Klein, 1989). These changes are to be accomplished through the following reforms:

- The basis of financial allocations to, and the organisation of, the hospital and family practitioner service are to be altered. Finance will no longer be allocated according to formulae designed to equalise the distribution of medical facilities and resources throughout the country. General Practitioners and health authorities will in future obtain money on the basis of their resident population (weighted for age and morbidity). General Practitioners will have a fixed global budget for the first time in their history as independent contractors with the NHS. They will be required to make contracts with hospitals (locally or outside their locality) to buy specific types and amounts of services for patients referred for diagnosis and treatment.

- New contracts are to be made with General Practitioners to require them to reach certain targets for specific forms of care (immunisations, ante-natal care, health screening), to make their practices more flexible and responsive to patients, to subject them to medical audit, and to link more of their remuneration to services provided as well as the number of patient registrations (capitation fees).
- An indicative drug budget will be fixed annually for each practice, and doctors will be expected to prescribe within their allocation, and answer for excessive prescribing.
- It is expected that many of the large acute and general hospitals will opt-out of District Health Authority control by becoming self-governing trusts; other hospitals and community units may also be able to become self-managing but remain within the NHS. These self-governing hospitals will receive their revenue on the basis of contracts made with Health Authorities and General Practitioners for providing specific numbers and types of services. Contract specifications will fix the price according to criteria and tariffs yet to be agreed about cost-per-case, caseload, waiting times, lengths of stay, etc. The self-governing hospitals will be permitted to borrow from the commercial money market to raise capital, and will be allowed to set their own salaries and working conditions for all grades of staff.
- Hospital consultants' contracts are to be changed to make them directly accountable to managers, and doctors are to be given managerial responsibility for resource use through clinical budgeting or resource management. More systematic medical auditing will be used to monitor doctors' clinical performance, and managers will be involved in the overview of these quality-control procedures.
- Health Authorities (at district and regional levels) are expected to exercise regulatory and coordinating functions. They will, for example, determine what the core of services will comprise, to which local patients will have guaranteed access, and which must be provided by self-governing hospitals. They will also monitor effectiveness, and stimulate competition and the drive for efficiency among alternative suppliers (General Practitioners, self-governing hospitals, directly-managed NHS hospitals, private hospitals) by setting the basic terms and conditions of contracts. The authorities themselves will be reformed (by reducing the number of lay representative members) in order to make them more business-like (Department of Health, 1989, Working Papers 1–8).

The underlying aim of all these measures is to create an internal market within the NHS, to create competition between providers, and thereby increase both cost-efficiency and responsiveness to consumers. Purchasers (General Practitioner budget-holders, and Health Authorities) will be in a strong(er) position to affect the type and quality of hospital treatments, it is believed, because money will flow with the patients. Providers (General Practitioners and hospitals) will in effect compete with each other to offer the best range and level of service. For General Practitioners there are real incentives to attract and retain registered patients, and for self-governing hospitals there will be real price competition as they strive to obtain contracts from General Practitioners and Health Authorities. Given greater local autonomy, and a requirement to earn revenue rather than simply receive a fixed financial allocation, health providers will have incentives to adopt a more positive commitment to service quality and cost-efficiency. The expectation is that ultimately consumers (patients) will benefit because of reduced waiting times and improved standards, and staff will be motivated to achieve higher levels of productivity.

THE IMPLICATIONS OF A MANAGED MARKET

There has been considerable political and professional debate about the desirability of these changes, and continuing arguments about their feasibility. The medical profession is divided about the consequences of an internal market, and there was a strong national campaign against the White Paper by the British Medical Association and other bodies. Predictions about the likely outcomes are bound to be speculative and limited, especially because there is little direct comparative experience from other health systems (where the public/private mix in any case is very varied). Nevertheless, there seems to be general agreement among informed commentators about the implications and probable effects of an internal market (Kings Fund Institute, 1989; Maynard, 1989a, 1989b; Robinson, 1988; A. Williams, 1989).

Firstly, in the primary care sector, where General Practitioners have chosen to become budget-holders, there will be incentives to avoid overspending and to maximise surpluses for reinvestment in the practice. In order to stay within budget, or to seek surpluses, General Practitioners may become more selective in accepting (or excluding) certain types of patient on their list (or may encourage them to leave).

High-cost and high-risk patients will consume proportionately more of the doctor's time and resources than other categories. The very young, the very old, and those with chronic and complex medical conditions requiring continuous and expensive drug treatments will, because of the specific nature of their needs and demands, require high levels of expenditure. There is then a risk of adverse selection, in which the inverse care law might apply: those in greatest medical need may receive the least, or poorer quality, provision if, for financial reasons, doctors avoid high-cost patients, or limit the treatment provided.

Further, in order to save money, in some cases General Practitioners may decide not to refer patients to hospital specialists, and instead try to treat them within the practice. It is also possible that General Practitioners, especially where the list size is large, will have even less time for consultations, and may under-treat patients. The restraint on prescribing (the indicative drug budget) may also lead to under-prescribing. Once contracts for specific services have been agreed with particular hospitals, and agreed by the District Health Authority, General Practitioners will inevitably experience a restriction on their traditional right to refer patients to any consultant in any NHS hospital. This changes the client–professional relationship, because the doctor is conventionally expected to provide the best care irrespective of cost, and this may entail referral to non-local specialists – but this freedom of referral is to be substantially reduced. At the same time, with the prospect of increased specialisation within and between hospitals, there will be a reduction in the range of clinical services available in a given locality. Even if referred to their contracted hospital, patients are likely to have to undertake longer and more expensive travel for care at that hospital.

More competition between doctors may yield a number of benefits if better and more comprehensive primary care is provided. However, there is also the probability that there will be increased variations in the type and range (as well as quality) of care made available in different localities and regions. Simply because of the demographic and socio-economic composition of local populations (and differences in morbidity, mortality, and consultation rates), some practices are more likely to experience budget deficits, or surpluses. Indeed, Maynard (1989a) has argued that in areas with affluent populations and patients able to subscribe to private health insurance, there will be more General Practitioners with budget surpluses, and vice versa. Given the differential ability of different social groups to articulate their needs, responsiveness to consumer demands may lead to further social inequalities and new social divisions in the use of health care services.

Within the hospital sector, self-governing hospitals will be competing for orders (contracts) placed by General Practitioners and the managers of District Health Authorities, in order to obtain revenue. There is uncertainty about which services are to be offered in all hospitals – so-called core services are to be defined by the District Health Authorities – but it is likely that there will be a move away from the all-purpose comprehensive district general hospital model. In seeking economies of scale, there is likely to be a concentration of specialties in only some hospitals. Others may choose to concentrate on services in which they claim a particular expertise and reputation. There will be more specialisation in acute care within and between districts, but this will necessarily reduce accessibility for resident populations. Given the incentive to generate income, self-governing hospitals may prefer to offer their most attractive service to patients referred from outside of their locality at a higher price. Those services, because they are more profitable, would expand at the expense of others.

Decisions about developments in services will in future be less influenced by the professional dominance of clinicians, because self-governing hospitals' executive boards and District Health Authority managers will enjoy increased control over budgets and strategic policy. The scope of general management is to be extended; employment contracts will be amended and consultants are to be made directly accountable to managers, and responsible for clinical budgets. Clinicians will be subject to regular medical audit, and managers will play a role in monitoring professional quality control, as well as evaluating cost effectiveness. These measures represent major changes in the structure of control in the NHS, and are likely to cause continuing disputes and bureaucratic–professional conflict.

The pricing of services is extremely complex and problematic, and has been the object of much research and debate in the NHS. It is unclear whether there is adequate information to allow price/quality trade-offs to be assessed by purchasers. Even if costing systems can be devised, there is still the internal problem of cross-subsidisation (revenue from relatively efficient or profitable units being used to subsidise less efficient or unprofitable hospital activities), and possible conflicts between different specialties and sections within hospitals over the allocation and recharging of costs. Moreover because self-governing hospitals will have to finance their capital charges, the prices of treatments in cities with high land-values will have to reflect those fixed costs. Hospitals with major teaching and research functions will also be in an invidious position, with higher than average costs which may not be fully recouped through contract prices. Competition between hospitals for staff may lead to increases in wage-costs, and be passed on in higher charges to customers.

In the internal market, the assumption is that efficient hospitals will attract more patients and thereby obtain resources to expand. The corollary must be that inefficient hospitals will face going out of business and thus closure. It is by no means clear whether this would ultimately be accepted politically, or indeed whether it is really feasible. In practice, both complete closure and major expansion are difficult because of the very large capital investments in hospitals. If outright closure is unlikely, hospitals will presumably be compelled to increase their efficiency (reduce costs) – but this will put pressure on quality and lead to a probable lowering of standards (King's Fund Institute, 1989; Maynard, 1989a).

Whether or not the new regime results in lower costs, or greater efficiency, one of the major objectives is to give more power to consumers. It is clear from the developments outlined above, however, that most patients will continue to be remote, or entirely absent from the crucial decisions on the supply and provision of services in the internal NHS market. Evidently General Practitioners will continue to act as the 'guardians' (Maynard, 1989b) for their patients not only in negotiating the content of primary care but in selecting hospital contract services. But their actions will be subject to Regional and District Health Authority supervision, and in effect general managers will function as intermediaries and gatekeepers, especially in bargaining with General Practitioners and self-governing hospitals about contract specifications and prices. The Health Authorities are expected to act as advocates of local populations, but they are currently non-representative and unelected, and under the new arrangements will have even less accountability to local communities.

Thus the accessibility, content, range, price and quality of health services will be decided through the intra- and inter-organisational politics of provider and manager bargaining, and not through consumer demand or preference. The internal NHS market will thus be a *managed* market, albeit one in which there will be a significant shift away from medical professional dominance of resource allocation and policy. Consumer choice may even be further diminished as doctors lose their influence, as patients are locked in to provider–

purchaser contracts, and as managers increase their powers as brokers, price-setters, and quality-controllers (for perceptive predictions of this, see Robinson, 1988; Social Services Committee, 1988b: paras 141–2, 171–2).

CONSUMERS, PRODUCERS AND MANAGERS OF HEALTH SERVICES

The social relations of consumption in the NHS are likely to be changed significantly by current government plans for an internal market. Two related objectives can be identified in these plans: increased efficiency and more responsiveness to consumers. The proposals form a part of a much larger programme of measures to restructure social policy and the welfare state, and a shift away from collectivism to individualism (Crouch, 1985; Flynn, 1989). There have been numerous attempts to control the growth of NHS expenditure, to improve its effectiveness, and to change the pattern of provision. In the 1980s, central government intensified these attempts, and extended its control over the volume of expenditure, the service priorities, and the management of health care delivery. There have been many initiatives and reforms – ministerial accountability reviews, performance indicators, cost-improvement programmes, competitive tendering, clinical budgeting and general management – intended to stimulate cost-containment and better value for money. The common trends in all these developments, and the most important in discussions of consumer choice, are centralisation, and the expansion of managerial control over medical professionals (Klein, 1983; Harrison, 1988).

Government policy in the 1980s and early 1990s has been geared to reducing state producers' power and enhancing consumers' individual influence, but as the preceding discussion suggests, it is difficult to specify the ways in which consumers will enjoy more choice or control. If implemented fully, the managed market will reduce doctors' and other health workers' autonomy, and subject it to closer and more stringent managerial control. Even if it is difficult to accept the basis on which professional definitions of medical need have been used in resource allocation and rationing, and whether or not these criteria and their outcomes are regarded as efficient or equitable or beneficial to consumers, it is even more problematic to identify the motives, interests and objectives of the general managers. Health service managerialism has grown throughout the history of the NHS, but since the introduction of general management in 1983, and with the White Paper proposals, managers' influence and prerogatives have been widened – but within a hierarchical system driven by central directives, and with a stress on cost-control and the application of commercial disciplines and values.

The impact of general management has been extensive, and according to many commentators, there has been a transformation from a classic administered bureaucracy into a managed service, managerial ideas have become the established orthodoxy, and there is an ongoing moral crusade to change the organisational culture of the NHS (Best, 1987; Davidson, 1987; Strong and Robinson, 1988). It is well-known that Health Authority members play only a limited role in policy-making, and that their influence is marginal relative to officials and professional advisors (Day and Klein, 1987; Ham, 1986). Recent studies of general managers have shown that one of their main concerns is to extend managerial authority over clinicians. Cousins (1987) observed that managers regarded NHS staff, equipment and plant as commodities and resources, and saw their own role as maximising efficiency in resource use. She also claimed that managers had become more assertive, authoritarian, and directive in dealing with all staff. Ferlie and McKee (1988) have argued that, recently, management imperatives have predominated, and that clinical supremacy is being eroded.

A study of general managers and directors of finance by the author showed that among district general managers dealing with budget crises and cost containment, much stress was laid on the necessity of extending managerial control over clinicians. In the hospital sector, many medical and nursing practices were regarded as obstacles to efficiency. However, in the climate of retrenchment, managers were confident that the influence enjoyed by doctors under the previous system of consensus management was being displaced – financial priorities were increasingly important, and enabled managers to challenge medical autonomy (Flynn, 1988). While agreeing that there has been a shift in the frontier of control between doctors and managers, Harrison (1988) argued that there is little direct evidence of changes in the substance of managerial–clinical relationships. Harrison *et al.* (1989) argue that hospital consultants still have a significant obstructive power, and that managers still inhabit a shared culture in which professional medical autonomy is challenged only rarely. Significantly, however, Harrison *et al.* note that managers *have* been able to assert their authority over clinicians in situations of financial crisis.

Evidently, then, through a variety of means, managers have enlarged their capacity and opportunity to influence local resource allocation, medical priorities, and, to an increasing extent, the delivery of services. What remains unclear is the nature of managerial goals and objectives, and how these might change in the new marketised NHS. Managers are accountable to superordinate line managers and District and Regional Health Authority chairpersons, and (like the latter) ultimately to the Secretary of State. The Health Authorities' representativeness has always been precarious and uncertain, and future changes in composition and functions will make their relationship to consumers even more ambiguous. Thus consumers (patients and prospective patients) are unlikely to be able to directly influence local managers, and those managers' allegiances and concerns are likely to be bureaucratic. Their contact with patients is minimal and very remote – because front-line health workers and gatekeepers deliver the service – and managers' primary future task will be to establish and regulate contracts within government-prescribed cash-limits and performance- and quality-indicators. Consequently, it is hard to see how managers will become responsive to consumer demands or preferences, and difficult to identify what model of health-care needs and priorities they will subscribe to.

CONCLUSIONS

This, then, finally returns us to the applicability of the market model in health care. It is generally acknowledged that demand for health care is theoretically infinite, and that some mechanism for rationing resources is inevitable. Prior to the 1990 proposals, resource allocation in the NHS tended to reflect medical professionals' definitions of needs and priorities, and consumer sovereignty had been ignored in favour of universalistic values of citizenship and equity. The proposed managed market will weaken professional dominance, and aims to make the suppliers of health care more attentive to patients as customers within the public sector. Whether it will succeed remains to be seen, but there are important limits on the acceptability and feasibility of the market.

For some, health care can be considered a commodity like other goods and services, and individuals should be allowed to determine the type and amount of personal consumption, and express their own choices, preferences and valuations, through the market. The conflicting view is that health has important externality effects, that patients cannot reliably know what their medical needs are, and that it is morally and ethically wrong to expect people to pay for care when they are ill – hence the financial risks should be shared, patients must defer to doctors' expertise, and services must be provided according to need, not according to ability to pay.

Thus, for example, Green (1988: 22), in advocating a competitive market and enlarged consumer choice, nevertheless recognises that health care is (partly) different from other kinds of economic goods, and so accepts that a remedial role for governments is justified. His recommendations are to maximise the extent to which individuals take personal responsibility for health care decisions, and reduce the monopolistic position of suppliers. By contrast, Mooney (1986) has stressed that few, if any, other goods or services have the unique combination of unpredictability, imperfect knowledge and externalities characterising health care. He argues that the agency relationship between doctor and patient cannot be equated with consumer sovereignty. What both approaches share is the inescapable observation that patients will almost always be *dependent* on medical professionals. The disagreement is about how that dependency is to be regulated, and how individual wants can be reconciled within the provision of collective goods.

Public sector consumerism reveals very clearly the contradictions between the market logic of efficiency and the welfare goal of equity, and also raises fundamental questions about who are the consumers and producers, and the nature of the relationship between them. Public services are not simply about meeting the needs and wishes of clients/customers, and doing so effectively and efficiently, they are also about making those services accessible, equitable, and accountable (Pollitt, 1988). Consumer preferences and producer incentives in such a context cannot be identical to those in a competitive commodity market. However, when they (or proxies for them) are introduced in the NHS internal market, it is likely that there will be 'greater inequality in access to health care, provision of health care of inadequate quality and cost inflation' (Maynard, 1989a: 2). If these outcomes do occur, then enhanced consumer choice will have been obtained at the cost of other values and objectives.

It is assumed here that the social relations of consumption in health are defined principally by criteria of dependency, need, accessibility and equity. Planned changes in the structure and operation of the NHS may indeed reduce the dominant influence exercised hitherto by medical professionals, but they will not thereby empower the patients, and they may have other regressive effects on the type, volume and standard of care made available. Medical producers will confront challenges by bureaucratic managers, whose relationship to consumers (patients and potential patients) is indirect and tenuous, and whose interests and priorities are opaque. Existing social divisions in health may be reinforced, and new ones emerge, as the pattern of supply and demand is established by managerial purchasers and professional providers. Consumer representation is unlikely to flourish in the new structure of power relations, as professional autonomy is eroded by bureaucratic control, and as consumer choice is mediated by managerial objectives and actions. Day and Klein are therefore entirely correct in their claim that an internal market will consolidate and intensify managerial control of the NHS. In assessing the changing relationships between consumers, producers and managers, they have argued cogently that:

> the new era will benefit the middlemen of health care: researchers, accountants, financial and management consultants, and others who profess expertise about efficiency even if they do not necessarily add to it (Day and Klein, 1989: 29)

It remains to be seen whether the internal market will be fully implemented, and what impact it will have on access to health services. Its effects on the social relations of production and consumption in health, and social divisions in general, are likely to be profound.

8 Patterns of Social Consciousness amongst the Middle Classes

Rosemary Crompton

INTRODUCTION

A common feature accompanying the development of capitalist industrial societies is the increase in the proportion of professional, technical and managerial employees amongst the occupied population. The actual extent of this apparent occupational 'upgrading' has been contested (Braverman, 1974; Crompton and Jones, 1984), but that there has been an increase in occupational complexity at the upper end of the hierarchy cannot seriously be doubted. This chapter will argue that, as the proportion of the occupied population in higher-level professional and managerial occupations increases, so does the heterogeneity of this grouping, and thus the diversity of social consciousness within it. Before developing these arguments, however, previous sociological commentaries on these occupational developments, focusing in particular on those relating to the 'service class', will be briefly examined.

In the 1960s, the expansion of such occupations was linked by liberal theorists, as part of a critique of Marxist predictions of class polarisation, to the coming 'end of ideology' in industrial (rather than capitalist) societies (Bell, 1974; Kerr *et al.*, 1973). The Marxist proletariat had long been associated with manual working-class occupations, thus the relative decline of these groupings, and the corresponding increase in middle-class or white-collar occupations, was seen by many as an empirical refutation of Marx's predictions. However, the class location of the burgeoning non-manual labour force was itself disputed. The lower ranks were widely held to have been 'proletarianised' (Crompton and Jones, 1984). Concerning the upper levels, there emerged a lively debate – fuelled by the outburst of educated radicalism in the 1960s and early 1970s – as to whether a new class, incorporating potentially revolutionary elements, was in the process of emerging (Gouldner, 1979; Ehrenreich and Ehrenreich,

1979). Although the increase in non-manual occupations had gained considerably in momentum after the Second World War, however, it was by no means a novel phenomenon. The Austro-Marxist, Karl Renner, had already coined the phrase 'service class' to describe these new middle classes, and this term has been taken up by a number of influential class theorists within British sociology.

THE SERVICE CLASS

Both Goldthorpe (1982; Goldthorpe *et al.*, 1987), and Lash and Urry (1987; see also Abercrombie and Urry, 1983) claim initial inspiration from Renner's (1978) work. However, although their descriptions of this putative class are apparently very similar, they arrive at radically different conclusions as to its significance for the development of contemporary capitalist societies. This is because their underlying approaches to class analysis are very different. However, as they both use occupations to describe classes, there is a superficial similarity in their arguments as they focus on the same occupational groups in their discussion of the service class.

Goldthorpe has developed a class scheme which, when applied to the occupational structure of industrial societies, divides it up into a number of classes of which the service class is one (Goldthorpe *et al.*, 1987). Within this scheme, service class occupations are those in which their incumbents are

> . . . typically engaged in the exercise of delegated authority or in the application of specialist knowledge and expertise, operate in their work tasks and roles with a distinctive degree of autonomy and discretion; and in direct consequence of the element of trust that is thus necessarily involved in their relationship with their employing organisation, they are accorded conditions of employment which are also distinctive in both the level and kinds of reward that are involved (Goldthorpe, 1982:169).

Service class personnel owe their positions to 'processes of bureaucratic appointment and achievement' (ibid:170). However, for Goldthorpe, 'classes' are not simply identified by the kinds of life-chances and employment relationships associated with particular sets of occupations. A 'class' can only be said to have emerged if 'specific social collectivities' have developed within the occupational structure *over time*, that is

> . . . collectivities that are identifiable through the degree of continuity which, in consequence of patterns of class mobility and immobility . . . have been associated with particular sets of positions (Goldthorpe 1983:467).

On the basis of his empirical research into male social mobility, Goldthorpe concludes that a service class has, indeed, emerged – a fact which is hardly surprising given the extent of occupational upgrading noted above. What, therefore, are the implications of the emergence of this class for the present and future development of capitalist industrial societies?

Goldthorpe concludes that, although the service class as he defines it encompasses considerable structural divisions, these are not more marked than those within the other classes, such as the working class, which are generated through the application of his class scheme. He concludes, therefore, that

> . . . while the service class can still be regarded as one *in statu nascendi*, the indications consistently are that its demographic consolidation is likely to be matched by a steady strengthening of its socio-cultural identity. It may be expected, like other classes, to contain within it segments that have the potential to be mobilized across a range of political ideology and action and, distinctively, to be a source of leaders and activists of all political colourations. But, we would believe, as the service class emerges as an increasingly important basis of collective action, it will be seen to constitute a primarily conservative force within modern society, so far at least as the prevailing structure of class inequality is concerned (Goldthorpe *et al.*, 1987:341).

Lash and Urry also point to the increase in professional and managerial occupations as evidence for the growth of the service class, which in their terms consists of 'those dominant positions or places within the social division of labour which do not rest upon material ownership'. These places enjoy superior work and market situations associated with the development of careers, and entry into such places is often regulated by the possession of credentials, either organisation-specific or general. However, although the occupations they identify are similar to those discussed by Goldthorpe, their realist approach to class analysis does not rest upon the application of a theoretical class scheme to the occupational structure. Rather, they argue that the 'causal powers' a class possesses which enable it to emerge as a social force identify the class, thus the *development* of the occupational matrix is the focus of their analysis. The service class, they argue, grew out of a struggle between already-existing capital and nascent managerial groupings. Once established, the activities of the service class serve to weaken the causal powers of the working class, given its role in the control and reproduction of this class.

Thus initially, the developing service class has an interest in the growth of organised capitalism; that is, a capitalism characterised by centralisation, deskilling of the labour process, monopoly, and mass organisations of both workers and employers. Lash and Urry's account of first the organisation, then disorganisation, of capitalism is complex, incorporating a range of technical, spatial, political and economic processes. It has obvious parallels with theses describing the transition from 'Fordism' to 'post-Fordism', as well as other currently fashionable 'binary histories' (See Piore and Sabel, 1984, and the discussion in Sayer, 1989). Lash and Urry's analysis, however, in contrast to some of these other accounts, gives a central role to the service class as far as the process of disorganisation is concerned. This is because the new class 'begins to have a dislocating effect on the relationship between capital and labour and an irredeemably disorganizing effect on capitalist society in general' (Urry, 1989), as the members of this class struggle to protect their own interests as well as playing an active role in the generation of new (non-class) social movements. The state becomes overloaded with the demands of their fragmented interests, and hence, further disorganised. In direct contrast to Goldthorpe, therefore, who has described the service class as primarily a 'stabilising force', Lash and Urry have argued that the service class has a profoundly *destabilising* impact in contemporary capitalism.

It is difficult to arbitrate between these two rather different conclusions because of the fundamentally different theoretical approaches to class held by the two sets of authors. Goldthorpe is concerned to establish whether sufficient numbers of particular occupations and employment statuses have 'crystallised' within the occupational structure over time. He judges that the evidence of this consolidation is sufficient to outweigh the consequences of any fragmentation within this grouping and concludes, therefore, that its emergence constitutes a force for stability. His approach to class analysis rests upon the identification of continuities within the occupational structure, discernible as a result of historical patterns of social mobility, which then have class labels attached to them. The occupational structure itself is taken as given (Marshall, 1990). In contrast, Lash and Urry view the structure of positions (or employment structure) as the *outcome* of class processes. They see classes as possessing economic, ideological, and organisational resources which account for their location in the occupational structure – as we have seen in their description, summarised above, of the growth of the service class (Lash and Urry, 1984:47). Two different problems, furthermore, are focussed upon in these different authors' explorations of the service-class concept; Goldthorpe is concerned with trends in occupational inequality, Lash and Urry with the future development of capitalist societies as a whole – an exercise which Goldthorpe might in any case be likely to reject given his opposition to 'historicism' (Goldthorpe 1978: 216). These problems are approached using different evidence, and different definitions of class. Not surprisingly, therefore, they have arrived at different conclusions. However, rather than engage in an extensive critique, it may be suggested that a more constructive way forward, as far as the analysis of the growth and significance of expert occupations is concerned, lies outside the service-class framework as such. Before these suggestions are developed, however, some more general issues raised by class analysis, as they relate to the service class in particular, will be briefly examined.

CLASS ANALYSIS AND THE SERVICE CLASS

Within both sociology and politics, there has been an extended debate concerning the theoretical origins of class processes. Neo-Marxists have tended to emphasise the significance of property and production relationships, neo-Weberians, the significance of property and market relationships. However, despite these theoretical differences, there would be general agreement that class processes have a significant impact on the characteristics associated with particular occupations, as well as occupational structuring more generally. For example, proletarian occupations may be held to lack autonomy, and, as we have seen, service-class occupations have long been associated with linear careers. Employers will have an obvious impact on structuring through their demands for particular kinds of labour, and occupational groups may seek to claim rights to particular kinds of skills, or reserve particular tasks for themselves. As a consequence of this close relationship between class processes and occupational structuring, sociologists have often treated the class structure as synonymous with the occupational structure. Two of the best-known examples of theoretical class schemes are Goldthorpe's neo-Weberian class scheme, which has already been discussed, and that developed by the neo-Marxist Erik Olin Wright (1985). However, although class processes have what is probably the single most significant impact on the structure of employment, they are not the only factors involved. The occupational structure also bears the imprint of a range of other variables such as gender, age, race, national peculiarities, and so on. The occupational structure is in a constant state of flux, as technological change, political and market fluctuations – indeed, what some might describe as the processes of 'class struggle' – reshape and restructure it. Thus any occupational class scheme will be constantly faced with what Abercrombie and Urry have described as the 'boundary problem'; that is, deciding which occupations should be located in which 'class' (1983:6–7. See also Crompton, 1989). The fluid and changing nature of the occupational structure means that the boundary problem, as far as occupational class schemes are concerned, is impossible to resolve conclusively. This does not invalidate the utility of such schemes, but it does mean that as theoretical measures of 'class', they can only ever be approximations.

The boundary problem lies at the root of those criticisms of 'service-class' theories that have emphasised the heterogeneity within this grouping. The point has frequently been made that the occupational groups comprising the service class have a wide range of potential interests which may often be in conflict with each other. One obvious source of difference is that between those members of the service class employed in the public, as opposed to the private, sector. These differences are clearly manifest in the distribution of political affiliations within these groups (Marshall *et al.*, 1988; Edgell and Duke, 1986). The service class is also markedly stratified by gender in that women predominate in a number of 'caring' professions (e.g. nursing, teaching, social work) which are also concentrated in public-sector employment. Child (1986) has argued that variations within the service class have important consequences for the capacities of different sections within it to respond to the problems raised by the advent of Information Technology. Savage *et al.*, (1988) have noted the growing cleavage between newer 'entrepreneurial' and established 'organisational' elements within the service class, and indeed, they also raise the question as to whether the development of these new and diverse groups undermines the usefulness of the application of a unitary 'class' concept.

Goldthorpe is fully cognisant of the extent of variation within the service class, but argues that they are not 'unusually marked' (Goldthorpe *et al.*, 1987:341) – that is, there is no more variation within the service class than within the other occupational aggregates he identifies within their class scheme. Therefore, *as he has defined it*, a service class is both growing, and consolidating its position in contemporary Britain in that the number of service class occupations is on the increase. He has argued that the service class will be primarily a conservative force as far as 'the prevailing structure of class inequality is concerned', that is, those in higher-level occupations will wish to maintain the level of material reward associated with these occupations, and ensure that their children occupy similar positions. Implicit in this argument is the assumption of a broad 'equality of condition' within the service class which its members have a common interest in preserving. However, if 'equality of condition' is nevertheless arrived at by a number of different routes, or stems from different sources, (as in, for example, the distinction between public- and private-sector employment), then it seems reasonable to raise the question of whether these diverse occupational locations can be said to compose a 'class'. Criticisms of Goldthorpe's position, however, would have to address the wider question of his definition and use of the class concept, rather than his discussion of the service class in particular (Hindess, 1987b, Crompton, 1989).

It is a central feature of Lash and Urry's arguments that the diversity of interests within the service class is integral to the 'disorganisation' of capitalism; to emphasise the differentiation and conflict within this grouping, therefore, hardly constitutes a criticism of their position. However, their account of the development of this fragmented class is in fact rather narrow, and this narrowness is reflected in their summary description of the role of the service class in the development of capitalism. In fact, the role of the service class is wider than that which they describe and, as a consequence, the 'causal powers' of elements within the service class may have outcomes other than the disorganisation of capitalist societies.

Lash and Urry argue that the development of Taylorism, or scientific management, plays a key role in the emergence of the service class. Taylorism is emphasised not only because of its impact on working-class labour processes and thus the causal powers of the proletariat, but also because of the manner in which it was implemented. The importance within Taylorism of verbalisation and written communications, together with the 'scientising' of the emergent managerial process, was a factor in the expansion of institutions of accreditation and thus the further development of the service class. Lash and Urry's emphasis on Taylorism in the development of the service class is further reflected in Urry's characterisation of this class as:

> [servicing] capital through meeting three functions: to conceptualize the labour process; to control the entry and exercise of labour-power within the workplace; and to orchestrate the non-household forms under which labour-power is produced and regulated.

Similarly, the causal powers of the service class are described as being:

> . . . to restructure capitalist societies so as to maximise the divorce between conception and execution and to ensure the elaboration of highly differentiated and specific structures within which knowledge and science can be developed and sustained (both citations from Urry, 1989).

It is not being disputed that Taylorism did have a crucial role in the development of the managerial stratum, particularly in the United States (Stark, 1980). However, features other than the struggle between existing capital and emergent management have also contributed to the development of the service class – for example, the development of civil administrations in emergent nation states, as well as rising standards of living which increased the level of demand for the services of independent professionals. Significant elements of the service class have played a central part in the rationalisation of the labour process and the separation of conception and execution. However, this hardly describes the full range of service-class activities (what about cultural production, the processes of government and decision-making, sports and entertainment?). In short, despite their emphasis upon the fragmentary nature of the service class, Lash and Urry's account of this class is, in fact, narrowly focussed in respect of both its emergence and causal powers. There is a constant tendency, in their account, to discuss industrial management as a proxy for the service class as a whole.

It may be argued, therefore, that neither of the two leading sociological theories of the service class have developed a satisfactory account of the significance of the increase of higher level and professional and managerial occupations for the likely future development of industrial capitalist societies. As occupations, administrative, professional, and managerial groups have considerably more to lose than their chains and may therefore be said to share some kind of interest in the continuing prosperity of capitalist industrial societies. However, their perspectives on how this aim may be best achieved may vary considerably, as may the *relative* advantage which different occupational groups derive from particular societal solutions. One theorist who has attempted to explore this diversity within the upper reaches of the occupational hierarchy is Wright (1985). His growing recognition of this occupational complexity, together with problems such as that of the class location of the non-occupied (or not employed), has been reflected in the continuing elaboration of his initial Marxist class map. However, as he himself has recognised, such elaborations have taken him further and further from his original objectives, to an extent that they may have been lost sight of (Wright 1989). If the boundary problem is taken seriously, as it has by Wright, then a proliferation of 'class' categories is likely to follow. Wright's example suggests that rather than attempting to continue to fit these diverse occupational groupings within the procrustean bed of theoretical class schemes, it might be better to start from an assumption of heterogeneity.

SOCIAL CONSCIOUSNESS AND THE MIDDLE CLASSES

The discussion that follows will explore a single issue – that of ideology, consciousness, or 'images of society'. It will be suggested that different elements within the service class may possess varieties of social consciousness which are at variance with each other, and which may give rise to substantial differences in their prescriptions for the organisation of societies more generally. The strategic positions which members of the service class occupy suggests that the actions deriving from their social consciousness might be likely to have a particularly significant impact on the course of events.[1] As we have seen, in their account of the service class Lash and Urry suggest that the 'servicing' aspects of this class in respect of capital are primarily (even solely) concerned with the regulation and reproduction of labour. However, the role of the service class also involves the work of conceptualisation and cultural production more generally, and at other levels besides that of the labour process.[2]

The study of working-class consciousness has long been of central sociological concern, as described, for example, in Marshall's (1983) review of the literature. Much has been made of the apparently fragmentary, and internally contradictory, nature of this consciousness, a factor which has been held largely responsible for the long-term failure of the working class to achieve its interests (Mann, 1970). In contrast, the consciousness of the dominant classes has been percieved as being of a relatively coherent and/or unitary nature. Indeed, it has been suggested, *contra* the 'dominant ideology' thesis, that the persistence and stability of the dominant classes rests existence of ideological cohesion within these groups, rather than a lack of cohesion amongst the subordinate classes (Abercrombie *et al.*, 1980). If the working-class Conservative has been treated as sociologically deviant, then the middle-class revolutionary has been regarded as an almost pathological type. However, the increase in the size and extent of professional and managerial occupations suggests that there is likely to be an increasing diversity of perspectives within this grouping.

A basic insight deriving from all varieties of class analysis (which is not being denied) is that the individual's experience of employment is likely to have a significant impact upon the way in which they percieve their world. The *relative* significance of the 'occupational effect' will be subject to considerable variation. For example, a range of studies in the sociology of work and occupations has demonstrated the differential capacities of occupations to socialise their members (Brown and Brannen, 1970). 'Class' is a term which is used conventionally to describe occupational aggregates, thus systematic variations in attitude by occupation – for example, as have been revealed in studies of voting behaviour – have often been used as an empirical indicator of class consciousness.

Occupation, therefore, has long been used as a proxy for 'class' but there are many other factors which shape individual and collective social consciounesses, and indeed, historical studies of class development have explored them in some depth (Thompson, 1968). Family of origin, or social background will have an important effect – which is one reason why Goldthorpe incorporates patterns of social mobility into his class analysis. To varying extents, individuals may hold religious beliefs which may be of considerably more significance in shaping their outlooks on the world than the work they do. Nationalism may be another powerful factor, as well as the more subtle 'societal' effect, the operation of which has been demonstrated through systematic cross-national research (Maurice *et al.*, 1986). Gender is of considerable importance in this respect. Empirical research has demonstrated the fragmentation of employment consciousness amongst working-class women as they juggle the demands of their employment and their domestic responsiblities (Pollert, 1981). The socialisation experienced by women, particularly that relating to the moral despotism of motherhood, will, as Purcell (1986) has argued, make it more likely that their world views will be characterised by an element of 'fatalism' than those of men. Gender is also manifest, through occupational segregation, in the structuring of the occupational order (Crompton and Sanderson, 1990), and, as has been noted, women have, historically, tended to be concentrated in particular service-class occupations such as nursing and teaching.

A wide range of factors, therefore, shape attitudes and perceptions but this discussion will focus upon the possible contribution of patterns of employment regulation, spatial mobility, and education within the middle classes which might be argued to give rise to distinctive patterns of social consciouness amongst these occupational groups. It will be argued that the exchange of expert labour (which is what service class employment involves) has problematic characteristics which give rise to a constant tendency to its regulation, which can take on different aspects. The significance of bureaucratic career structures to service class occupations has already been noted; such career paths may be associated with varying patterns of geographical mobility which give rise to different patterns of involvement in community and region. Professional and managerial employment is likely to involve extended experience of education. The experience of higher education has itself been argued to have a discernible impact on social consciouness, as in, for example Inglehart's exploration of 'post-materialist' perspectives amongst the better-educated (Inglehart, 1981; see also Rootes 1990).[3]

In the initial development of this exploratory framework, the outline strategy will be informed by that of Lockwood's influential account of the generation of working-class consciousness. For the most part, he argued, individuals

> visualise the . . . structure of their society from the vantage points of their own particular *milieux*, and their perceptions of the larger society will vary according to their experiences . . . in the smaller societies in which they live out their daily lives (Lockwood, 1966: 249).[4]

The rapidity and extent of communications, and the pace of change, within the 'global village' have increased enormously in the quarter of a century since Lockwood outlined his model, but such proximate elements of socialisation are still likely to be of central importance as far as the individual is concerned. In the remainder of this chapter, therefore, an attempt will be made to pull together some of the existing empirical evidence which might indicate the locus of systematic variations in social consciousness amongst different elements within the service class.

EDUCATION

As with the debates relating to ideology and 'images of society', it is with the impact of education upon the *working* class that sociologists have been most concerned. In the years following the reforms instituted by the 1944 Education Act, which made secondary education free for all, the liberal debate was dominated by the question of why, despite a notional equality of access, working-class children failed to gain the full benefits of the education system as measured by entry into selective schools, examination results, access to higher education, and so on (Halsey *et al.*, 1980; Marsh and Blackburn, this volume). From this perspective, the school was implicitly regarded as a liberating institution as far as working class children were concerned, that is, as incorporating benefits and advantages which were somehow being denied because of lack of access. During the 1970s, however, there developed alternative perspectives (often informed by Marxist critiques) which emphasised the role of the school as a repressive, rather than a progressive, institution in respect of working-class youth (Bowles and Gintis, 1976; Willis, 1977). When educational institutions were not instilling the requirements of the dominant ideology, they were ensuring that working-class children learned how to fail, or alternatively rebel, but still ultimately reproduce their working-class position in society.

Such arguments tended to obscure the fact that, despite the supposed negative impact of education, social mobility statistics demonstrate that a substantial minority of children of working-class origin have become service-class adults (see Payne, this volume). On the basis of his empirical research findings, Goldthorpe has argued that, for men at any rate, such mobility has not resulted in the growth of dissident elements within the upper echelons of the occupational hierarchy (Goldthorpe *et al.*, 1987). Political orientations (which might be taken as an empirical indication of social perspectives) within the service class continue to be substantially influenced by the route taken into it, in that the upwardly mobile are less likely to be Conservative supporters – a finding which is confirmed for both men and women by Marshall *et al.*'s (1988) recent work. However, as we have seen, Goldthorpe argues that this evidence does not give support to

> theories . . . of the emergence of a 'new class' from among the swelling ranks of higher-level white-collar employees which would represent . . . a major source of socio-cultural dissidence or of moral and political radicalism

within 'post-industrial' or 'late-capitalist' society' (Goldthorpe *et al.*, 1987:340).

It is not necessary, however, to adhere firmly to the view that such radical elements *are* present in order to recognise that a wide diversity of social origins, which will be mirrored in diversity of educational experience, will be likely to contribute to the heterogeneity of views among the upper occupational groups in society.

The implications of these developments could only be properly explored in another paper, and the remarks that follow, therefore, should be regarded as preliminary suggestions. They are relevant only to the English case, as national variations in educational systems might be expected to have different consequences as far as their impact on particular groups are concerned.[5] This discussion will be restricted to the impact of the school system. However, it could be argued that post-school education, in universites and professional institutions, is at least as important to the development of social consciousness. In the next section of this paper, an attempt will be made to tap into these sources through the identification of 'professional' and 'clan' modes of regulation of expert labour.

In some contrast to the absence of commentary relating to the impact of education on middle-class youth as a whole, one area which has been investigated is that of the private or 'public' schools. As total institutions, their role in the perpetuation of the English elite can hardly be questioned. Although the public schools have produced some notable elite deviants,[6] they can be expected to systematically inculcate assumptions and perspectives conducive to the production and reproduction of the material and power resources of the dominant social groups in society (Bourdieu, 1973).

However, as recent decades have demonstrated, there is room for considerable dispute as to how capitalist society may best be managed. The public schools are hardly likely to be hotbeds of revolution, but the values they espouse are likely to be closer to the aristocratic norms of *noblesse oblige* than the active promulgation of unbridled market capitalism with all its negative consequences for the social order as a whole. For example, Crouch (1986) has argued that 'gentlemen's agreements', operating through networks such as the elite London clubs and other informal networks, have always characterised the operation of British capitalism. This gentlemanly code enjoins '. . . a certain restraint on the maximization of immediate self-interest for the sake of maintaining a wider unity' (Crouch, 1986: 194), operating, he suggests, as a 'mild functional equivalent' of corporatism. Paradoxical as it may seem, therefore, it might be suggested that the public schools are more likely to support 'organic', rather than highly competitive models of society. Recent political and journalistic commentaries (for example, that surrounding the recent Neil/Worsthorne libel action) have emphasised the difference between the 'old' Conservatism (i.e. Worsthorne; public school, Garrick club) associated with the gentlemanly ideal, and the 'new' (i.e. Neil; Scottish high school, Glasgow University), characterised by the upwardly mobile (the title of Tebbit's memoirs), aggressive, entrepreneurial factions within the Conservative party.[7] Although this faction may be currently dominant, it would be a mistake to assume that old-style Conservatism has gone forever.

In respect of the state education sector, the empirical evidence available tends to lend support to the arguments of the radical theorists rather than those of right-wing critics – such as, for example, Cox and Boyson (1977). Studies of educational attainment and mobility, cited earlier, have demonstrated that on average, middle-class children do better out of state education than the working class. As far as the impact on the social values of the service class is concerned, it may be suggested that the experience of the state education system may have a contradictory impact. The successful, self-made, upwardly mobile entrepreneur (and these may include those in expert occupations who pursue occupational, rather than organisational, careers) may forcefully reject the weakly liberal middle-class values which permeate much of the state sector. Those who have 'made it' often have scant sympathy with those who have not, and such attitudes may be coupled with a marked antagonism towards those at an unfair advantage – and these would include members of the establishment or 'gentlemanly elite'. On the other hand, those who have benefited as a result of the provision of universal education might be more likely to favour universalist provision more generally. As far as the state system is concerned, the experience of post-school education and employment might be more crucial for the development of the attitudes of their products than those of the public school system. Thus the state educated who train for and enter occupations characterised by professional norms of 'institutionalised altruism'(discussed further below) might be expected to adhere to universalism; indeed, this group probably constitutes a major source of dissent, as far as government policies are concerned, amongst the contemporary service class.

It is important to stress that, although education is probably assuming an increasingly important role in the process of allocating individuals to occupations, a substantial minority in higher-level positions in Britain have always had little in the way of formal qualifications, and this feature is likely to persist. I have emphasised that the fluidity of the occupational structure will constantly throw up new occupations which will be performed, at least initially, by the formally unqualified, and the downward spread of the title of 'manager' means that many who possess the title (for example in the retail trade, or the leisure and entertainment industry) will have little in the way of academic qualifications.

THE REGULATION OF EXPERT LABOUR

The exchange of expert labour has always contained within it potential problems, in that the purchaser (on the assumption that he or she is a non-expert) is not in a position to make a firm judgement of the quality of the expertise being purchased. Consumer protection may be sought in a number of ways. If the product is material (a piece of complex machinery, a house or building), then its quality and performance may (in theory at least) be checked and tested. Expertise may be 'demystified', that is, skills broken down, subject to controls through routinisation and fragmentation, and so on. Braverman's influential account of 'deskilling', for example, is an account of the application of such strategies to craft employment in the late nineteenth and early twentieth century (as we have seen, Lash and Urry argue that the 'service class' emerged out of this process of the separation of conception and execution within the labour process). Even where the product is not material, processes of evaluation may be relatively easily developed. Whether a company is profitable or not is apparent from dividend payments and other measures of return on investment; in education examination pass rates may be monitored, as may the proportion of successful cures, bed throughputs, and so on in health care. Demystification and monitoring often go hand in hand, as the former is usually necessary in order to achieve the latter. Nevertheless, as the example of 'scientific management' suggests, the destruction of old skills often involves the creation of new ones, and a stable situation is unlikely to be permanently achieved. The client (purchaser), therefore, will always be at risk of some vulnerability in relation to new generations of experts.

Consumers may seek to secure expert services by offering a high level of material rewards. This could be seen as simply reflecting the market value of the experts' services, others might want to suggest that the determination of rewards is a consequence of the structurally determined power of both the experts and those who employ them (Johnson, 1980). However, relatively short-term trends (for example, the demand for deep-sea divers following the discovery of oil in the North Sea, or the creation of new occupations, such as computer salespersons, in technologically advanced production sectors) will ensure that there will always be some scarce expert occupations for which market based explanations provide the best account of their levels of material reward. Even in a capitalist market society, however, there is no such thing as a completely unregulated market for labour. This is in part because of the possibilities of malfeasance, or bad faith, but also because in a society characterised by a complex division of labour, a high level of cooperation is necessary to achieve production and reproduction. Not surprisingly, therefore, strategies other than those involving direct control have always characterised the exchange of expert labour. Of particular significance to the development of different perspectives amongst expert labour is the manner in which purchasers – and the experts themselves – have sought to morally regulate the circumstances within which expert labour is exchanged.[8]

Two major patterns may be detected in respect of this moral regulation; first 'professionalism', which is articulated largely at the level of the occupation, and second, organisational corporatism or the 'clan form', which is articulated largely at the level of the organisation. 'Occupation' is being used here in a rather loose fashion to include modes of regulation which encompass entire institutions. A major example would be the civil service in Britain, where 'professional' modes of regulation prevail (Perkin, 1989: Chap. 8).[9] The moral regulation of professionalism has been described by Merton (1982) as 'institutionalised altruism'; that is, as the norm that

> . . . professionals should do everything they can for a client, to a degree even at the expense of maximising their own distinct interests. Correlatively, the norm proscribes professionals acting in ways that will result to their advantage, and not only monetary advantage, when this is at the expense of clients (Merton, 1982: 115).

As Merton argues, the norm does not have to be universally adhered to in order to be demonstrated to exist.

Moral regulation at the level of the organisation has been extensively explored within the Durkheimian tradition associated with the sociology of work – for example, in the work of Elton Mayo and the 'human relations' literature. The 'organisation man' (or woman) is a standard figure in writings on management. Ouchi (1980), (drawing explicitly on Durkheim's work) describes the 'clan' as an organisational form where individual and organisational interests overlap, brought about through socialisation, cultural identity, or a combination of both. An oft-cited example of this strategy in respect of expert labour is that of Japanese management systems. Expert labour is recruited young, on the assumption that it will have a job, or be otherwise protected, for life. Such labour is trained by the recruiting organisation, and the skills aquired are general, rather than more narrowly focussed, as in the 'professional' model. As with the norm of institutionalised altruism, it would not be difficult to locate examples of instances where the organisational reality will be far removed from the organic 'clan' model; indeed, a fundamental criticism of the approach to organisations associated with 'human relations' and derived approaches is that they have consistently ignored fundamental *conflicts* of interest which also structure organisational processes (Clegg and Dunkerley, 1980). Nevertheless, this does not mean that strategies of 'normative involvement' (Etzioni, 1964) are never effective, nor that many individuals are not substantially affected by them. Such kinds of involvement have been historically associated with bureaucratic career structures.

Professionalism and organisational incorporation are not necessarily in conflict with each other, although Blau and Scott (1963) have argued that 'professional' and 'bureaucratic' 'orientations to work' are indicative of different levels of organisational commitment. For the purposes of this discussion, however, the point to be made is that a greater emphasis upon one or the other might have different outcomes as far as the development of social consciousness is concerned. Successful organisational incorporation suggests that the expert employee will become identified with his or her employing organisation, whose interests might be seen as superseding those of other potential claimants such as those of family, clients, community, or nation. In contrast, the ethic incorporated in the ideology of 'professionalism' stresses the importance of universalistic standards (of service) as integral to the protection of the interests of the client. Thus it might be expected that the ideology of professionalism may be more likely to result in less emphasis on purely sectional interests than those of the 'clan'.[10]

Both professionalism and organisational incorporation, however are expensive to administer and may not always be successful as regulatory mechanisms. Direct regulation of experts may be attempted through either deskilling or performance monitoring, strategies which are aquiring some prominence in the current context given the present (Conservative) government's commitment to 'market forces' as their preferred mode of regulation (for example, the removal of the optometrists's monopoly to sell spectacles, the introduction of 'opting-out' and other forms of quasi-markets in the Health Service (see Flynn, this volume), the attempt to force competitive bidding for undergraduates upon the universities, and so on). It is paradoxical that such policies create a demand for more experts in performance monitoring, such as accountants, lawyers, and human resource managers. Even in the absence of such policies, the pace of market developments and new occupations associated with technological change implies that at any one moment, some experts will remain unregulated except by the market.

SPATIAL MOBILITY

Geographical mobility has long been regarded as an integral element of the middle class linear career. Following Gouldner's (1957; 1958) development of Merton's (1965) distinction between 'cosmopolitans' and 'locals', Blau and Scott have distinguished empirically, in a workplace context, between 'professional' and 'bureaucratic' orientations to work, orientations which are associated with different patterns of occupational and geographical mobility. A professional orientation, they suggest, will be associated with the mobility necessary to the pursuit of an occupational career, as the 'itinerant professional moves from place to place seeking ever more interesting, prestigeful, and perhaps even more profitable positions' (Hughes, 1958:136). In contrast, the bureaucrat is more committed to his or her employing organisation, and is less likely to be mobile. In British sociology, the most influential discussion of patterns of middle-class mobility has been Watson's (1964) distinction between the geographically mobile 'spiralist' and stationary 'burgess' elements within the middle class, a distinction which supplied a paradigm for empirical research on the middle classes through the 1960s and 1970s (Bell, 1968; Edgell, 1980).

The link between social and spatial mobility has recently been examined in some depth by Savage and his colleagues (Savage 1988; Savage *et al.*, 1988). They demonstrate that the extent of geographical mobility has been declining in recent decades, although it is still greater amongst the higher socio-economic groups. Savage argues that the downturn in spatial mobility is linked to a decline in the extent of organisational careers within the professional–managerial group. Organisational careers, he suggests, incorporated geographical mobility as individuals moved through internal labour markets spread around the different locations of large national and multinational companies. Such career/mobility patterns he associates with the 'service class' as conceptualised by Renner and Goldthorpe. Using Wright's (1985) class typology, he argues that these old-established elements within the 'service class', whose causal powers rested upon organisational assets, are in decline. However, there has been an increase in the 'occupational' elements within the service class, that is, individuals who rely upon their skill assets to move freely between employers. Therefore, Savage *et al.* argue:

> . . . the main growth class in contemporary Britain is a new service class based in small private sector firms, often in the service sector . . . the *new* service class is that with . . . skill assets. This class has distinctive economic and political practices. Economically, it is highly mobile between employers and into self-employment. Politically, it is attracted to a politics of conservation and consumption-oriented issues, reflecting its use of one area as a base for job-hopping (1988:471–2).

That is, Savage and his colleagues suggest that these newer elements within the professional–managerial grouping will use the market powers deriving from their scarce skills in order to bypass the geographical mobility requirements associated with traditional bureaucratic careers.

It would be possible to argue with some of the detail of Savage's arguments – for example, the extent to which the 'old-style' organisation man (or woman, although the individual concerned would usually be a man) was absolutely required to be geographically mobile may be called into question. Head Office concentration in industries such as insurance companies and building societies, and the concentration of many functions in London and other metropolitan centres, have facilitated 'organisational' careers which do not necessarily require geographical mobility. However, it is not necessary to be in complete agreement with Savage's empirical conclusions in order to recognise that his work provides evidence of the persisting distinction between locally and nationally based elements and orientations within the higher levels of the occupational structure.

The sociology of the middle classes (rather than of the service class in particular) has, therefore, suggested at least two axes which might differentiate their social consciousness. These axes may be combined, in a highly schematic fashion, to give the categories shown in Table 8.1.

Table 8.1 The fragmentation of social perspectives within the middle classes

Geographical mobility	*Occupational regulation*		
	None, or Market alone	*Professional*	*Clan*
Mobile	Uncommitted	Universalists	Organisationally incorporated
Not mobile	New locals	Old locals	Organisational locals

Templates for the *uncommitted* could include well-publicised figures such as James Goldsmith, or Ian MacGregor, whose activities span even national boundaries. A more modest example is to be found in Forrest and Murie's (1987) description of the 'housing career' of a 'spiralist cosmopolitan', which gives a detailed description of a process of financially advantageous job- and housing-hopping which has been associated with the substantial rise in house prices over the last two decades. The uncommitted, as their label implies, will not have strong links with occupation, organisation, or locality. Detailed research evidence is not available as far as their social consciousness is concerned, but it may be suggested that, as they may have derived considerable personal advantage from the political and economic policies which have characterised the last decade, they are likely to be sympathetic to arguments relating to the superiority of 'market forces' in the regulation of human affairs.

In contrast *universalists*, it may be suggested, might be expected to espouse 'corporatist' type prescriptions at the societal level, given that their occupational socialisation has itself tended to stress universal standards of provision for 'clients'. They may include an important sub-category identified by Forrest and Murie, that is public sector employees in professional or medical careers (ibid: 354–5).

The *organisationally incorporated* might be anticipated to have a 'bureaucratic' (Blau and Scott, 1963) orientation to work and thus manifest preferences and views congruent with the requirements of their employer (usually private capital). They would include long-term, senior employees of major, often international companies such as IBM, ICI, and so on. Despite the fact, therefore, that individuals might sometimes move between employers, this grouping might be expected to manifest a commitment to the persistence of large capital and the conditions necessary to achieve this. The need to flood a valley, or remove a settlement, for example, might be regarded as an unfortunate necessity but a necessity nevertheless.

The *new locals* are those identified by Savage as the new, skill-based 'service class'. As he suggests, they are likely to be active in the protection of their 'locality resources', and might as a consequence find themselves in conflict with organisational locals (see below) as well as the representatives of larger business interests. Pahl's (1965) work on English commuter villages, and Newby's (1977) on rural communities, suggests that these groups may find themselves resented by established populations.

Old locals include the middle-class professionals, identified by Watson as an element of the 'burgess' category. To the extent that 'old locals' possess a sense of *noblesse oblige*, there might be other tensions arising between new locals and 'older' or more traditional middle-class groups. For example, community oriented local professionals (particularly if this category is seen to incorporate occupations such as head teachers, or members of the clergy) might be in favour of opening a factory, or keeping open a mine or quarry for the sake of employment and thus the local 'community', whereas new locals might be in favour of keeping out or closing down such units in order to enhance regional amenities.

Organisational locals, given their embeddedness in region or community, might be drawn into opposition to capital as far as local issues are concerned, that is, as Urry (1981) has suggested, local social issues might cut across apparent 'class' interests, 'service' or otherwise. Organisational locals remain unresearched in a community context, but would include many in the lower reaches of the occupational hierarchy, including those described by Bell as 'blocked spiralists' where 'often explicit in their apparent lack of further ambition was the realization that promotion would involve geographical mobility which in their eyes was undesirable' (Bell, 1968: 40). Other examples would be those whose careers had been made within a single bureaucratic organisation – as, for example, the case of the insurance managers at 'Lifeco' (Crompton and Jones, 1984).

The discussion has focussed on employment, but small-scale entrepreneurs should also be included in discussions of the middle classes. There will be some overlap, and movement between the uncommitted, 'new', and 'old' locals, and thus more heterogeneity in the social perspectives of this group than might be anticipated given their location in relation to the market processes of capitalist society (Mason, 1991).

Table 8.1 has been developed as a heuristic device through which to begin the task of exploring the processes which may structure different social perspectives within the middle classes, rather than as a watertight system of classification. If suitable quantitative measures were to be developed and applied to the middle class (defined in occupational terms) there would doubtless be many examples of individuals falling into the 'wrong' boxes, or failing to fit into any of them. Nevertheless, if the categories proved to bear no relation to empirical reality, then little would have been achieved in this discussion. However, there is some recent evidence which does point in the general direction of the argument that has been developed above. Savage's recent (1991) secondary analysis of the 1987 British General Election survey demonstrates that Professional SEGs (so classified) were less likely to vote Conservative, and more likely to vote Labour or Alliance even when factors such as social mobility and sector of employment were taken into account. Indeed, the professional 'inheritor' (that is, the professional son or daughter of a professional father) was actually less likely to vote Conservative than the average. Given the policies of the different political parties, this evidence suggests that as a mode of occupational regulation 'professionalism' is more likely to be associated with a universalist perspective.

CONCLUDING REMARKS

The very simple point being made in this chapter is that, as the proportion of the occupied population in higher-level professional and managerial occupations, and thus the heterogeneity of this grouping, increases, so too does the diversity of social consciousness within it. Goldthorpe has argued that nevertheless the service class will somehow act in its own 'interests'; Lash and Urry, that the service class is a contributory element in the development of 'disorganised capitalism'. It is not being denied here that occupational groups *do* have a general tendency to act in their own interests, nor that competition within a 'class' is likely to result in fragmentation and disorganisation. However, it is being argued that the very diversity which is recognised by both authors may as a consequence produce groupings who do not always act in their own narrow self-interests, as well as those who would produce powerful arguments (and actions) in the direction of the *organisation*, rather than the disorganisation, of capitalism. Such organised forms may, in keeping with established practice, be described as 'corporatist'. The development of corporatism at the level of the nation state, as Crouch (1986) has argued, is a result of a complex meshing of specific historical factors including the nature of the break between traditional institutions and secular liberalism; (whether it was sharp, gradual, or never properly achieved), the manner in which labour was brought into a legal status, and so on. Such arguments, as well as those such as Lash and Urry's account of first the organisation, then 'disorganisation' of capitalism, should make us reject any attempt to develop a single-factor explanation as far as complex historical phenomena are concerned. It would not be sensible, therefore, to suggest that, having 'disorganised' capitalism, the service class can 're-organise' it, and that is certainly not being argued here.

The more modest point is being made that, rather than there being a linear trend in the particular direction of 'disorganisation', both 'organising' and 'disorganising' tendencies are present in modern capitalist societies, and that these are discernible in the variety of social perspectives that may be identified within the heterogeneous grouping which has been described as the 'service class'. As recent critics of 'binary histories' have stressed (Sayer, 1989; Lovering, 1990) the extent of post-Fordism, flexible specialisation, disorganisation, and so on, may prove, as were reports of Mark Twain's death, to have been exaggerated (Gilbert *et al*., 1991). Like Cronus, the free market has always had a tendency to consume its own offspring. One consequence is that, in reality, there is no such thing as a completely unregulated market society. As well as producing its own gravediggers, the capitalist division of labour has also produced its own regulators.

This discussion also has implications for the future research agenda in British sociology. Our knowledge of British society, as well as our capacities for important work such as cross-national comparisons, has been enhanced enormously by developments in the collection and analysis of large scale survey data. However, many important concepts (such as, for example, the theoretical occupational class schemes devised by Goldthorpe and Wright) which are essential to the analysis of survey data are themselves derived from the findings of intensive case study work. Important aspects of 'work' and community situations (e.g. autonomy and discretion, or the extent of social networks), which are held to be significant for the purposes of classification, can only be studied *in situ*.

When Lockwood wrote his now-classic article analysing 'sources of variation in working-class images of society', he argued that '. . . on the basis of existing research, it is possible to delineate at least three different types of workers . . .' (1966: 250). That is , he was able to draw upon an established tradition of workplace, locality, and community studies within British sociology which enabled him to build up a composite picture of the 'working class'. Today, the sociologist is not in such a fortunate position. The relative lack of empirical research on the 'middle class' holds the place of an almost standard observation in sociology textbooks. Perhaps of even more concern, however, is the fact that the tradition of community research, established in the 1950s and 1960s, that Lockwood was able to draw upon appears to have all but disappeared.[11] In British sociology, such work was much influenced by anthropology. By the 1970s, it was being increasingly criticised for its descriptive and atheoretical character, and even its descriptive value was challenged on the grounds that the researcher's attention had often been focussed upon an atypical backwater, rather than being concerned with the mainstream of modern society. Contemporary studies of locality (rather than community) (e.g. Harloe *et al.*, 1990) cannot be subject to the same criticisms, but it might be argued that a necessary emphasis on national issues has tended to de-emphasise the close investigation of the minutiae of social life which was one of the strengths of the earlier tradition. Case-study work can often be slow and painstaking, its findings may not be dramatic and they are always liable to the criticism that they are somehow 'unrepresentative'. It has provided, however, a bedrock for British empirical sociology. Watson's distinction between 'burgesses' and 'spiralists' was first articulated in 1957, on the basis of empirical research carried out some years earlier, and is still in use today. This can be seen as a tribute to the quality of this early research, but perhaps it also suggests that, at least in the area of class and community analysis, our sociological foundations are in some need of renewal.

Notes

The author would like to thank those who have made valuable contributions to earlier drafts of this chapter. They include Chris Rootes, Gordon Marshall, John Urry, Mike Savage, Roger Burrows and Cathie Marsh.

1. To suggest that ideas may influence the course of history is not to abandon materialist explanations altogether. However, particularly at the level of the nation state, it is obvious that ideologies may have a profound impact upon populations which have significant effects in both the long and short run. Consider, for example, the history of Iran over the last two decades.
2. For example, Cain's (1983) empirical study of solicitors revealed that, far from being primarily concerned with the regulation of the working class, as had been suggested by radical critics of the legal profession, they were, rather, 'conceptive ideologues' engaged in the work of advice, translation and interpretation on behalf of their middle-class clients.
3. Some features, such as housing tenure and ownership, which have been argued to result in markedly different perspectives amongst those in 'working-class' occupations (Saunders, 1984) may not be of as much significance as far as professional and managerial occupations are concerned, as it may be reasonably assumed that the vast majority will be owner-occupiers (see also Savage *et al.*, 1990a; 1990b; this volume).
4. Lockwood's article gave rise to a number of empirical studies (for example, Newby, 1977; Davis, 1980) which have often been critical of Lockwood's formulation. However, it is his general approach to the analysis of consciousness, rather than his conclusions, which is being followed here. It may also be noted that Sabel (1982), although seemingly unaware of Lockwoods' work, follows similar principles in his exploration of workers' 'world views'.
5. For example, in France, private education is regarded as of lower status and quality than that offered by the elite lycées, in contrast to that available in the top English public schools.
6. For example, the group surrounding the defector to the USSR, Kim Philby.
7. This passage refers to a recent (1990) court case in which the editor of the Sunday Times (Andrew Neil) sued the editor of the Sunday Telegraph (Peregrine Worsthorne) for libel. Worsthorne had written that Neil's attendance at particular nightclubs was not an appropriate lifestyle for the editor of a serious newspaper. Neil won the case.

   Norman Tebbit was until 1987 a minister in Thatcher's neo-liberal administration.
8. These general points may of course be made in respect of the labour contract more generally, as is discussed at some length in Fox (1974).

However, it is nevertheless reasonable to argue that they are particularly relevant as far as expert labour is concerned. The notion of 'moral involvement' has been usefully explored by Etzioni (1964).

9. I have recently argued at some length that the long-standing sociological distinction between 'professions' and 'managers' should be dissolved (Crompton, 1990). It should not be thought, therefore, that an emphasis upon the difference between professionalism and organisational corporatism is an attempt to bring back distinction through the back door. In this discussion, the emphasis is being laid upon 'professionalism' and 'organisational corporatism' as strategies of moral regulation, rather than as being associated with specific occupational 'types'.
10. The link between 'professionalism' and what may be described as 'welfare' or 'corporatist' alternatives to the organisation of modern capitalism can be traced back to Marshall's development of the concept of 'citizenship' (1939; 1951), and was forcefully stated by Halmos (1970) at a high point of the post-war consensus. A recent development of a similar argument may be found in Perkin (1989). Discussions such as those of Halmos and Perkin may be criticised for both their over-simplified (and over-optimistic!) arguments, but nevertheless, neither can the trends they identify be dismissed as of no importance.
11. For example, Young and Willmott (1957); Dennis *et al.* (1957).

9 *thirtysomething* and Contemporary Consumer Culture: Distinctiveness and Distinction

Frances Bonner and Paul du Gay

INTRODUCTION

This chapter examines the use of the title of the American TV programme *thirtysomething* as a name for a particular service-class fraction – the new petite bourgeoisie. It is concerned with the way the characters in the series both reflect and promote the distinction of this social group. A major focus is upon their characteristic 'investment orientation to life' – what Rose (1991) has termed 'the enterprising self' – and how the series acts as a vehicle for its promulgation. The TV programme is investigated in an attempt to discover which aspects have facilitated its title being appropriated, and how it can now be applied to people who do not necessarily resemble those depicted in the show. It is not our intention to celebrate or to pan the programme itself, rather we wish to concentrate upon it as the locus for the discussion of certain key socio-cultural shifts. In particular we will focus on several contemporary issues of consumption and lifestyle.

The programme was first screened on ABC in the USA in 1987 and in Britain on Channel 4 early in 1989. It is set in Philadelphia and traces events in the domestic and occupational lives of eight friends of the appropriate age. The central couple are Michael, an advertising executive, and his wife Hope, a consumer journalist. They are the moral locus of the show and have a young daughter, a dog and a house they are doing up. Michael is one half of a creative team in an advertising agency with his friend Elliott, who so far during the three series has been married to, separated from and reunited with, Nancy, a book illustrator, with whom he has two children. The other characters are unmarried: Gary, Michael's college friend, an unsuccessful academic; his partner Susannah who works at a welfare centre; Melissa, a photographer and Michael's cousin; and Ellyn, Hope's old friend who works for City Hall. Various work mates, lovers and family members intermittently appear. The plots most often concern domestic relationships, though they may move outside.

It is generally agreed that one of the major effects of recent patterns of economic restructuring and social change has been the expansion of a 'service class' in most western capitalist societies (Abercrombie and Urry, 1983; Crompton, this volume; Goldthorpe, 1982; Lash and Urry, 1987; Savage *et al.*, 1988). Whilst the term does have a distinct advantage over the conventional categorisation 'middle class' in that it explicitly excludes some forms of routine non-manual labour (such as clerical work), this still leaves a bewildering array of administrative, managerial and professional workers lumped together in this putative 'service class' (Crompton, this volume; Savage *et al.*, 1988: 457).

In the UK, rather than becoming an increasingly cohesive class 'for itself', as Goldthorpe (1982), for example, has suggested, Savage *et al.*, believe that the service class is becoming more fragmented. They argue that there is a 'growing fragmentation at the top of the social hierarchy which is only clouded by continual reference to *a* service class' (1988: 457, our emphasis). Alongside the traditional service class whom they locate in the higher echelons of public bureaucracies and large private companies, the authors perceive 'a new service class' which is 'very much the product of the last decade or so'. As Thrift (1989), for example, has argued, this is a class that has increasingly absorbed and disseminated the idea of competitive individualism inherent in the spread of an 'enterprise culture' (Burrows, 1991; Keat and Abercrombie, 1991).

This new service class clearly corresponds to two social groupings delineated by Lash and Urry, and Featherstone (following Bourdieu): the 'new bourgeoisie' and the 'new petite bourgeoisie' (Lash and Urry 1987: Featherstone 1987; Bourdieu, 1984). Common to both of these class fractions are values firmly rooted in consumer culture. It is they who are deemed to have benefitted most from the 'Thatcherite revolution', and from whose ranks the decade's mythic (anti-) hero, the Yuppie, sprang.

The Adoption of the Term

The term 'thirtysomething' entered the public domain in Britain very soon after the initial screening of the series. Particular lifestyles and groups of people were identified, usually snidely, as 'thirtysomething'. An especially noticeable use of it was in a report on plans for a Home

Office campaign to engender a sense of civic responsibility in that group of opinion-leading 25–40 year-olds who were deemed to have benefitted most from 'ten years of the Thatcher revolution' (Dobbie, 1989: 5). The group, described as 'Britain's thriving thirtysomethings', was to be told to stop thinking about themselves and start helping others. Since this time (August, 1989), the use of the term has become much more widespread, though the pejorative implications are still usually available.

Lantos' early article on *thirtysomething* describes it as a 'show written by yuppies, about yuppies, for yuppies' (1987: 50). Although this was a common term for the characters at the time, it was an uneasy fit as few if any of them are particularly upwardly mobile, nor, despite appearances, are they demonstrably conspicuous consumers. After this, descriptive terms varied in a way which indicated an inability to define the group depicted and targeted, until the nomenclature problem was resolved by the adoption of the term 'thirtysomething' itself. It appears in serious and flippant articles and programmes throughout newspapers, magazines, radio and TV (e.g. Hersch, 1988; Mower, 1989). It is also beginning to appear directly in advertisements, like one urging readers to 'celebrate being 30 something' by starting a Sun Alliance savings plan. There no longer appears to be any need for explanation by reference to the TV show – an indication that it has achieved wide recognition within the public domain. In so doing it has become stripped of much of its initial specificity. No doubt this was in part due to its ability to name increasingly important socio-cultural shifts which could no longer be encompassed by reference to the term 'yuppie'.

THE DISTINCTIVENESS OF THE PROGRAMME

One of the factors involved in making the term 'thirtysomething' so apt for adoption as the name of the group that had outgrown so many names, was that the programme was a particular mix of the generalisable, like the title itself, and the distinctive, especially in generic and visual terms. As an American programme being viewed in a British context, the distinctiveness may well appear in different aspects on either side of the Atlantic.

Reading reviews from both countries, it becomes obvious that the American ones are much more dominated by questions of reality and verisimilitude. The main bases for these judgements depend on the programme's concentration on the minutiae of life. On the one hand the programme is adjudged real because it deals with aspects of domestic life not often mentioned on US TV, like diaphragms, and the continuity of medical insurance when a couple is separating; and on the other it seems real because of its meticulous attention to the details of the objects meaningful to the generation it both depicts and targets. In part this means using brand names and showing identifiable branded merchandise. Not only are neither of these particularly novel in the UK, but the brand names would not necessarily carry the same, or any, resonances. Such reality is not the basis of the programme's appeal for the British, but the locating of the value and the pleasure of the programme so emphatically in objects is important.

One way in which the programme is distinctive in Britain is generically. It is a particular mix and inflection of soap-opera, melodrama and sitcom, with not all that much of the last. Some parts of the situation recall the old American family sitcoms, but the important mix is the soap-opera/melodrama one. This has made *thirtysomething* a very attractive programme to advertisers (and hence to TV programmers) because it can deliver what are described as 'good demographics'. In the USA, it attracts middle-class, high-income women between 18 and 49, (Lippman, 1989: 1). The Channel 4 ratings, which teeter between 2 and 2.5 million, may not seem of themselves very good, but these are changing times for TV schedulers and advertisers who want access to those with disposable incomes rather than to large audiences dominated by the aging poor as is the case with the 17 million audience for *Coronation Street*, for example (Markosky, 1989).

The ABs which figure significantly in *thirtysomething* audiences have not generally watched much TV and when they have, overwhelmingly chose BBC in the UK and Public Broadcasting in the States. In the USA, the attempt by major networks to target specific economically desirable groups by paying attention to something other than gross ratings is quite recent – *L.A. Law*, *Hill St. Blues* and *Moonlighting* were some of the first. *thirtysomething* joined these in addressing a wealthy, better educated, visually literate audience. It was distinguished from them by its setting, its dominant domesticity and its pace.

Generic Distinctiveness

The word 'domesticity' immediately evokes the genres soap opera and melodrama, both of which terms are frequently used pejoratively, the first in particular connoting all that advertisers after specific audiences were avoiding. Arguably worst of all, they are both seen as women's genres. A soap is a melodrama in a particular form – episodic, with many characters, open-ended and with several narratives of basically the same importance being pursued at any one time with abrupt cutting between them. The circularity and lack of distancing markers are believed to make soaps characteristic of female narrative (Curti, 1988: 159).

While *thirtysomething* attracts an audience more female than male, this was not the intention of its creators and in its promotion it depends very substantially on not appearing to do so. In fact, most interviews given by Marshall Herskovitz and Ed Zwick, the writers, producers and directors of the show, emphasise that what motivated and continues to direct them is the experience of being fathers (Lantos, 1987). Absolutely central to the generic distinctiveness of *thirtysomething* is its presentation of, and appeal to, the male. Yet if men are traditionally defensive in admitting to watching soaps, they are even more resistant to admitting to watching melodrama with its aura of 'women's weepies'.

Joyrich (1988) has demonstrated at length how suited melodrama and TV are as she notes the migration of melodrama from its initial televisual home in soaps into most other genres. The domestic setting of television viewing combines with the continuing repetitive nature of most TV drama (series and serials) to result in attention being turned from the adventures and actions even of the traditionally most masculine forms like police shows and Westerns, onto the characters and their interactions. Melodrama becomes pervasive and it is especially difficult to maintain the distinction between melodrama and soap. The traditional hallmarks of melodrama involve high emotionalism and stark ethical conflict. As Brooks (1985: 15) explains, it developed in the nineteenth century to 'become the principal mode for uncovering, demonstrating and making operative the essential moral universe in a post-sacred era.' Although both the emotionalism and the starkness of the ethical conflict have been muted, these are still characteristics of *thirtysomething*.

Torres (1989: 87), writing specifically of *thirtysomething*, has pointed out how central to the programme are the recent issues dominating melodrama: 'the constitution and consolidation of the family, the maintenance of the suburban home, the regulation of sexuality, the display and displacement of emotion.'

How, given this, could *thirtysomething* still be considered distinctive? For Torres the answer lies in the exclusion of male subjectivity from classic domestic melodrama and its inclusion, or attempted inclusion, in this instance. Her final generic description is that it is 'male domestic melodrama'. Medhurst (1989: 39), on the other hand, writing shamefacedly about his fondness for the programme, terms it a 'chamber soap' because so little happens. Perhaps the compound 'chamber melodrama' is a better encapsulation. It makes an unsatisfactory soap because it is too leisurely and usually there is only one dominant narrative per episode, yet the episodic and open-ended nature are maintained.

The expansion of melodrama to (re-)address the male viewer is facilitated by a move television has already contributed to – the expansion of consumption from a female activity to a feminine-marked, but non-gender-directed one. All viewers are now addressed as consumers, but this is still a feminised position. Compounding this is the way that, as theorists like Houston (1984) have noted, the television viewer too is situated as feminine – in part by the process by which television itself is continuously consumed. Joyrich's suggestion that melodrama can help ease this threatening feminisation by its appeal to moral and experiential truths (1988: 147), may help explain both why melodrama has invaded so many other television genres, and the appeal of the masculinised melodrama itself. One of the ways in which melodrama is modified by Herskovitz and Zwick in the attempt to attract both men and women and particularly the desired better-educated, wealthier ones, is by appealing to their perceived self-conscious, self-aware, visual literacy. They are the people who grew up with television, who like to play with popular cultural allusions. There have now been a substantial number of American TV programmes which exploit references to other popular cultural texts – *Moonlighting* and *Quantum Leap*, for example – but few are as thorough-going as *thirtysomething*. The references are on at least three levels: diegetic (i.e. within the narrative) – the characters refer to cultural products when talking to one another; structural – the programme itself often moves into a format modelled on another cultural product, as in the presentation of a quarrel from four different points of view based on a technique in Akira Kurosawa's film *Rashomon*; and at the production level where the producers' love of and dependence upon the Frank Capra film *It's a Wonderful Life* has led to their production company being named Bedford Falls, after the town in which the film was set.

Watching *thirtysomething* can often become a spot-the-reference game. Precisely what these references do other than incorporate and exclude viewers as they catch or miss the allusions is another question. Their main function is undoubtedly to generate the warm glow of recognition, the pleasure at being so personally addressed. When they succeed, they tie the viewer more tightly into acknowledging the similarity between themselves and the characters. But what apart from this does Jimmy Stewart in *It's A Wonderful Life*, for example, do? Are we to transpose the lesson he learns, that every individual contributes something to the whole, that no life is worthless, into this particular fiction? That we might be intended to do just that is indicated not only by the fact that sometimes within the fiction characters learn by the excursions into referentiality, but also, and this is a point which will be expanded on later, by the use some American therapists are making of the programme outside the fiction, particularly in their marriage counselling work (Hersch, 1988).

Visual Distinctiveness

The visual distinctiveness is particularly noticeable if it is contrasted with other American, rather than British programmes. It is composed and shot far more cinematically than televisually. Shots are held longer, characters wander in and out of shot and there are fewer close-ups, especially the two-shot close-up so typical of soaps. There is also a greater manipulation of focus and depth of field.

The importance of this is in its contribution to another distinctive visual characteristic – the cluttered *mise-en-scène*. The sets on most TV programmes are the result of recognising that given the size and resolution of the TV image, comparatively spartan sets with minimal decoration are adequate. This is changing generally, but even so the interiors in *thirtysomething* are crowded with things and often also with people. When there is a group scene in Hope and Michael's kitchen, as there frequently is, it provides a dense crowded visual experience. There are far too many objects and sometimes people, to consciously identify; nor are things orderly. The resultant impression is one of excess, and this is a characteristic of melodrama agreed on by both pejorative belief and scholarly study. Brooks' subtitle even calls melodrama 'the mode of excess'. The excess is however variously located: it may be an excess of effects over cause elevating the importance of Fate or Destiny (Neale, 1986: 7), an excess of emotionalism, or visual excess. Feuer, examining a number of different views on film melodrama, comments

> how despite the changing theoretical stances all see excess not merely as aesthetic but as ideological, opening up a textual space which *may* be read against the seemingly hegemonic surface. (1984: 9, our emphasis)

She argues that in prime-time soaps (like *Dallas* and *Dynasty*), the visual excess acts expressively not subversively. The same is at least partially true of *thirtysomething*, though it may be that the visual excess, like the programme's other excess – of Talking about Problems – pinpoints the most telling moments, those available for particular investment, including the affective.

Mulvey (1987: 77) has commented that in the women's film melodramas, *mise-en-scène* 'provides the central point of orientation for the spectator.' The things and the people shown surrounding them are important. It is highly significant that when the character Ellyn was being shown to be behaving foolishly, the writers chose to demonstrate her lack of control and moral irresponsibility by a display of temper directed at a kitchen appliance owned by Hope and Michael. It allowed no room for doubt that she had *gone too far*.

The leisurely pace, the greater number of medium or long shots and the greater depth of field all encourage the audience to dwell on the objects held within the *mise-en-scène*, and, as well as carrying a heavy weight of meaning within the programme, objects carry particularly strong symbolic value for the *thirtysomething* group. Yet while viewers can check their ownership of commodities similar to those shown in the programme, it cannot reasonably be argued that the *thirtysomething* characters engage in conspicuous consumption. They are not often shown shopping (and even more rarely buying things) and when they do, they buy a very limited range – mainly food, toiletries and things for the children. The things which serve to place them socially so distinctively have already been bought, are already in place. As Mower wrote in an article on the group, not the programme, they

> will encourage the growth of services, which are what you want when you have all the clothes, furniture and hi-fi gear you need, but still can't run your life. (1989: 21)

The visual and generic distinctiveness also focus desire on the family and emotional life. All the devices used to highlight the objects are also deployed on the people in their object-laden settings. We do not, however, want to suggest, as so much contemporary journalism does, that families, especially children, function as things or accessories. They function here, as do friends, as emotional loci. The emotions of the characters are essential to the forward drive of the narrative. Even when there is a significant event, as for example when Michael and Elliott's company goes bankrupt, it is not action which constitutes the plot, but emotion, as the characters' poignant memories of their first job and their setting up independently are explored. Indeed actions may be referred to but then apparently forgotten, while emotions are painstakingly examined. This proclivity is intensified by the constant concentration on the minutiae of life and by the overall generic centrality of emotions. As Joyrich says of TV melodrama in post-modern times:

> History and memory are allowed to wander as emotion provides the only stake, a situation giving free rein to consumer fantasies. With the elision of history comes the promotion of the image (of both the commodity and the self) which is now personal and self-referential. (1988: 141)

The flashbacks in *thirtysomething* where characters recall formative moments (although they seem in memory to be already what they will become) usually focus on past possessions but do so, in illustration of Joyrich's assertion, to reconstitute and re-present an emotional state.

'THIRTYSOMETHING' AND THE 'NEW' SERVICE CLASS FRACTIONS

In many ways, as Terri Minsky (1987) has argued, the occupational placement of the characters in *thirtysomething* is not televisually distinctive. It is merely the modern day equivalent of, rather than a distinctive break with, the white-collar, middle-class occupations assigned to the central characters of a variety of US sitcoms in the 1950s and 1960s.

After all, Minsky continues, 'What was Rob Petrie of the *Dick Van Dyke Show* but the head writer for a variety show? Didn't Samantha Steven's husband Darin, work in advertising in *Bewitched*?' However, if the performance of a white-collar, middle-class service occupation is something *thirtysomething*'s characters share with many of their televisual predecessors, what is it, then, that makes today's characters so different, so (un) appealing?

In attempting to provide an answer to this question, we want to move beyond a narrow consideration of the service occupational placement of the characters in the series.

Instead, we argue that the term 'thirtysomething' delineates a particular service class fraction – the new petite bourgeoisi.e. – and that the characters in the series are best viewed as both reflecting and promoting the distinction of this social group.

We believe that *thirtysomething* is best viewed in relation to the 'habitus' of the new petite bourgeoisi.e. (Bourdieu, 1984). As an expanding class fraction, this social group attempts to legitimate its own particular tastes and lifestyle(s), especially through its central involvement in the production and dissemination of consumer culture imagery and information.

According to Bourdieu (1984: 359ff), the new petite bourgeoisie includes 'all occupations involving presentation and representation' and occupations in all organizations providing symbolic goods and services. Thus, members of this class fraction work predominantly in marketing, advertising, design, public relations, radio and television production and journalism.

As we mentioned earlier, the characters portrayed in *thirtysomething* fit the bill more than adequately here. Michael and Elliott work in advertising, Hope is a consumer journalist, Nancy illustrates children's books, Melissa is a professional photographer, Ellyn does some form of PR work for City Hall and Gary is on the cusp of academia and social work. In addition, almost all of the minor characters in the series also have typical new petit bourgeois occupations.

Bourdieu (1984: 357) goes on to argue that these occupations do not always bestow upon their holders the quantity of economic capital they felt entitled to expect 'by reference to an earlier state of the relationship between qualifications and jobs', and, often, in comparison with their original social capital and social origins. Thus, the new petite bourgeoisie has experienced, in one sense, at least, an 'interrupted trajectory'. This is represented in *thirtysomething* by a fear most of the characters have , especially those who are consistently negatively coded, of not being as economically successful as their parents. Such anxiety cannot be simply brushed aside under the rubric of 'Yuppie angst', however, for it does have material foundation. Whereas in 1950 a median-price house cost the average US wage earner 14 per cent of his or her gross monthly income, by the mid-1980s this had increased to 44 per cent (Fallows, 1990:17).

In one episode of the series, for example, Gary, a failed academic and the character least divorced from the 'cultural inheritance' of the late 1960s and early 1970s, comes face to face with the responsibilities of imminent fatherhood. Wanting to buy a house for the new family and needing anyway to replace the apartment tied to his academic job, Gary goes to view a newly built suburban housing complex with the happily married Michael. Michael explains that the house Gary's parents bought for 'twenty-seven grand' when they were first married (which is the basis of Gary's expectations) would now cost at least $200,000. When Gary bemoans the lack of space, character and authenticity of the apartment he has just been shown, Michael is dismissive:

> **Michael:** Oh that's right, I forgot, I'm sorry, you're not buying into any of this bourgeois crap about making a home for the woman you love or seeing that your kid has it better than you.
> **Gary:** Better? This isn't better.
> **Michael:** No, but this you can afford. Let me tell you something Gary, this is much better than a lot of people can manage.

This scene not only compares Gary with his parents, but also relates the anxiety to his prospective child as well. At the same time, Michael's 'words of wisdom' here, both reflect his role as one half of the emotional and moral centre of the show, and also promote the idea, inherent to the series as a whole, that the only problems facing the new petite bourgeoisie are interpersonal ones. He advises Gary not to 'look at the buildings . . . [but to] look at the people'. The exchange, especially the comment 'welcome to the economy, bud' also serves to frame Gary, and those of his ilk, as hopelessly outmoded romantics, unaware of the all pervasive, and 'natural', presence and influence of a market that cannot be 'bucked'.

Nonetheless, if the new petite bourgeoisie suffers from an 'interrupted trajectory' in an economic sense, how then does it attempt to extend or re-establish this trajectory? According to a number of commentators (Lash and Urry, 1987; Featherstone, 1987; Turner, 1988), it does so through a strategy of 'cultural libertarianism' – a disruption of cultural conventiality – by applying 'the cultivated disposition to not-yet-legitimate culture' (Bourdieu, 1984: 357; 370). In other words, this new class fraction imbues certain cultural objects with a new status as part of an attempt to rehabilitate their own careers. And they do this through their work as 'cultural intermediaries', as 'taste creators'.

As Bourdieu puts it:

> Seeking its occupational and personal salvation in the imposition of new doctrines of ethical salvation, the new petite bourgeoisie is predisposed to play a vanguard role in the struggles over everything concerned with the art of living, in particular domestic life and consumption, relations between the sexes and the generations, the reproduction of the family and its values. (1984: 366–7)

It is immediately noticeable that all these 'struggles' take place in areas traditionally defined as female. They are also, and not coincidentally, the central themes of *thirtysomething*. As we have already demonstrated, however, these very same issues are those that have preoccupied recent melodrama. We would like to stress here that *thirtysomething* can be seen to provide a particularly salient name for the new petite bourgeoisie in part because it provides a site where the feminised values of the group and the masculinised form of melodrama coalesce. It also draws attention to the generational specificity of this new class fraction. The new petite bourgeoisie has been shaped by the inheritance of being the first post 'youth culture' generation. It is this class/generation formation that has acquired both the 'knowledge of popular cultural codes and conventions and the economic and cultural space with which to play with them' (Clarke, forthcoming). This 'knowledge' and 'playfulness' is now a significant component of contemporary popular culture, encompassing a variety of (postmodern) cultural practices – a seemingly random juxtaposing of signs, ironic self-referencing and a playfulness with conventions and genres, to name but the most obvious.

As we noted earlier, *thirtysomething* exhibits all of these cultural practices (which, in turn, go someway towards defining the series' televisual distinctiveness). At the same time, however, these practices are also an integral component of the distinction of the new petite bourgeoisie. As Lash and Urry, for example, have argued, the new petite bourgeoisie

> use postmodern cultural goods to challenge traditionalist culture. That is . . . postmodern cultural objects are in the 'ideal interests' of the new middle classes, who, in their rise, will benefit from the extent to which the whole of society comes to share their valuations of such cultural forms. (1987: 288)

Rather than being a simple extension of traditional middle-class, white-collar television shows, as Minsky (1987) argues, it is the particular class fraction/generation mix which *thirtysomething* captures and names that makes the show so different, so (un) appealing. Indeed, Minsky implicitly admits this elsewhere in her article. As a mid-thirty-year-old 'middle-class' symbolic intermediary, she acknowledges that the series does touch a nerve. In particular, she recognises that *thirtysomething*'s elaborate re-articulation of a variety of popular cultural texts (the *Dick Van Dyke Show* included) is analogous to her own cultural practice as a 'pop' journalist on *Rolling Stone*:

> there's one important thing we don't get from these shows. Because we like to talk, we're always looking for new material. We quote song lyrics, memorable movie lines. . . gossip about people we've never met. The trouble is you can't do that with today's yuppie television. They're quoting us. (Minsky, 1987)

Therapeutic Selves

According to the co-creators of the show, by narrowly focussing 'on the issues of our lives – and the lives of our friends and contempories' (Lantos, 1987), in 'just turn[ing] the camera right around on us, on the little moments, the everyday events' (Minsky, 1987), *thirtysomething* has given a class fraction/generation a vehicle for its own promulgation. The show has 'stimulated a community of feeling which strikes a nerve' (Lippman, 1989). Nonetheless, by concentrating so markedly (and melodramatically) on the emotional and the personal, *thirtysomething* rarely attempts to allude to a world beyond that of its characters (unlike Hill Street Blues or St. Elsewhere, for example). This has not gone unnoticed by some reviewers. Ella Taylor, for example, argues that the series has become so 'engrossed in its own claustrophobic detail' that its characters'

> connection to public life is severed altogether, or reduced to a trite shorthand of pop-cultural icons. . . that casually cue us into time, place and generation, and than shrink back into the politics of the personal (quoted in Torres 1989: 90–1).

Ken Olin, the actor who plays Michael in the series, responded implicitly to this charge in an interview with a US paper when he argued that

> nobody on this show is presuming that the problems of these characters are as serious as the problems of the homeless and the mentally ill and the

> tragedy of war. . . but that is not to say that this generation doesn't face a set of issues that is valid too. (quoted in Torres, 1989: 91)

Olin's comments seem to suggest that the problems facing thirtysomethings are precisely not those of poverty or homelessness. They also reflect the series founding assumption that the most pressing problems facing this class fraction are interpersonal ones, and enact *thirtysomething*'s tendency to express 'what are primarily ideological or social conflicts in emotional terms' (Joyrich, 1988:131). Even when Herskovitz and Zwick attempted to address this criticism by (confused) reference to the ozone layer, or by expanding Gary's work at the Project (the welfare agency), the internality of the programme persisted.

According to Joyrich (1988: 138), recent TV melodrama has emerged as a 'therapeutic' discourse, which attempts to produce the real in the form of authentic emotion and ethical imperative. As we mentioned earlier, the 'therapeutic' potential of *thirtysomething* has already been acknowledged in the US where the series is being used by an increasing number of therapists in their work:

> therapists are finding that the show speaks with a clear and sometimes painful voice to a generation of 'thirtysomethings' that is struggling with feelings of uncertainty while pursuing the American dream. (Hersch, 1988: 62)

For Bourdieu, the 'therapeutic' is an integral component of the new petit-bourgeois 'doctrines of ethical salvation'. It forms part of this class fraction's opposition to the 'repressive morality' of the traditional dominant classes and also provides a discourse through which the new petite bourgeoisie can resolve the

> essential ambiguity resulting from the discrepancy between the (symbolically) subversive disposition linked to their position in the division of labour and the manipulative or conservative functions attached to the position, between the subjective image of the occupational project and the objective function of the occupation. (1984: 366)

In other words, the 'therapeutic' is functional in that it resolves a problem for the new petite bourgeoisie. The promotion of an ethic of lifestyle and pleasure allows them to reconcile their objective role as servicers of capitalist culture with their subjective aspirations to lead a 'good' life and make the world a better place.

The deployment of such 'skilfully ambiguous' therapeutic discourse within *thirtysomething* is readily admitted by the show's creators. They believe that the series provides people in a similar position to themselves (and especially those in therapy) with 'a language' with which to deal with their personal problems (Hersch, 1988: 63); in Joyrich's terms it

> helps us place ourselves in a confusing world – its insistence on the validity of moral or existential truths and its faith in the reality of the stakes creates a space from which to act. . . (1988:147)

The dialogue between Hope and Michael in a scene from the last episode of the second series provides a good example of this. In many respects, the whole scene is an attempt by the show's creators to provide a definitive reply to the criticisms that reviewers like Ella Taylor have made of the show's navel-gazing tendencies. Here, Michael constructs a very skilful (but also very ambiguous) defence of the lifestyle Hope and he lead, the morality of which his wife is temporarily questioning. Although he asserts the primacy of the family, his and the creators' unease is encapsulated in his projected comment to his daughter when she becomes a questioning 14-year-old.

> Sorry about the ozone layer sweetheart, but we were a little focussed on your pre-school.

Although Michael's 'defence' is alternately self-aware and self-mocking, in the end it simply enacts *thirtysomething*'s melodramatic tendencies by collapsing a socio-political 'outside' onto a familialised and domestic 'inside' (Torres, 1989).

According to Hersch *thirtysomething* works best as therapy on 'the age groups it depicts':

> like the characters on the show, they [the patients/clients] worry about how to have it all, how to remain close to friends and family who are doing very different things, wondering whether they are selling out and what being 'grown up' is really all about. (1988: 62)

Indeed, for the creators of the show, *thirtysomething* is a channel for 'talking out' their own problems. They see the characters as mirroring their own dilemmas:

> they want to be free, but they want to have families. They want leisure time, but they want lots of money. They think of themselves as independent, but they all own the same cars and coffee makers' (Lantos, 1987: 50).

We argue here that *thirtysomething* can be seen to promote a particular view of 'self' – the 'consuming' or 'enterprising' self – and a particular orientation towards life, what Featherstone has termed 'an investment orientation':

> An approach to life which is characterised by a 'why can't I have my cake and eat it' attitude quests for both security and adventure. The new narcissism where individuals seek to maximise and experience the range of sensations available, the search for expression and self-expression, the fascination with identity, presentation and appearance makes the new petite bourgeoisie a 'natural consumer'. (1987: 65)

The characters in *thirtysomething* both reflect and promote this 'orientation to life'. They attempt to make a project of themselves. In other words to work on their emotional world, their domestic and conjugal arrangements,

> their relations with employment and their techniques of love-making, to develop a 'style' of living that will maximise the worth of their existence to themselves. (Rose, 1991)

Under this 'regime of the self', individuals are encouraged to become 'entrepreneurs of themselves' (Rose, 1991). However, the 'right' to an autonomous act of choice entails a parallel 'obligation' to accept responsibility for the consequences of the choice made. In other words, in making a project of one's life, the individual must take full responsibility for the failures as well as credit for the achievements.

The need for self-improvement through self-government, and the consequent balancing of rights and obligations, is central to the lives of the characters in the series. Life is not complete for them, nor is it 'healthy', unless they are continually seeking to 'have it all'. As one commentator has put it, 'the implication of *thirtysomething* is that if you are not blazing a trail of professional glory, agonising over balancing a career and a family, or endlessly dissecting emotions to the core, then the world has passed you by' (Lippman, 1989). Consequently, if a character in the series appears to be reneging on their 'life project', then you can be sure that another character, or characters, will quickly remind him or her of their 'obligations', thus insuring that the bandwagon keeps rolling.

Mid-way through the second series, for example, Michael and Elliott's advertising business goes bust. After a brief period of unemployment in the wake of the bankruptcy, Michael is offered a job at Pressman's, a mass market hardware chain. Concurrently, DAA, a very prestigious advertising agency, begins making overtures to him and to Elliott. Michael, disliking Drentell, the agency head, and suspicious of the actual prospects of a job, is unwilling either to begin negotiations with DAA or to accept Pressman's offer. He remains unemployed, exasperating Hope until she confronts him about their debt and his inaction:

> **Hope:** . . . we are digging ourselves deeper with every cheque and I don't see you trying to get a job. I mean if not this one then something else. I mean this is just not the way it was supposed to happen. Not for us.

This scene represents one of the few occasions in the series where Michael is negatively coded. He is portrayed, here, as a man failing to live up to his responsibilities. As such, not only is he doing his family a disservice, he is also betraying his sense of 'self'. Through a lack of 'enterprise', he is allowing both his own, and, consequently, Hope's, 'rising trajectory' to be needlessly interrupted. Hope's almost predestinarian 'this is not the way it was supposed to happen. Not for us' is a secularised call to return to the path of salvation. Needless to say, it is a call that Michael recognises and quickly heeds. The scene proves to be a turning point, and shortly afterwards Michael visits Drentell, thereby guaranteeing himself (and Elliott) a suitably 'creative' job, and hence re-establishing the trajectory.

Indeed here Hope's direction to Michael calls to mind the wider role of the new petite bourgeoisie in enunciating how its own members as well as others should conduct themselves. This feature is not only integral to the class fraction's view of itself but essential to the wider propagation of the lifestyle(s) it advocates.

CONCLUSION

Viewer responses to the programme have been equivocal both in the US and the UK. Torres' comment that it is 'so compelling, so repellent' (1989: 102) would seem to apply in both places. The melodrama in *thirtysomething* serves to generate an intensity of response, though not necessarily of pleasure. While for some viewers, the programme's portrayal of the domestic and emotional life of the (American) new petite bourgeoisie provides considerable enjoyment, for others this is not the case.

Grossberg (1987) has written about the televisual excess left over after the generation of meaning and available for affective investment. Not only is *thirtysomething* generically excessive, but it also provides a variety of excesses – visual and narrative (especially in the stories presumed to continue in the 'real time' between the weekly episodes). It should not be surprising then that it incites such a strong emotional response.

As we have had cause to note, the 'investment orientation to life' espoused by the new petite bourgeoisie may well be in the 'process of creating the perfect consumer' (Featherstone, 1987). For this class fraction is ideally positioned to act as 'a transmission belt' (Bourdieu, 1984: 365) and to drag into the 'race for consumption and competition' all those from whom it is attempting to distinguish itself. In fact, one of the defining features of the new petite bourgeoisie is precisely its sense of legitimacy in educating others in 'how to live' by a 'symbolic action' which not only produces the need for its own goods and services, but also, in the long run, legitimates itself and the life-style(s) it puts forward as a model.

It is not our contention that the television programme *thirty-something* is an example of the new petite bourgeoisie consciously engaged in educating others in this way. The adoption of its title as the popular name for the social group reveals however that it provides a way of thinking about their increasing socio-cultural prominence and influence. Melodrama, with its long tradition of enunciating moral positions, is serving once again to simplify the complex realignment of relations between social groups.

It seems possible that part of the dislike, to put it no stronger, for the programme, frequently expressed by reference to the characters' self-obsession, derives from the self-perceived tutelary role of the class fraction and their symbolic representatives in the TV melodrama. Resentment at being instructed about the desirable way to live (with its characteristic consumer practices) by those already living it may be expressed through contempt for the programme.[1]

Note

1 As we go to press it has just been announced that *thirtysomething* is to be discontinued. A sign of the times? [eds]

10 Class Differences in Access to Higher Education in Britain

Catherine Marsh and
Robert M. Blackburn

INTRODUCTION

Access to higher education in Britain is still confined to a relatively small proportion of the population, and the existence of social inequalities is unmistakable. There have, nevertheless, been important changes in the last 30 years. There has been a considerable expansion of provision, with changes in the method of financing students. This has been accompanied by a marked reduction in gender inequality as women have taken up a larger proportion of available places. However, the changes in class inequalities are more problematic and more difficult to assess. It is this question that we address here.

The problem of differential access to higher education entails structured inequality based on occupational stratification as well as inequality relating to consumption, and it is not possible to separate them. Contrary to some contemporary revisions of Weber's ideas on status, consumption does not provide an alternative to class analysis, let alone a replacement. To be sure, a simple class dichotomy between capital and labour is not sufficient to analyse the inequalities in higher education but the alternative is not necessarily to turn to differential consumption; all contemporary theories of class or stratification treat occupations as crucial in differentiating relations to the means of production and location in the labour market, and the associated inequalities embrace patterns of consumption. Education clearly illustrates the integrated nature of class and consumption because of its pivotal position in the reproduction of social inequality. It is well established that class is strongly associated with the consumption of higher education and in turn that higher education is a major determinant of access to higher level occupations.

Unlike secondary education, higher education is not compulsory. Therefore there is an element of 'choice' involved. This gives some plausibility to the argument that consumption tastes are decisive (Murphy 1990). However, this ignores the social context in which tastes are formed, the relevance of preferences in relation to what is possible and the constraints on choice, all of which are more strongly socially differentiated than aspirations.[1] Of particular relevance to higher education are the provision of places, the numbers competing for them and the differential opportunities. Class factors exert an important influence on opportunities both in the prior preparation in secondary schooling and in the ability to meet the financial costs.

All these factors have been changing, with the result that it has been difficult to assess changes in inequality. The available evidence and analyses have been very important in debate and policy formulation, but the inability to deal with the complexity of the changing situation makes all previous interpretations questionable. One response to the ensuing uncertainty has been to claim that legislation intended to widen opportunity and lessen financial constraints has had no effect. If indeed such structural changes have been without effect we may well doubt their relevance, and this opens the way for arguments giving choice a central role. Thus trends in inequalities, rather than just an observed association between background and consumption, are crucial. It is essential to establish whether or not inequalities changed in response to circumstances, and especially in response to legislation. It would, of course, be sociologically naive to expect specific legislation to so disrupt the processes of social reproduction as to produce dramatic changes,[2] but if circumstances are relevant, some changes should be discernible. We propose to demonstrate that this is indeed the case.

In this chapter we will challenge the view of the New Right that tastes and consumption styles are distinct components of the structure of social inequality. We begin by outlining a reconceptualisation of social class, and then ask how class differentials in educational advantage have been affected by social policy designed explicitly to equalise chances across social groups. Answering this question will get us into quite technical water, but the effort is worth it, because at the end we will be able to provide, for the first time, definitive answers on the relationship between occupational and educational advantage. It is these answers which constitute the challenge, by contradicting the arguments giving centrality to tastes and consumption styles and demonstrating the relevance of class-based policy.

THE MEANING OF CLASS

Where we part company with conventional class analysis is in the conceptualisation and measurement of the structure of social inequality. Rather than defining a set of discrete classes we take the structure to be a continuous hierarchy of social advantage.

Class analysis is concerned with real differences of advantage and experience. However, the 'classes' themselves, however defined, are sociological constructs, and not only is there no agreement on the number or location of the boundaries but the criteria used to define them allow variation within class categories. Such lack of class homogeneity itself suggests the possibility of continuous measurement. Furthermore, the occupational groupings are normally treated as constant, which creates problems with changes over time since the social meaning of being in an occupation may alter with variations in the occupational structure. In particular all schemes show a pattern where the membership of the top class grows and that at the bottom shrinks, which gives strong reason to doubt whether the meaning of being in either class has remained unchanged. Considering the top class, for example, it would be difficult to maintain that the social advantage of membership, relative to the rest of the population, has not declined as the class has more than doubled its share of the population. Social closure, in the professions for instance, is supposed to operate to prevent just such a dilution of power based on exclusiveness, but there has nevertheless been a great expansion of professional occupations.

An exception to constant definitions is the Registrar General's (OPCS) scheme of social classes. This has been revised for every census this century, and often in quite fundamental ways. The revisions appear to take some account of the effects of the changing occupational structure (see below), but this does not help; it merely creates uncertainty. So when examining changes in the class location of the population across time, it is hard to know how much of the apparent change is the artefactual results of changes in the measuring instruments used and how much represents real change in the social world.

All the theoretical problems associated with class categories stem from treating them as real, discrete and internally homogeneous groupings, when in fact they are more or less sociologically appropriate and convenient divisions in a structure of inequality. Underlying the class groupings is a single dimension of stratification.[3] There are variations in different aspects of inequality, such as education and income, and although they are related the correlation is not perfect. However, it is conceptually and methodologically justifiable to attempt to identify a single underlying dimension of relative social advantage.

The measure we use here is the Cambridge Scale (Stewart *et al.*, 1980; Prandy, 1990; Blackburn *et al.*, 1990). To identify a scale of social advantage, it was necessary to select theoretically significant criteria of differentiation. Friendship and marriage choices were selected as the Cambridge Scale criteria. The theoretical justification was that marriage and friendship choices represent instances of equality in advantage; or put the other way, the less likely different types of people are to interact, the greater the social distance between them. The occupation of the marriage or friendship partner was used as a means of identifying different types of people. Multi-dimensional scaling tests to see if this did provide a structure of stratification revealed a clear single dimension. Thus the scale is a continuum of inequality which is not created by sociological fiat but derived from the data of social interaction. Furthermore, while the method would allow for significant groupings into 'classes', no evidence for such discontinuities was found. The initial version has been refined to its present form but the theoretical basis remains the same (Prandy 1990).

This still leaves open the question of whether the scale does in fact provide a useful measure of social inequality, in relation to the sort of factors that are generally, and rightly, regarded as significant in class analysis. This has been convincingly established by Prandy (1986; 1990), who demonstrates particularly strong relationships with a wide range of variables, from voting to indices of health status. However, for our present purposes the requirement is more limited and more specific. We require that the scale should provide a continuum of advantage which relates to educational selection and underlies the class groupings sociologists traditionally construct. In an earlier paper (Blackburn and Marsh, 1991) we showed that, in relation to entry to secondary schools, the relationships of the Nuffield classes could be re-created effectively by choosing cutting points on the scale to create 'classes' of similar magnitude. More importantly, we found a progressive relation between height on the scale and entry to selective secondary education. Here again, as shown in Figure 10.1, we find a clear relationship, at least in the top half of the stratification structure which accounts for the great majority of higher education places. (See below, for an account of the data used and the definition of higher education.) As we would expect, there is no clear trend among the tiny proportions in the lower half. (It is interesting to note that the hint of an upturn at the bottom of the stratification distribution which we first noted in attendance at selective secondary schools is clearly in evidence again for attendance at higher educational institutions: we need to consider whether the explanation suggested there also applies here.)

Figure 10.1 Percentages attending higher education by father's occupational level (Cambridge Scale score in 5% groupings)

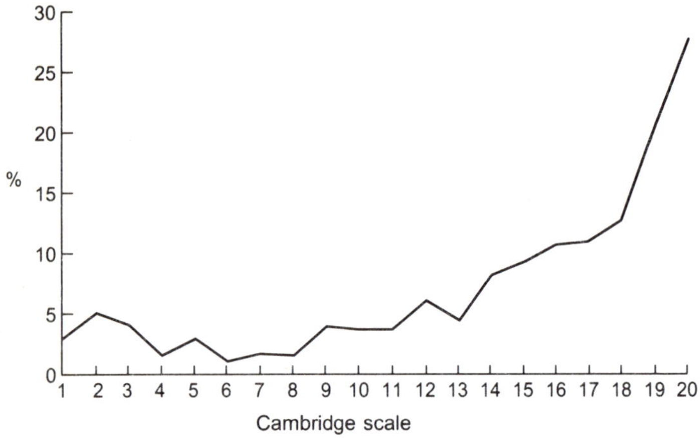

Source: SCELI 1986 surveys

On theoretical and methodological grounds we consider the use of the continuous measure is preferable. For the specific question of access to higher education it is clearly appropriate. Therefore we shall use it in the following analysis. This will allow us the option of dividing it up into 'classes' in whatever way is most useful.

Before moving on it is worth considering the meaning of what is being measured by the Cambridge Scale. Since it uses a relational approach it is, in a sense, a measure of lifestyles. It might, therefore, be thought that it is measuring status or 'consumption' rather than class. It might also be suggested that, since the formation of friendships is influenced by educational experience, there is something circular about relating the scale to education. Both views are similarly misconceived.

The relationships involved are relations of equality in a structure of inequality which covers all aspects of social life, including work, leisure and education. Of course friendship and education are related for they are part of the social life of an unequal society. It is the structure of just this inequality which the scale seeks to capture. It uses occupation as an identifying indicator, and then constructs the dimension of social advantage by examining people's lifestyles in social relationships. It thus integrates traditional concerns with 'class' and 'status'. In practical terms the scale relates equally well to variables conventionally associated with either 'class' or 'status'.

CHANGES IN CLASS INEQUALITY IN HIGHER EDUCATION

A major difficulty inheres in the study of social change: if all the goalposts are moving at once, seemingly simple questions, such as how have class differentials in access to education changed over time, become very difficult to answer. In essence this involves the same problem as sociologists face when trying to make comparisons across cultures: if too little is comparable between societies then the task of comparison itself is vitiated. Ideally we would like to be able to use John Stuart Mill's method of difference: holding everything constant except for one thing which varies. Since this cannot be realised in practice, and there are so few social situations in which we can even approximate it with controlled experiments, we have to rely on drawing conclusions from the complexity of natural variation. Higher education is no exception.

Higher education denotes courses above the standard required for the Advanced ('A') level of the General Certificate of Education in England and Wales, or the Higher Grade in Scotland, or the Ordinary National Certificate or Diploma. There are three main locations for pursuit of such courses: universities, polytechnics and other colleges and institutes of higher education, and the Open University. In the analysis which follows, all those who have obtained a degree or equivalent qualification in any of those institutions are grouped together with all current students on a degree course.[4]

Since, unlike secondary education, entry to higher education is not compulsory and depends on the acquisition of entry qualifications, there is no precise way of measuring the demand for places. However, the numbers in the relevant age group may be taken as a guide, and changes are certainly relevant to the competition for places. There has also been a general upward movement in demand, partly reflecting changes in the schools but largely a response to expanded provision of places: supply has generated demand, indicating that the potential demand from those who would have liked higher education was greater than the level of applications. At the same time the changes in provision must be seen as significantly altering the intensity of competition. Finally, in considering class inequality we need to take account of class sizes. If the top class has been growing, as all traditional measures indicate, we would expect it to increase its share of places.[5] On the other hand, it is not possible for the proportionate share of places going to each class to remain proportional to class size, and only in the limiting case (the corresponding change in the number of places available) can the proportion of each class gaining places remain unchanged. As we shall see, all these changes make for difficulties not only in the interpretation but also in the measurement of changing inequalities.

We shall now attempt to unravel these complexities. After reviewing some of the existing literature on access to higher education, some analysis of a survey conducted in 1986 will be performed, to examine how the association between class and attendance at higher education institutions has varied over time. In addition to changing provision and competition we shall pay attention to financial arrangements affecting students. If we can show that propensity to undertake higher education expands at lower levels of the social hierarchy when suitable opportunities are created – an argument much doubted of late – we shall have dealt an important blow to the view of consumption classes as formed around different tastes.

THE ROBBINS AND ANDERSON PRINCIPLES

Lord Robbins' name is indelibly linked with the expansion of higher education in the 1960s. He chaired a committee, established in 1961, to review the pattern of full-time higher education in Britain and to advise on its long-term development. Although the committee was staffed like a Royal Commission, its status was that of a special Departmental Committee of the Treasury with special input from the Prime Minister.[6] The committee reported in 1963.

As supplement to its report, the Committee sponsored some of the finest policy-oriented social research ever conducted in Britain. The Committee's research team was headed by Claus Moser, an able statistician and a passionate communicator.[7] In the words of a historian of government–university relations, 'The text of Robbins supplied the brass and wind: Moser's figures the strings' (Carswell, 1985: 29). Some of the detailed evidence about the effect of class background on attendance at university which Robbins considered is discussed below.

Robbins is accorded the responsibility for initiating the rapid expansion of higher education in the mid- and late-1960s, on the basis of the principle in his report that

> courses of higher education should be available for all those who are qualified by ability and attainment to pursue them, and who wish to do so. (1963a: paragraph 31)

The Robbins principle was endorsed by all governments until 1980.

However, history has perhaps accorded Robbins too much credit for the expansion. The seven famous Robbins universities might be better named the Murray universities after the name of the now forgotten chairman of the University Grants Committee who had already approved their establishment at the end of the 1950s (Carswell, 1985; 17).

Moreover, in terms of long-term effect on the structure of the higher education system, the Anderson Committee's Report (Anderson, 1960) on the ways of funding students at university predated, and was every bit as important as the Robbins Report. The Anderson Committee had been charged with the task of tidying up the *ad hoc* existing arrangements for supporting students. The methods for financing students at university before the 1960s were very similar to those for selective secondary schools before 1944; some universities, predominantly Oxbridge, had funds of their own to distribute, but the basic system was one of competition based on 'A'–level results for state or county scholarships.[8]

The Anderson Committee decided that the whole system should be swept away in favour of a uniform system of national entitlement: students should get a grant sufficient to enable them to undertake full-time year-round study, subject perhaps to a parental means test. The committee was divided about this last point, but the parental contribution was in the end implemented for the non-fee component of the grant.

A system of financial support was thus established for all full-time students at universities immediately before the great expansion of student numbers and types of higher educational provision, and was never reconsidered thereafter until the mid-1980s. As Carswell puts it:

> The Anderson Committee said that everyone who could get into full-time higher education should have a grant. The Robbins Report completed the edifice by saying that everyone who wanted higher education and reached the required standard should have a place to go. (1985: 25)

Both principles were formulated without consideration of the other, and between them, they constituted the foundation of a high-cost higher education policy for two decades.

In the 1980s, the Conservative administrations tried on more than one occasion to question this system. The value of the student grant was allowed to erode to the point where the Anderson principle of allowing students to pursue full-time year round study was undermined. Also, several attempts were made to devise a scheme of student financing with a central loan component to them. To date these have faltered, either because of the administrative difficulty of such schemes or because of their political unpopularity among sectors of society which traditionally support the Conservative party. Nevertheless, as we write, a limited loans scheme is being introduced.

In the discussion on student loans, many claims have been made about the consequences for distributive justice of different methods of student support – from the National Union of Students claiming that universal grants especially benefitted working class and women students, to Conservative politicians arguing that it was unjust for the mass of tax-payers to support an elite through an education which would bring them so much financial benefit in the long run.

The claims of the National Union of Students are important, and we believe well-founded, but their validity is not obvious. It is certainly true that the number of women students has risen since grants were introduced (though this does not necessarily establish a causal link), but the position of working-class students (male and female), which is our present concern, needs further scrutiny. In the universities, universalism has gone hand in hand with elitism; Britain has a very small university sector in comparison with other industrialised countries. The private sector in Britain has never seemed willing or able to mount any sort of competition to the state-financed institutions of higher education, perhaps suggesting that the state institutions were already doing such a good job of creaming-off an elite for intensive and costly endowment with valuable qualifications that the private sector could not compete. Indeed, sympathetic commentators on the welfare state have suggested that the principle of universalism, when used to distribute higher education resources to a small minority, may have produced a tertiary education system which is not defensible on egalitarian grounds (O'Higgins, 1987: 16).

There is a paucity of good evidence. What was the effect of the Anderson–Robbins system on equality of access? To what extent did meritocracy become the new principle of distribution of higher education places? Did the expansion of the late 1960s improve the chances of students from lower-class backgrounds? These are questions that have not been satisfactorily answered.

PAST EVIDENCE OF CLASS INEQUALITY IN ACCESS TO HIGHER EDUCATION

In this section, evidence is assembled from various existing sources on changes in class inequality in access to higher education. First, series of official statistics are examined. Next, the results of surveys conducted at different points in time are set alongside one another. Finally, comparisons are made between different age cohorts of a single cross-sectional survey. There are problems attached with each of these methods, as we shall see.

Evidence from Official Statistics

As far as applications for university places are concerned, statistics produced as a by-product of the administrative processes involved in admission yield a certain amount of interesting data. The application form asks, 'What is your father's/mother's occupation?' and answers are coded to the Registrar-General's social-class scheme.[9] From the UCCA Statistical Supplements trends in admissions can be compared across time. There is, however, a major drawback. The data only relates to candidates for admission; compositional percentages can be calculated (the percentages belonging to each class among those admitted) but not risk percentages (showing the proportions of each class who gain admittance to university).

These data reveal a strong correlation between attending university and social class. Moreover, the percentage of students who come from professional backgrounds has been rising. But, then, so has the proportion of these people in the population, and so far as we are aware, no attempt has been made to correct for this. In order to arrive at risk percentages, one would need to divide the numbers attending university in each social class by estimates of the size of the eighteen-year-old population in that class. Such a procedure would be open to numerator–denominator biases which could prove quite large, since class-coding can vary widely and there is no regularly published data on population size within class categories.

One interesting thing that does emerge from the UCCA statistics is that the association is largely due to the strong correlation between class and 'A'–level score. Within each 'A'–level score group the proportion of university applicants who are successful is virtually identical for each social class. There are, however, class differences, which have changed, in the acquisition of 'A'–level qualifications.[10]

Unfortunately, no comparable official statistics are available for polytechnics and other parts of the higher education structure.[11]

Glass and Robbins

The question of access to higher education was thoroughly researched in 1961–2 in monumental surveys conducted by Claus Moser to inform the deliberations of the Robbins Committee. As is often the case, data had to be combined from different sources in order to answer particular questions.

In order to get evidence about whether social class differences were changing over time, the committee compared their estimates of the class distribution of those entering university in 1960 with the class distribution of university entrants found in Glass's social mobility enquiries (Glass, 1954).

Robbins presented the information shown in the top of Table 10.1 as evidence that the rise in the participation rate had produced no change in class differentials. But there are great difficulties with this comparison. The Glass enquiry was conducted in England and Wales, whereas the 1960 data referred to Great Britain. The class schemes varied; Glass used the Hall–Jones scheme, whereas the data which Robbins assembled were coded to the Registrar General's scheme. The 1960 data were obtained retrospectively from respondents at the age of 21, whereas the average age of the Glass respondents was much older, and thus took older students into account. The numerator and denominator for the 1960 data were based on different surveys and thus potentially open to numerator–denominator biases. Both tables restrict attention to boys going to university, but by 1960 the expansion of places for girls and the growth of Colleges of Advanced Technology should surely have been brought into the picture. These problems are not unique to this comparison; they are typical of the difficulties that beset those who are forced to study social change by compiling data from different sources.

Table 10.1 Percentage of boys attending university courses by class background and time: Glass and Robbins' data

Father's occupation	*Age 18 in* 1928–47	1960
Non-manual	8.9	16.8
N=	(449)	(1,674)
Manual	1.4	2.6
N=	(1,045)	(4,549)
RP	6.4	6.5
D	0.075	0.142
tau_B	0.182	0.257
gamma	0.741	0.767

Source: Robbins (1963b: 54)

However, even if none of these problems existed, an analytic difficulty of some importance would still remain: how is the association in two tables to be compared when the marginal distributions in the tables vary? The statistic Robbins used to demonstrate no change is the ratio of the proportions (RP): he divided the percentage attending higher education among those from non-manual backgrounds by the percentage attending from manual backgrounds, and arrived at a figure of 6.4 for the earlier period and 6.5 for the 21-year-olds surveyed in 1960. However, if any of three other measures of association had been used, (the difference of proportions (D), Kendall's tauB or Yule's Q (gamma)), an increase in the association between class and access would have been demonstrated. While none of the measures is unaffected by changes in the marginal distributions, the fact that three indicate an increase at least casts serious doubt on the Robbins conclusion.

In our earlier papers (Blackburn and Marsh, 1991; Blackburn *et al.*, 1990), this technical problem was discussed in some detail; measures of association can be shown to be differentially sensitive to changes in the marginal distributions of tables. To the extent that these changes represent real social change – such as expansion of places at elite educational institutions – an investigator might be tempted to decide that this did not pose an interpretive problem. Unfortunately this is not so, for the different measures behave in different ways, indicating that real and artefactual[12] changes are compounded. To the extent that the measures of association are responding to changes wrought by social scientists in their class schemas, however, there is even more cause for alarm. The expansion of professional and managerial occupations over time is real enough, but claims of a resulting rise in net social status or relative advantage should be viewed with suspicion. For instance, given that social class is correlated with measures of ability, as the jobs at the top end of the social spectrum expand, they will come to occupy a different portion of the ability spectrum, and any changes in the correlation between class and attendance at various forms of selective education could just be artifacts of these shifts.

We have proposed a way round these problems which we shall be using again. However, there are too many differences between the Glass and the Robbins data for it to be worth trying to correct for these difficulties in this instance.

Evidence from Oxford Mobility Survey

A more satisfactory way to gather data to study social change is to collect retrospective information from people and to infer processes of social change by considering changes across age cohorts. In this manner many differences of procedure, sampling, coding schemes used and so on can be brought under control.

This is the technique used by Halsey *et al.* (1980) in their study of access to various forms of privileged education. They analysed a subsample of the 1972 Oxford mobility data, restricting themselves to men who were less than 60 in 1972, and who were resident in England and Wales at the age of 14 (and at interview). They coded all occupations to a slight variant of Goldthorpe's seven-fold class schema, a discrete classification scheme constructed on the basis of employment relationship. These classes were then grouped into three larger categories: the service class, an intermediate class and the working class. Although Goldthorpe himself says that there is no inherent ordering in the class scheme, in fact it exhibits ordinality even in the full seven-fold version (Marsh, 1986).

Table 10.2 Percentages of boys attending university courses by class background and time: Halsey *et al.*'s data

Fathers occupation	*Age 18 in* 1931–40	1941–50	1951–60	1961–70
Service class	7.2	15.9	23.7	26.4
Intermediate	1.9	4.0	4.1	8.0
Working class	0.9	0.9	2.3	3.1
N=	(1,846)	(1,879)	(1,856)	(2,246)

Source: Halsey *et al.* (1980: Table 10.8)

Halsey *et al.*'s findings on the class background of the men who had attended university are shown in Table 10.2. (They do not explain why they restricted their attention, in a survey done in 1972, to universities alone.)

Cross-classifying attendance by class by time in data drawn from one standard survey database represents a great advance over the kind of inferences that Robbins was able to make. Halsey *et al.* rightly observe that, in contrast to the situation following the 1944 Education Act, Robbins did manage to increase provision in line with the post-war baby boom. However, their statements about what this table shows in terms of changes in class inequalities are open to question.

They argue that 'the fastest *rates* of growth went to the working class but the largest *absolute* gains to the service class' (1980: 193). The first part of the statement is not borne out in this table, where the fastest rate of growth between columns 1 and 2 is among the service class, between 2 and 3 among the working class and between 3 and 4 among the intermediate class. The second half focuses on how the increase in places between each cohort was shared out between the classes, but merely reflects the larger pre-existing share of the service class.

They also note that the availability of university places grew faster than the number of qualified applicants between the first and second cohorts. Then the numbers with qualifying 'A'–levels kept pace with the number of university places in the third cohort and grew faster than the number of places in the final cohort, and they observe that in these circumstances 'the working class was less able to hold onto its previous gains so that the distance between classes increased' (Halsey *et al.*, 1980: 189). However, once again the evidence they present does not really support the interpretation; it shows the greatest gains of the service class relative to the working class occurred between the first and second cohorts (1980: Table 10.9, 189). Apart from these and the previous remarks they come to no conclusions about changing class inequalities.

A NEW ANALYSIS OF CLASS DIFFERENTIALS IN ACCESS TO HIGHER EDUCATION

It has not been possible to draw any definite conclusions from previous research on changes in class differences in access to higher education. We now present a fresh analysis which makes quite clear what the pattern of changing inequality has been during the past 40 years. To achieve this we use an approach – marginal fixing – where the effects of changes in the marginal distributions are controlled.

Data

In this section, the strategy adopted by Halsey *et al.* – using retrospective data on qualifications from a single sample of people – is repeated on a different, more recent dataset; one, moreover, where the experience of both boys and girls and the whole of higher education can be considered.

The data comes from the ESRC-funded Social Change and Economic Life Initiative (SCELI). Interviews were conducted with one thousand adults between the ages of 20 and 59 in six urban labour markets in Great Britain in 1986: Aberdeen, Coventry, Kirkcaldy, Northampton, Rochdale and Swindon.[13] Although the six labour markets differ considerably, the characteristics of this sample taken together are very similar to those of the country as a whole.

Respondents were asked what qualifications they had, and these were coded to the 15-category GHS scheme.[14] For those with higher education we put together those who reported that they had a degree or a teacher-training diploma with those who said that they were currently full-time students studying for a degree; failure to include current students would have led to a bias in the proportion with higher qualifications in the youngest age-group.

Real Changes in Circumstance

Many processes of social change have occurred in the lifetime of these SCELI respondents, and they can be reflected in the distributions of different variables by age.

In order to study social change, the respondents were divided up into four age groups covering equal periods of ten years. The groups represent, roughly, periods of growth or decline in the number of 18-year-olds and associated demand for places. As Figure 10.2 shows, the size of the 18-years age-group in Great Britain has fluctuated quite a lot. Following a steady decline corresponding to the falling birth rate of the 1920s and 1930s, there was an increase culminating in a particularly sharp rise reflecting the delayed birth of babies in 1946. After this the numbers dropped back somewhat, but then, as Robbins had foreseen, throughout most of the 1970s and on into the 1980s

Figure 10.2 Number of 18-year-olds (Great Britain)

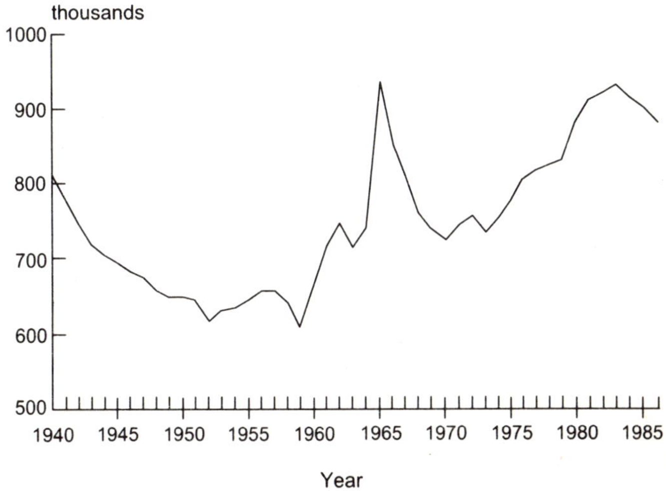

Source: For years prior to 1961, Annual Abstract of Statistics; for 1961–86, AUT (1983: Table 1) (whose source is cited as the Government Actuary's Department).

there was a long sustained rise in the size of the 18-year-old population. These large demographic fluctuations have had major consequences for the unlucky members of the boom generations and for the lucky members of the less populous bust generations, consequences in educational, social and labour-market experiences (Easterlin, 1987) which must be included in any account of changes over time.

The oldest cohort were 18 between 1945 and 1954, cohort 2 were 18 in the 10 years from 1955 and 1964, cohort 3 benefitted by being 18 in the period of expanding provision and for the most part, the population decline from 1965, and the youngest group were 18 in the period of steady growth between 1975 and 1984. For present purposes we shall ignore precisely when each respondent started their college education, and assume that all behaved like the majority and went straight from school. (Any misallocation will be slight and simply tend to produce small underestimates in the observed changes and so does not affect the argument).

Table 10.3 shows that there are substantial changes in this dataset both in the numbers in different age-groups and in the class background and educational experiences of these age-groups. The two younger groups contain substantially more people than the older groups. These younger groups are also more likely to have fathers who had professional and administrative jobs (Registar General classes I and II); and the proportion with a degree is markedly higher than in the older two age-groups. Despite the rather specialised nature of the sample, these changes tally reasonably well with what we would expect from other national data sources. Thus the sample numbers are in keeping with the trends shown in Figure 10.2 in the numbers of 18-year-olds in Great Britain across time.

Data on the numbers attending higher education are harder to come by. The university statistics are quite well documented, but it is much harder to obtain consistent time series on those attending all forms of higher education. Ideally, one would like to obtain data on those new home undergraduates embarking on any full or part-time higher education degree course in a particular year, but, to our knowledge, such a dataset has not been compiled on a consistent basis over a long period of time. Figure 10.3 shows the total numbers attending full-time higher education courses (i.e. both home and overseas, both undergraduate and postgraduate); higher education has been defined to correspond with the meaning given to the term by Robbins and the definition cited earlier.

Table 10.3 Changes in marginal distribution by age

	Age 18 in			
	1945–54	*1955–64*	*1965–74*	*1975–84*
N=	(992)	(1,114)	(1,669)	(1,581)
Percentage with fathers in professional or administrative jobs	20.1	22.5	22.8	28.7
Percentage with a degree	3.0	6.1	9.5	8.2

Source: SCELI 1986 Surveys

From the point of view of access, the numbers need to be expressed as a proportion of the numbers who were available to attend in order to know whether the chances for any individual of getting in to higher education were going up or down in that time. One conventional way to arrive at this idea is to express the numbers attending as an age-participation rate: to divide the newcomers each year by the total 18-year-old population in that year.[15] Since the student numbers in Figure 10.3 are totals for the whole of higher education, they have been multiplied by 0.31 to arrive at an estimate of the numbers who were first-year undergraduate home students[16] before dividing them by the 18-year old population in each year.

Figure 10.3 reveals that while student numbers have grown throughout the period under consideration, the chances of any particular 18-year-old securing a place at an institute of higher education only increased up to the end of the 1960s and marginally to 1973. Thereafter, the rise in the number of higher education places in the 1980s barely kept place with the rise in the number of 18-year-olds, and even fell for a time. So the relative proportions with a degree in different age groups as shown in Table 10.3 do seem broadly in line with national figures.[17]

Finally, external sources confirm that there has been long-term change in the occupational structure. This much is well known from sources such as the Population Census (see Figure 10.4a). The occupational and class schemes have varied in each census, however. It is interesting to note that a more consistent method of classifying jobs has shown more change (Figure 10.4b). Similarly the Nuffield

Figure 10.3 Attendance at higher education

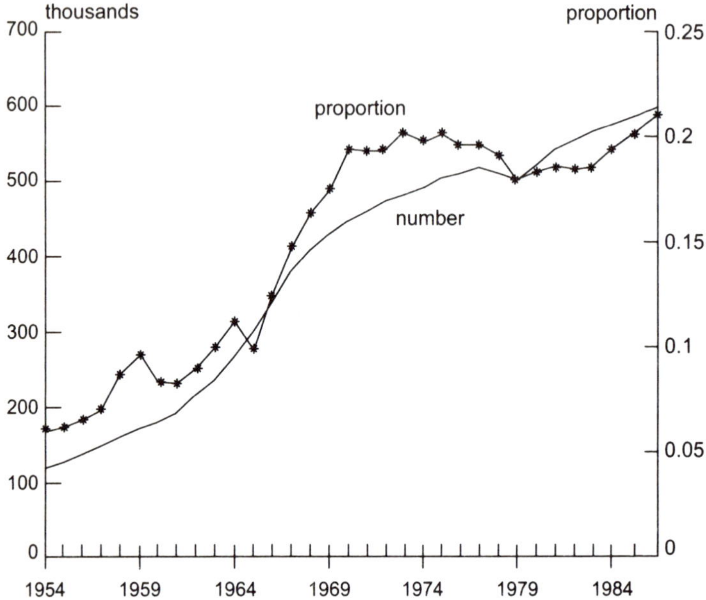

Sources: For 1954–62, Robbins (1963b: Table 46), for 1963–8, Educational Statistics for the UK (1968, *Department of Education and Science*) (multiplied by 0.97 to arrive at a GB estimate); for 1969 and 1971–4 Education Statistics for the UK (1975) (× 0.97); for 1970, Statistical Bulletin 9/85, *Department of Education and Science* (July, 1985); for 1971 and 1977, Statistical Bulletin 17/83, *Department of Education and Science* (July, 1985). Values for 1976 and 1978 were interpolated.

classes show greater growth at the top. It seems that the periodic changes in the official scheme have the effect of partially compensating for the changes in size that have taken place.

So we may conclude that we get a reasonably secure picture of national trends in the marginals of surveys of this kind. Moreover, since the data are drawn from a single survey as opposed to a series of official statistics or national surveys, we benefit from homogeneity of survey procedures; of population sampled; of variable definitions; of coding schemes and so on.

Figure 10.4a Class structure in censuses

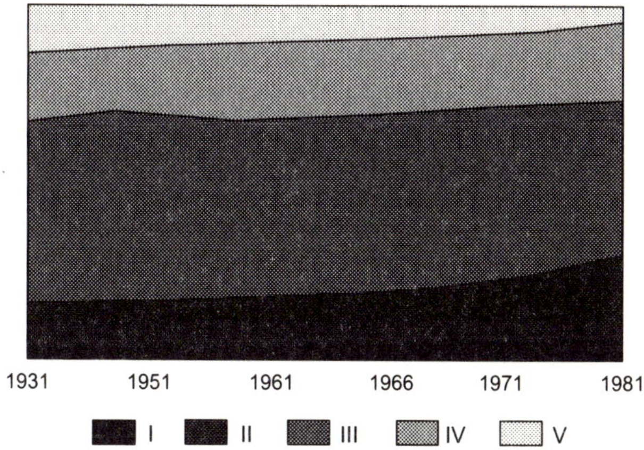

Source: Census data

Figure 10.4b Class structure in the FES

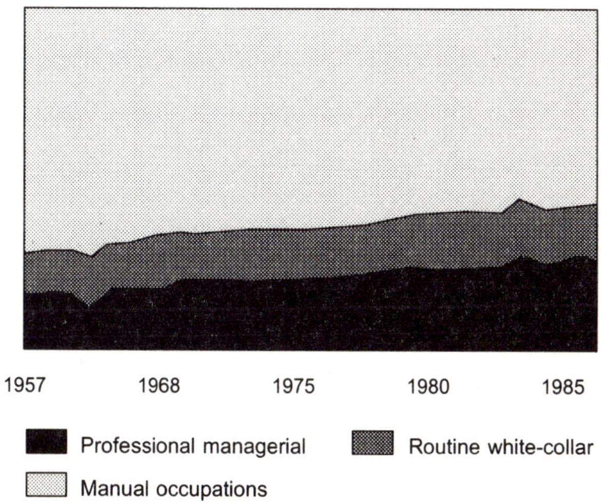

Source: Family Expenditure Surveys

Changes in Class Inequality

Given that demography, places in higher education and occupational structure were all changing in the post-war years, how can we make meaningful comparisons across age-groups? The tables that we will construct will have different marginal distributions and these will affect the measures of inequality that we choose to summarise the changes. As we have argued in previous papers, the solution is two-fold. First, for variables such as social class, where it is reasonable to believe that the groupings are in fact relatively arbitrary divisions of an underlying continuum, we should ensure that the marginal distributions of class are held firmly under control. In particular we shall match the marginals of class and places in higher education. The justification for treating 'class' advantage as a continuum in this respect was established earlier (see Figure 10.1). Then, we shall investigate inequality by a series of different coefficients of association, giving preferential treatment to Kendall's tau_B especially since, when we have matched the marginals, this can be given the most consistent interpretation across tables (Blackburn and Marsh, 1991).

In the first place, however, we show in Table 10.4 the data in a 'naive' manner, ignoring the problem of varying marginal distributions. In this table, respondents have been classified according to the Registrar General's class of their father's job; this has been dichotomised into classes I and II versus the rest, as these are predominantly the groups who have sent their children to college. In the table, the proportion getting higher education qualifications by class background is shown for the four different age-groups.

Four different measures of association are shown at the foot of table 4: RP′ (the ratio of proportions adjusted to ensure that the result lies in the range 0–1), Kendall's tau_B, D (the difference of proportions) and gamma (Yule's Q). The results they produce are not consistent. If we look at changes between cohorts 1 and 2, which fell before the Robbins expansion period, the measures agree that there was rising inequality, but RP′ suggests that inequality rose very little. Between periods 2 and 3, immediately after the Robbins expansion, all measures except D show a decline; D suggests that very little changed. In the final period, the measures entirely fail to agree: RP′ and gamma suggest that inequality increased, tau_B suggests that little changed and D tells us that, if anything, inequality fell.

Table 10.4 Percentage of respondents getting higher education qualifications by class background and time: (i) Registrar General's classes I+II versus the rest

	Age 18 in			
	1945–54	*1955–64*	*1965–74*	*1975–84*
Classes				
I+II	9.6	18.8	21.7	18.3
N=	(199)	(250)	(380)	(454)
Classes				
III–V	1.9	3.1	6.6	4.8
N=	(793)	(864)	(1,289)	(1,127)
Measure of				
Associations	*RP′*	tau_B	*D*	*gamma*
	0.64	0.17	0.08	0.70
	0.66	0.26	0.16	0.75
	0.50	0.21	0.15	0.59
	0.59	0.22	0.13	0.63

Source: SCELI 1,000 Surveys, 1986

By now we should be fairly familiar with these sorts of inconsistencies. They reflect the difficulty in measuring social trends which has encouraged the sceptical view that nothing really changed. They were noted above in Table 10.1, and the same sort of inconsistencies were found with respect to secondary education (Blackburn and Marsh, 1991). Since the statistics respond differently to changes in the ratio of one marginal to the other, it is important to ensure that the inconsistencies are not an artifact of changes in the marginals – in the stratification structure in relation to the number of available places.

In Table 10.5, therefore, we show the result of matching the marginals to make the relative size of the top 'class' in a two-class structure equal to the proportion of places at higher educational institutions in that cohort. In other words, as the output from higher education institutions expands, we cut the continuum of advantage up to allow a correspondingly larger top segment to be defined. The highest class, after all, has (in Britain at any rate, if not elsewhere on the continent of Europe), been defined as the professional and managerial class. Holding a degree is one major qualification for entry into those jobs. So it is quite reasonable theoretically to think that as the output of trained personnel expanded, the size of a top class should be allowed to expand. There are also sound statistical reasons for adopting this procedure. By matching the marginals, we avoid artifactual differences in the *possibility* of finding a perfect correlation, since in each cohort all four measures can occupy the full range from 0 to 1; and tau_B can be interpreted as a product–moment correlation coefficient giving an undistorted measure of explained variance.

Matching the marginals defines a much smaller top class than in Table 10.4. In other words, if all the children of RG social class I and II parents had wanted higher education, there would not have been enough places to accommodate them.

Table 10.5 Percentage of repondents getting higher education qualifications by class background and time: (ii) matched marginals

			Age 18 in	
	1945–54	*1955–64*	*1965–74*	*1975–84*
Upper class	13.5	26.2	25.4	28.0
N=	(33)	(72)	(161)	(128)
Lower Class	3.0	5.3	8.4	7.2
N=	(1,001)	(1,045)	(1,533)	(1,472)
Measures of associations	*RP'*	tau_B	*D*	*gamma*
	0.67	0.10	0.11	0.67
	0.72	0.21	0.21	0.73
	0.53	0.17	0.17	0.58
	0.58	0.20	0.21	0.67

Source: SCELI 1,000 Surveys, 1986

Table 10.5 now tells a clearer story: all measures agree on the direction of change of inequality in each period. However, they still differ as to the magnitude of the rise or fall. We shall give preference to tauB, which in principle should now be the same as the difference in proportions. (The small numerical differences reflect the impossibility of perfect marginal matching because of clustering at the points of the Cambridge Scale.) They have been graphed in Figure 10.5.

Figure 10.5 Inequality measures: matched marginals

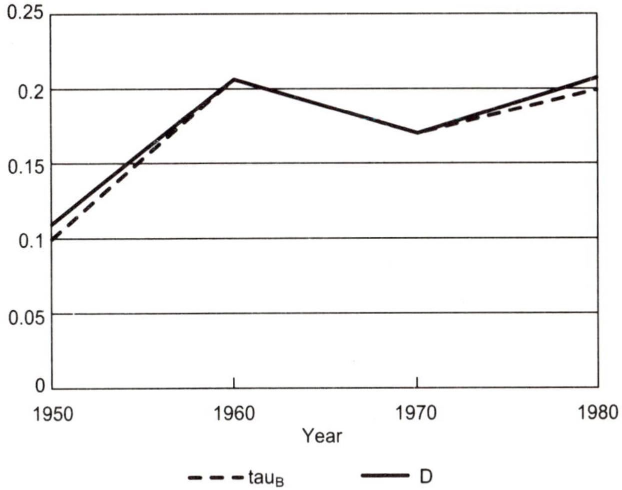

Source: SCELI 1000 surveys, 1986.

From figure 10.5 we can see that inequality was rising most sharply between the first two cohorts. It then fell between the second and the third, but rose once more (although not as sharply as previously) in between the third and fourth cohort. Considerable confidence can be placed in these results: they are not the result of changes in the marginal distributions.

DISCUSSION

How are these results to be interpreted? It is not plausible to attribute them to changes in tastes. Rather they must be seen as following from changes in circumstances, in which social policy played an important part but was influenced by the level of competition for places (whose main cause was demographic). This can be seen if we go back to the marginal changes discussed earlier.

The changes between the first two cohorts occurred in the period before Robbins. In this period before universal grants were established, the number of 18-year-olds was fairly static: although student numbers were rising, places were being taken disproportionately by the children of professional and managerial parents, and class inequalities widened. Carswell (1985) asserts that no child in the pre-Robbins era was denied a place at university because of inability to pay, but provides no evidence for this. Perhaps it is true that children from other classes did not get as far as applying for a university place that they could not see how to finance, but evidence from the next cohort belies the truth of Carswell's claim.

In the period after Robbins, the trends in inequality were reversed: the number of 18-year-olds was greater but the number of higher education places more than kept pace – the number of places per child was rising, as a result of social policy intervention.[18] As with secondary education (Blackburn and Marsh, 1991), universalism coupled with expansion brought about a decline in inequality.

Between the third and the fourth cohort, the number of 18-year-olds was climbing but the number of places levelled off, thus leading to a decline in the places per pupil. Even with universal access, class inequalities tended to re-assert themselves under these conditions, and the trend towards equality was turned around. Universalism in the context of declining resources per head led to a reassertion of old class differentials. Crosland's (1956) argument that socialism's best chance was to redistribute through growth is given resounding support from these findings.[19]

It should be noted that universalism has never been complete in higher education. There has always been an element of means-testing for student maintenance grants (which has increased in recent years). This tends to work to the disadvantage of the middle levels of the stratification structure – those who have to pay but can least afford it. This may possibly account for the slight upturn in the proportion with degrees that we noted in the lowest stratification positions in Figure 10.1, since these students would get the full grant. As with secondary education the net effect is likely to be to increase inequality. Since higher education is not compulsory there is also an opportunity cost of foregone earnings which is more significant where parental incomes are low, though at the very lowest levels the maintenance grant may seem a reasonable alternative. These factors have helped to sustain class inequalities in higher education. Nevertheless the policy of (near) universalism plus expansion did reduce inequality, and without it the present level of inequality would have been far greater.

It should also be remembered that in this analysis the university and other higher education sectors have been collapsed together. It could be the case that there are important differences between the two sectors in trends in their class composition. Unfortunately, the data we have analysed here did not differentiate between the two sectors.

However, taking all degrees together, it has finally been possible to establish the pattern of changing inequality. In this the effect of social policy is clear. The combination of universal grants and expanding opportunity achieved a narrowing of class differentials; but when provision failed to keep pace with potential demand the increased competition led to a return to greater inequality. This is a lesson of relevance for the current discussion about the financing of students in higher education. Under conditions of falling numbers of 18-year-olds, the universalism inherent in the Robbins–Anderson principle offers the opportunity for returning the trends to declining class inequality. But without it, it is likely that class differences in higher education will continue to widen.[20]

Social stratification, unlike geographical stratification, is a fluid process and the components of each stratum require to be replenished each generation. Education is a key institution in the process of assigning people to different locations in the hierarchy; it is an integral part of the structure reproducing differential social advantage. It would, therefore, be surprising if parents higher up the stratification hierarchy did not attempt to exploit their advantage to provide their children with an education appropriate for passing on the social advantage. However, the strong relation between parents' class and gaining a degree does not necessarily preclude explanations in terms of consumption tastes. To rule out such explanations, as we explained at the outset, it has to be established that changes in inequalities are related to changing circumstances affecting advantage. This has now been done. We have shown that universalism in financial support reduces social barriers in times of real growth of resources. In times of static or declining real resources, the role of education as a means of passing on social advantage from one generation to another comes more to the fore. Whatever else, it cannot be argued that social advantage is irrelevant to gaining the benefits of higher education. Such a cynical position was only possible while the relevant data analysis was inconclusive.

Notes

1. In a survey of parents who held some sort of bank account in 1990 (around 90 per cent of the adult population had accounts), 85 per cent said they would like their children to go on to higher education

(*Independent*, July 16, 1990) and there were virtually no differences in preferences between parents in different income groups (private communication, Legal and General).

2. The limited power of legislation to produce changes may clearly be seen in relation to race and sex inequalities, but the persisting degree of inequality can hardly be attributed to tastes for being victims of discrimination.
3. Most class schemes recognise this, at least implicitly, as the classes are hierarchically ordered.
4. There are, of course, differences in prestige between degrees from different institutions which would be interesting to take into account if the data were available. However, the simple division between those who obtain degrees and those who do not is important, and is sufficient for present purposes.
5. Murphy (1990) takes such an increase as evidence of increased inequality without considering changes in class sizes.
6. Carswell (1985) gives two reasons why the Robbins Committee was never a Royal Commission. Having experienced loss of control at the hands of over-zealous Royal Commissions in the Victorian era, the universities themselves would not have supported a new Royal Commission. And the University Grants Committee feared that such a Royal Commission might have turned into a standing committee whose power might have usurped its own.
7. He went on to become head of the Government Statistical Service.
8. Scholarships awarded by Oxbridge also carried entitlement to state scholarships, with the value of the Oxbridge scholarship deducted.
9. The method is rather crude, being based on one simple question rather than the three usually asked on major government research surveys, but Rudd (1987) has shown that more careful research on students accepted in 1984 produced substantially the same results.
10. Halsey *et al.* (1980) present information in their Table 10.9 on the proportion of people with 'A'–levels or equivalent in each class who went to university. The numbers involved are quite small, but there is an interesting suggestion that a reversal in the correlation between class and the qualified participation rate has occurred over time. Among Halsey *et al.*'s oldest respondents, working class people were much less likely to get 'A'–levels, but having got them were more likely to use them to go to university. Among their youngest group, however, qualified working-class people were less likely to go to university than those from higher classes. It seems that the expansion of opportunity has led to a greater growth in the number of working-class pupils gaining basic entry qualifications than in actually gaining entry.
11. It could well be that the decline in the relative proportion of qualified working-class people entering universities (Note 10) has been offset by higher proportions elsewhere.
12. Artifactual changes are those occurring in a measure for technical reasons rather than changes in what is being measured.
13. The sample design was a two stage stratified random sample drawn from the electoral roll, with correction for non-electors. The response rate

varied between 75 per cent and 77 per cent in the different localities. The original sample was designed to yield a disproportionately high number of people unemployed at the time of the survey; in the analysis which follows the data have been reweighted back to the true population proportions.

14. For details of this scheme see the annual reports of the General Household Survey published by the OPCS.
15. The other popular way is to calculate a 'qualified participation rate', i.e. the proportion of people obtaining school qualifications which would permit entry to college who in fact go. But since the rate is so high, and class differentials are insignificant once qualifications are taken into account, we stick with the age participation rate.
16. In both 1979 and in 1987, first year undergraduate home students formed 31 per cent of the total numbers in full-time higher education (*DES Statistical Bulletin* 4/89, Table 5).
17. We cannot explain why almost twice as large a proportion of the age-group appear to have attended a higher education course in the calculations for Figure 10.2 as say they have a degree in the figures in Table 10.3. However, for our purposes it is the relative changes that are crucial in influencing conclusions we draw about changes in relative advantage.
18. The number of 18-year-olds rose dramatically for one year in 1965, slightly outstripping the expansion of places, but this has little effect on the overall pattern of inequalities.
19. Once again, this is a result similar to that for secondary education. It is worth noting that the other measures considered here (RP′ and gamma) present a picture of greater influence for social policy, by suggesting a bigger fall in inequality and a lesser turn around as competition increased. While the measures we have prioritised must be regarded as more reliable, the others certainly give no reason to doubt the effects of social policy.
20. Unfortunately, the SCELI sample does not contain people from the cohort who were 18 in the 1940s and early 1950s. An analysis of class inequalities in access to higher education in that period would be very instructive, as the age-group size was declining as now and no universal maintenance grants were available.

11 Competing Views of Contemporary Social Mobility and Social Divisions

Geoff Payne

INTRODUCTION

Social divisions and social mobility go hand in hand. Social division implies distinctive memberships, so that measurement of exchanges of members becomes one of the ways of identifying the boundaries, the permeability, and the permanence of the divisions. Movements between origins and destinations pre-suppose origins and destinations that are socially divided. The classic manifestation of this link has been between social class and social mobility, although the logic of mobility analysis can be extended to movements of other kinds. Recent developments in the study of social mobility itself have, for example, incorporated insights drawn from labour-market, gender, race and life-course studies (Payne, 1989a). Movements between consumption sectors, such as housing tenure, and household levels of material well-being, have also been explored (Dale, 1991; Savage *et al.*, this volume).

As well as evolution from within, there has also been an external critique of the sociology of mobility, class and inequality. Among writers on the New Right, Flew (1976, 1982) has argued that innate differences between individuals explain educational and occupational achievement, while Hiskett (1988) claims that inheritance of private property actually promotes social and economic mobility. The neo-liberal strand of the New Right has argued that over-emphasis on immobility and the rigidity of the class structure reflects a refusal to recognise the dynamics of an enterprise culture (Dawson, 1981; Marsland, 1987). A more neo-conservative strand of thinking (e.g. the Hillgate Group, 1986) attacks sociology as a whole for its general assumption that Britain is 'a class-structured inegalitarian society' (Rawling, 1990).

Two recent publications from Peter Saunders have argued that conventional sociological wisdom about class and mobility in contemporary Britain, 'the Westergaard and Resler view' (Saunders, 1989: 3) is seriously wrong:

> Very rarely have sociologists accepted the possibility that Britain might be a fairly open society, yet this is the direction in which the evidence points us. This does not mean that Britain is a meritocratic society . . . Yet having said that, it would be just as fatuous to conclude from this that Britain is a closed society in which a dominant class perpetuates itself while excluding others from its privileges . . . Sociology reproduces its own myths and continues to shut its ears and eyes to any development in psychology or molecular biology which might lead us to question this resolute commitment to social determinism. (Saunders, 1990a: 77–8, 83)

The Saunders' view is at once one of greater social fluidity, and of a mobility contest in which many of the prizes go to the most able competitors.

This interpretation of his position is not intended to be pejorative. It is perfectly consistent to argue that there is high social fluidity, and that those who succeed have greater capacities, provided one makes appropriate assumptions about the proportions of the able and less able in society. Nor does Saunders' argument deal only with fluidity and ability: in full, his position is more complex. He acknowledges the strength of the barriers of racial, gender and class exclusivity (Saunders, 1990a: 77), and that access to educational qualifications is crucial, not least for the grammar school generation which grew up taking state support for granted (Saunders, 1989: 4). He accepts the structural forces at work in mobility:

> technological change and the shift in employment from industry to services has expanded the number of higher positions . . . and some degree of upward mobility is thus inevitable. (Saunders, 1990a: 69)

In other words, he is not replacing sociological with psychological explanations, as Marshall and Rose have implied (Marshall and Rose, 1989: 4) but rather introducing extra psychological and economistic reasons to explain why one person rather than another similar person should be mobile, why there may be finite limits to mobility rates, and why continued structures of inequality may be 'natural' and 'legitimate' – the latter terms being drawn from neo-liberal writers such as Nozick and Hayek (as well as, interestingly, Durkheim).

Although, at present, Saunders' ideas have appeared in relatively simplified expositions, his contribution is an important one. Because it draws on ideas from other disciplines, and is couched in an aggressively ideological fashion which attacks mainstream sociology for being left-wing biased, there is a probability that his work will not receive the serious consideration it deserves. If we leave to one side the rhetoric of 'left-wing' and 'bias', we can engage Saunders' position at three levels: the ideas which are the source of his perspective; the evidence he adduces to support his view of mobility; and the significance and causal explanations he attaches to this alternative evidence.

IDEAS OF SOCIAL MOBILITY: THE MOBILITY PARADIGM

Rather than talking about bias, it would be more accurate, if less dramatic, to say that social scientists work on social divisions within established paradigms of methodological and conceptual assumptions, sometimes keeping closely within them, and at others using parts of the paradigm as a scaffolding for the construction of new models. Within any such paradigm – and it can be argued that mobility does indeed operate within widely-agreed frameworks – there is the possibility that the set of ideas creates

> systematically distorted communication through which orthodoxies come to be perpetuated without anybody necessarily realising or intending it. (Saunders, 1989: 3)

In other words, an unconscious bias may emerge, a point also argued by Pawson (1990) in his observations on the exchanges between Saunders and Marshall and Rose. It may also be true that in the construction of a paradigm, explicitly political assumptions are involved, but that in itself does not necessarily invalidate the paradigm in its subsequent operation. Again, the orthodoxies may be collectivist, or the original writing politically inspired, but that is not the same as claiming 'left-wing bias'.

We can illustrate this by an examination of mainstream mobility research, starting with Glass's *Social Mobility in Britain*. The 1949 LSE study was a paradigm-setter in several ways, not only producing the empirical evidence which was the central connection between mobility research and class analysis in this country for a quarter of a century, but also stimulating a proliferation of national studies, throughout the 1950s and 1960s. In this sense, and equally important, in the methodological pre-empting of definitions, data-collection, and modes of technical analysis, Glass and his colleagues established the modern mobility paradigm (see Payne (1987a: Chapter 6; 1989b) for further details).

We can examine *Social Mobility in Britain* with four questions in mind: what was its political orientation? does its methodology lead to an unconscious bias? why did the results of the study have so much influence, and can this be attributed to political or unconscious bias?

Turning to the first of these, Glass's interest in mobility and social divisions was originally both very focused and historically specific: 'the formation and structure of the "middle classes"', and the consequences of the 1944 Education Act – 'which so far as social stratification is concerned, is probably the most important measure of the last half-century' (Glass, 1954: 3–4). His focus on the professions and the higher civil service led him to make a general study of all classes, but only for the sake of background comparison (ibid: 4–5). There was little discussion on class boundaries, consciousness, integration or structural rigidity in the book, and the extensive data received scant interpretation. Class differences were discussed almost exclusively in the context of education. School reform would reduce the effect of family background, 'mobility will increase, and probably increase greatly' (ibid: 24):

> With a fluid social structure there is more likelihood that positions requiring high ability will in fact be held by individuals who possess high ability . . . there may, as a consequence, be less feeling of personal frustration and a greater possibility of social harmony (ibid: 24–5).

Are we to see this as a political statement, and does it reflect conscious or unconscious bias? First, it clearly *is* political, being concerned both with the formation of elites and with one of the pillars of post-war welfare policy normally associated with the Attlee government (the wartime passage of the 1944 Education Act notwithstanding). However, Glass's work hardly merits the label 'left-wing': Kreckel (1973) among others has criticised it for its narrow, 'Fabian' orientation, and while Goldthorpe has tried to show that Glass was concerned as much with equality of condition as with equality of opportunity, closer reading of the text shows the latter's real concerns at the time have more to do with the reduction of social conflict (Glass, 1954: 26–7; Goldthorpe, 1987 *et al.*: 23). Glass's writing was essentially meritocratic with its aim, as shown in the above quotation, being social harmony; more Durkheimian than Marxist.

The second legacy of *Social Mobility in Britain* was methodological. At the centre of the statistical development associated with the text was the Index of Association, which effectively compared observed mobility against the *statistical* concept, 'perfect mobility'. Perfect mobility is the condition of no association between origin and destination, akin to a value of zero for a correlation coefficient. The condition of no association is widely used in a number of statistical techniques. The word 'perfect' means 'absolute', not 'perfection' or 'morally desirable', although as MacKenzie has argued about eugenics and Pearson's correlation coefficient, the intellectual framework of ideas is related to the measures devised in research practice. It *may* be true that Glass' general interest in a more meritocratic society provided the impetus to create a statistical measure based on the standard of no association. However, even if its origins were political, the subsequent uses of such measures by a variety of sociologists is not then automatically political:

> the point is not that the techniques . . . necessarily continue to reflect, in their contemporary use, the conditions of their origin. (MacKenzie, 1979: 38)

Much subsequent effort has gone into refining the Index of Association, along lines directly equivalent to other statistical analyses, and this has been carried out by sociologists of every political hue (Bibby, 1975). Present usage is as apolitical as that of chi-square, which is also based on the comparison of observed values and those expected under a hypothesis of no association.

Indeed, a genuinely left-wing position would arguably call not for a statistic based on the limited goal and standard of 'no association', implying merely meritocracy, but rather a statistic based on a state in which as many middle class children as possible were *debarred* from middle class occupations, to make way for positive discrimination in favour of children from the working class.

It follows that the development and use of mobility measures based on the standard of no association do not sustain Saunders' claim that

> in the idealised world of left sociologists, people's destinies should be randomly determined . . . The principle of relative mobility depends upon a comparison between actual mobility rates and an ideal norm in which people's starting points have no effect on where they end up. Goldthorpe and the Essex team will not accept that the system is open until such time as destinations are randomly related to origins. (Saunders, 1989: 4)

Saunders' leap from a conventional statistical approach, utilised by social scientists of *all* political persuasions, to a politically motivated and ideologically determined 'test' on the part of his chosen adversaries must, to say the least, lack credibility. It does no service to his allied claim, that Goldthorpe and the Essex team place more emphasis than is warranted on measurement of relative mobility, rather than absolute mobility, a point which is discussed below.

On the other hand, Saunders might have been on slightly stronger ground had he explored the way in which Glass's findings were subsequently incorporated in the sociology of class in Britain. With the benefit of hindsight, it is now clear that Glass' mobility tables are completely fallacious, and yet they have been largely taken at face value. The problem with the tables is that the class distributions of fathers and sons are the same, whereas from census and other sources it can be shown that there was a historical expansion of middle class occupations during this period. Furthermore, class differentials in fertility at that time should also have created differences between the reported distributions, because middle-class fathers have fewer children, so a random sample of children picks up fewer children reporting middle class fathers than there actually were middle-class fathers in the previous generation (Payne 1987a: 110–15). Despite doubts expressed about the distributional symmetry of the Glass mobility tables from at least the early 1970s, the results of the LSE study became totally integrated into the body of sociological knowledge, and proved resilient to critique.

The explanation *may* be that the picture of low mobility reinforced politically-biased pre-conceptions about Britain as an unequal society. But it equally well owes as much to the professional self-esteem of a budding group of academics in a new discipline: sociology could for the first time in the 1950s and early 1960s speak on the basis of empirical scientific facts against the mere common sense of the man in the street or the unreliable opinion of the self-seeking politician. Another, and equally powerful explanation lies in the dominance of the LSE in the early post-war years, and its subsequent seeding of new sociology departments with its graduates and Glass's co-workers (Payne, 1987a: 90–1; Payne *et al.*, 1981: 23–4). It should also be remembered that the dearth of sociological studies of Britain in that era was such that any one contribution was likely to make a much greater impact on our body of knowledge than in present times.

Whichever explanation is favoured, it is not unreasonable to suggest that there was a widely agreed reading of the evidence on mobility and how it related to certain features of the class structure as the major social division in British society. This secondary paradigm operated alongside the statistical one that we have already discussed: it is within these paradigms that Goldthorpe among others has worked. If that constitutes unconscious bias, only the radicals among us in every field of sociology can claim to escape it.

This applies not only to British sociology but also the sociology of other nations in which mobility research took place in response to Glass's work. It must not be forgotten that writers such as Lenski (1958), Lipset and Bendix (1959), or Blau and Duncan (1967) have all worked in much the same tradition. They share a *sociological* mode of explanation, but no-one would seriously claim from these, or their other writings, that the named researchers were members of the political Left. They were operating in a context of intellectual currents concerned with a Cold War demonstration of the moral and functional superiority of social democracy and liberal capitalism. Blau and Duncan see America not as exceptional, but only as being in the vanguard of societies in their fundamental trend towards a system based on universalistic values. As Goldthorpe observes, Blau and Duncan view the USA as having:

> a type of stratification which has no inherent tendency to give rise to distinguishable collectivities of any kind with which individuals might identify or which could provide a basis for socio-political mobilization. . . a highly open form of stratification is that functionally most consistent with a liberal-democratic order. (Goldthorpe *et al.*, 1987: 16–17)

By comparison, Lipset's doubts about high rates of mobility being destabilising show his more conservative position.[1]

It is true that these illustrations are drawn from American rather than British sociology, but national sociologies do not exist in total isolation. In Britain, almost no empirical research into mobility rates *per se* took place between 1949 and 1972: the mobility paradigm was sustained from abroad and from writings which used Glass's data in their treatment of class (Payne, 1989a). The point of these illustrations is that sociologists of quite different political stances, and also using different conceptual frameworks for much of their sociology, nonetheless shared two elements in common. First, the questions of openness and how mobility, opportunity and the political order interact are not the province of any one political hue of sociologist: people of all shades of political opinion wish answers, even if the answers they seek are diffferent. Second, all of these politically different mobility writers have started with the same basic assumptions. Talent is assumed to be broadly, if not uniformly or randomly, distributed across the population. Social processes are then assumed to intervene to allocate people to social destinations which do not necessarily reflect the original capacities of the individuals. The important problem is to identify these sociological processes of allocation. It is this which lies at the heart of the supposed 'unconscious biases' that focus on discontinuities and collective explanations, rather than on equality and individualistic explanations. As we saw above, even Saunders uses a sociological approach to the core questions, whatever his detailed objections.

It would, of course, be equally as simplistic to attribute *all* of the British interest in class and mobility to this underlying paradigm. Glass set up a political debate about mobility, the upper middle class and education. The Oxford study took this on another generation, perhaps more directly in Halsey's work than in that of Goldthorpe. The work of the latter, and of Marshall *et al.*, explicitly relates to the political interest and theoretical focus of their authors. The choice is therefore whether we see the political dimension as *the* explanator, or whether we take a wider view, including the set of elements that comprise the paradigm, to provide a more rounded, if less straightforward, explanation.

IDEAS OF SOCIAL MOBILITY: A NEW ALTERNATIVE

Saunders raises three objections to the conventional interpretation of social mobility: that mobility analysis ignores improvements in quality of life; that it makes unstated assumptions about the desirability of high rates of mobility; and that it fails to tackle the problem of legitimacy and limits to inequality. Each of these redefines the dominant mode of thinking about social divisions.

The first of these objections draws on Hayek's (1960) analogy of the 'moving column': in capitalist societies

> there are always people at the front and people bringing up the rear, but the whole column is always moving forwards, and everyone benefits. (Saunders, 1990a: 48)

This movement is driven by the entrepreneurs' self interest: their attempts to make money through innovation do not all need to succeed for productive power and the wealth of society as a whole to expand:

> a few entrepreneurs become rich, some others fail and go bust, and meanwhile the rest of society grows more affluent as it gains by their efforts. (Saunders, 1990a: 53)

The outcomes for the individual of the market process may depend heavily on luck in Hayek's model (rather than meritocratic ability in Saunders' view) but the dynamic nature of capitalism lies in the incentives it offers to 'those with talent and enterprise to use it in pursuit of material wealth. *Capitalism is dynamic because it is unequal*' (Saunders, 1990a: 53, original emphasis).

While this can be used as a justification for an unequal society, its special relevance for social mobility is not so much the upward mobility of the few successful entrepreneurs, or the downward mobility of those who fail, but rather the 'spin-off' of rising standards of living for the population. Here Saunders is on firmer ground. Manual workers in this country now expect to own a car, and a television, to occupy a dwelling of several rooms in good physical condition, to take a holiday abroad, to have several sets of clothing. Such a life style (even if still not available to more than, say, three-quarters of households) would in 1950 have been associated with the middle or upper middle classes, who made up about one quarter of society. In less than a single lifetime, manual workers have in consumption terms been upwardly mobile, 'even while we're standing still' (to misappropriate Spike Milligan's remark about growing old). If one compares 1921 with 1991, the contrast is even greater. Because we have continued to think of mobility as class movement in a monolithic way across a single dimensional social divide, we have ignored the very real change in material experience for the working class, a change which however imperfectly also extends to improved health, access to education and political rights.[2]

It follows that mobility analysis may be impugned in two ways (although Saunders does not develop his ideas in this way). First, the idea of indexing a person's origin and destination by occupation is weakened if the *meaning* of being, say, a manual worker is not the same at origin and destination. Historical comparisons become unreliable. Second, the significance of lack of upward mobility is lessened: to remain in the same relative position is still to experience improvements in the quality of life. Arguments about class formation and the growth of a class consciousness based on a sense of disadvantage (such as those found in Goldthorpe's work) seem to be less powerful. The underlying social divisions have fragmented: 'a model based on class alone is inadequate to account for changed circumstances.

This is not to say that upward mobility is irrelevant – on the contrary, Hayek and Saunders' positions call for there to be both inequality and a striving for achievement across that structured framework. Saunders (1989: 3; 1990a: 75–80) in particular argues that upward mobility has increased by implication due to the development of capitalism:

> capitalism always entails inequality between top and bottom. We saw earlier how neo-liberals such as Friedrich Hayek defended capitalism precisely on the grounds that . . . everybody benefits from economic expansion. This is an argument which is never considered in key works like those of Goldthorpe or Marshall and his colleagues, for they are concerned only with relativities and never with absolutes. (Saunders, 1990a: 81)

His interpretation of improved absolute mobility rates is thus combined with improved conditions of living in general, to argue that mobility analysis has misrepresented what is happening in contemporary Britain. This alternative view cannot be easily dismissed, even if the explanation for the changing conditions may be disputed.

SOME EVIDENCE ON SOCIAL MOBILITY

Improved rates of absolute mobility are central to Saunders' second objection to conventional interpretations of mobility. He uses Goldthorpe's data to show that

> the British class structure is more open and fluid than (Goldthorpe) had imagined, and that social mobility rates have increased over the years (1990a: 80) . . . The class system has actually become more fluid. (1989: 3)

The main evidence supporting this view is Goldthorpe's critique of the 'three theses' of social closure, buffer zone and counter mobility:

> 16 per cent of males born into the working class make it to professional, managerial and administrative positions and 15 per cent of males born into these top classes move in the opposite direction' (Saunders, 1990a: 78).

Sixteen per cent becomes 24 per cent by 1983, while the percentage of people trapped in the working class for a second generation drops from 60 to 53 per cent. The Essex survey is also quoted as showing that 'one-third of people in classes I and II had started out in classes VI or VII' (Saunders, 1990a: 80).

The claim that 'there is evidence of considerable fluidity and movement across the whole range of the occupational scale' (Saunders, 1990a: 78) is dependent on simple or absolute measurements of mobility, both upward and downward. Saunders criticises Goldthorpe and Marshall *et al.* for underplaying such direct mobility, and relying instead on the idea of relative mobility, which compares the chances of people from different origins of gaining advantageous destinations:

> The principle of relative mobility depends on a comparison between actual mobility rates and an ideal norm in which peoples' starting point have no effect on where they end up. Goldthorpe and the Essex team will not accept that the system is open until such time as destinations are randomly related to origins. (Saunders, 1989: 4)

We have already seen this runs together the idea of statistical independence and socialist equality, but how strong is the empirical evidence? While at one level, the extent of fluidity is a matter of judgement, the choice of measures and cut-off points have to be open to inspection and justification. There is no *one* measurement, least of all in a complex and statistically sophisticated area like the analysis of mobility tables.

Therefore to use the idea of statistical independence as a reference point is a procedure that can be justified by appeal to a battery of tests and research outside of the immediate topic. In contrast, to assert that social fluidity is high because 24 per cent of professionals were born the sons of manual workers is to make an arbitrary judgement. It happens to be a judgement with which the present author personally has some sympathy, given his assumptions about the inherent difficulties of obtaining professional qualifications in *any* society. However, that arbitrary judgement can only be legitimated by comparing the figure of 24 per cent with some other standard. For example, as professional and similar jobs comprise about 26 per cent of all (male) employment (Goldthorpe and Payne, 1986: 4), then the sons of manual workers are close to obtaining their 'fair share' of what is available. On the other hand, as the sons of manual workers make up 56 per cent of the population, it could be argued that they should do better than 24 per cent: the point is that whichever view is taken, a point of comparison – such as no association between origin and destination – is needed.

However, neither Goldthorpe nor Marshall *et al.* are actually using such a straightforward comparison. Their operationalisation of relative mobility (in which people of different origins would have different chances of arriving at a given destination, compared with their chance were there to be statistical independence of origins and destinations) is not a simple disparity or odds-ratio read directly from the mobility tables. Instead, it is usually a calculation of relative chances under one crucial condition, namely that mobility can be sub-divided into two kinds. The first kind is seen as relating to changes in the occupational structure: the expansion of non-manual occupations creates, through the distribution of destinations, new mobility opportunity. If one is really interested in whether social policy modifies opportunity for upward mobility, then such structural mobility is noise in the system (see Marsh and Blackburn, this volume). The proliferation of indices of mobility over the years testifies to the dominant paradigm's attempt to sort out structural mobility from the second type, that which reflects outcomes of class competition over opportunity. Although Pawson (1990) is right to chide mobility and class analysts for an over-eagerness to leap from mobility rates to the success or failure of the British welfare state, this interest is an entirely legitimate one (Marsh and Blackburn, this volume), even if there are other ways of asking mobility questions than differentiating actual mobility as experienced into two logically separate categories.

The latest version of this differentiation is log–linear modelling, in which a series of terms are added or subtracted from a model; the object is to inspect the strength of factors by seeing how closely each model approximates to the observed mobility table. In a model which uses birth cohorts to represent change over time,[3] and which contains origins and destination distributions (and therefore their changes over time) relative mobility does not change significantly. In other words, if we control for structural change, the remaining patterns of mobility are virtually invariant in Goldthorpe and Marshall *et al.*'s data.

Why do they choose this way of presenting mobility? First, it must be seen as a natural continuation of the paradigm and its interest in what controllable social processes like national education policy promote or retard mobility and thus reproduce or dismantle the core social division. Second, if we are interested in equality of opportunity we need to include some kind of comparison. Third, this generates an intellectually fascinating paradox: absolute rates increase, relative rates stay constant (Payne, 1990). And fourth, and here Saunders has at the very least circumstantial evidence to support him, *relative mobility constancy is less discomforting to a traditional 'class' perspective than is the rise in absolute mobility rates.*

If one returns to the key introduction of log–linear modelling in mobility analysis (Hauser *et al.*, 1975a, 1975b), the original argument can be read in two ways. One is the way Goldthorpe has taken it (and Marshall *et al.* have followed, since they wish to compare their results with his). On the other hand, for some questions of mobility, if relative mobility rates can be treated as a constant, then we should stop worrying about such an insignificant factor, and concentrate on the things which really do change historically – the structures of origins and destinations and the mobility associated with them. In particular, if we are interested in the causes of mobility, we cannot ignore one type once we have separated it (or to be more accurate, minimised it) in our discussion of how much mobility there has been. Although Saunders may be wrong in his assumption that this is entirely due to political bias, he is nevertheless correct to raise doubts about the Goldthorpe position.

So what are we to make of such statements, quoted by Saunders against their respective authors, such as

> There have been no changes in social fluidity (Marshall *et al.*, 1988: 137)

or

> No significant reduction in class inequalities has in fact been achieved (Goldthorpe *et al.*, 1987: 252)?

Clearly they must be explicitly hedged in by the crucial condition that these claims apply to a model which contains structural mobility as a quite separate effect.

SOME EVIDENCE ON SOCIAL MOBILITY: A RECONSIDERATION

On the other hand, if one resorts to a much simpler statistical level, and works directly from the mobility table, both straightforward absolute and relative rates of mobility can be calculated from the actual structures. In this analysis, then, relative mobility is used in a different sense than that adopted by Goldthorpe or Marshall *et al.* In addition, we can use the two studies as a means of obtaining a chronological picture of changes in mobility rates, as one comes 12 years after the other. This is an improvement on cohort analysis, for the reasons already indicated in Note 3. While we cannot entirely escape the problem of personal judgements about the meaning of the numerical values we calculate, we can re-examine the claims of the New Right about equality of opportunity by looking at these changes in rates of male mobility.

The data used in this section come from the published reports of the two studies in question, together with Goldthorpe and Payne's re-analysis of the 1983 British General Election Study (BGES). The latter is included to improve the comparability between the two studies, because among other methodological limitations, the class schema has evolved from 'old' to 'new'. It would of course be interesting to include data on female mobility, but at present there are no equivalent time-lapse data-sets available.[4] Table 11.1 (on the following pages) sets out in detail the core numerical information for the reader's convenience: successive tables re-present these data in different forms.

The comparisons of most interest at the outset are between 1972 and the 1980s. If we take the old schema on the left of Table 11.1, we see that the percentages for the cells relating to upward mobility are all higher in the BGES 1983 table. The same is true if we look at the equivalent cells for the three new schema tables on the right hand side of Table 11.1. These differences in absolute mobility are summarised in Table 11.2; 'upward mobility' combines for each panel of Table 11.1 the cells relating to class III–V origins/class I and II destinations, and class VI and VII origins/class I and II and class III and V destinations, while downward mobility includes the cells relating to class I and II origins/class III–V and VI and VII destinations, and class III–V origins/class VI and VII destinations.

Here we see that Nuffield reported 32 per cent upward mobility and 17 per cent downward, as compared with 37.7 per cent and 14.7 per cent in the BGES 12 years later. Alternatively, on the new schema, Nuffield found 31 per cent upward and 16.6 per cent downward, whereas the two later studies found 35 per cent and 36 per cent upward, and 16.1 and 19.1 per cent downward, respectively. On all these indicators, there is more upward mobility, thus supporting the argument that there is increasing equality of opportunity and not supporting the view that Britain continues to maintain the same high levels of class rigidity. A similar conclusion can be drawn from comparing the movements from the manual working class into the service class in each sample. Again, the proportions remaining

Table 11.1 Male mobility across three classes in recent English studies; shown in percentages

Old schema

(a) Nuffield 1972

		Destinations			
		I and II	*III–V*	*VI and VII*	N =
origins	I and II	58.8	26.0	15.2	**1,242**
	III–V	27.6	36.7	35.7	**3,105**
	VI and VII	15.5	27.2	57.3	**5,087**
	N =	**2,372**	**2,848**	**4,214**	**9,434**

(b) BGES 1983

		Destinations			
		I and II	*III–V*	*VI and VII*	N =
origins	I and II	65.1	24.7	10.2	**204**
	III–V	34.4	38.3	27.4	**372**
	VI and VII	21.5	31.2	47.3	**598**
	N =	**390**	**378**	**406**	**1,174**

New schema

(a) Nuffield 1972

		Destinations			
		I and II	*III–V*	*VI and VII*	N =
origins	I and II	57.7	23.2	19.1	**220**
	III–V	31.2	13.9	37.0	**433**
	VI and VII	16.0	22.7	61.2	**867**
	N =	**401**	**386**	**733**	**1,520**

(b) BGES 1983

		Destinations			
		I and II	*III–V*	*VI and VII*	N =
origins	I and II	62.0	22.2	15.8	**210**
	III–V	34.2	34.3	31.5	**347**
	VI and VII	23.6	23.8	52.6	**616**
	N =	**394**	**313**	**466**	**1,173**

(c) Essex 1984

		Destinations			
		I and II	*III–V*	*VI and VII*	**N =**
Origins	I and II	60.0	20.0	20.0	**100**
	III–V	34.8	30.4	34.8	**233**
	VI and VII	20.1	28.8	51.2	**299**
	N =	**201**	**177**	**254**	**632**

Sources: adapted from (a) Goldthorpe *et al.* (1987: 45, Table 2.1); (b) Goldthrope and Payne (1986: 11, Table 7); and (c) Marshall *et al.* (1988: 77, Table 4.8).

Table 11.2 Summary of male absolute mobility; shown in percentages

	Old schema	*New schema*
	(a) Nuffield 1972	
Upward mobility	32.1	31.0
Downward mobility	17.2	16.6
Immobile, service class	7.7	8.6
Immobile, manual class	30.9	34.9
Service to manual moves	15.2	19.1
Manual to service moves	15.5	16.0
	(b) BGES 1983	
Upward mobility	37.7	35.0
Downward mobility	14.7	16.1
Immobile, service class	11.3	11.1
Immobile, manual class	24.1	27.6
Service to manual moves	10.2	15.8
Manual to service moves	21.5	23.6
	(c) Essex 1984	
Upward mobility	–	35.9
Downward mobility	–	19.1
Immobile, service class	–	9.5
Immobile, manual class	–	24.2
Service to manual moves	–	20.0
Manual to service moves	–	20.1

Sources: as Table 11.1.

immobile in the manual working class also decline across the decade; the old schema figures dropping from 30.9 per cent to 24.1 per cent and the new schema figures falling from 34.9 per cent to 27.6 per cent and 24.2 per cent.

We need to balance this picture by looking at downward mobility and immobility in the service class. Saunders calls downward mobility 'the *real* test of openness' (1989: 3, original emphasis). The BGES data suggest a smaller decline in downward mobility (i.e. 16.6 per cent to 16.1 per cent) while the Essex data show a small rise (16.6 per cent to 19.1 per cent). The flow from service to manual class shows the same difference in the two studies: 19.1 per cent drops to 15.8 per cent in the BGES, against a rise to 20.0 per cent in the Essex data. Since the changes are small, it would be safer to say that there is little evidence to support the thesis of greater openness on the 'real' test nominated by Saunders. When it comes to immobility in the service class, or in other words the intergenerational securing of a privileged position, both the later studies show small increases. It follows that the early support for increased openness from upward mobility rates has to be weighed against the rival evidence from downward mobility and inheritance of service class status.

At the same time, it must also be recognised that the changing structures of the mobility tables increase and decrease the 'risk' of individuals being found in one cell or another. For example, as the manual class contracts, there is a smaller risk of downward mobility, whereas as the service class expands, there is a greater risk of both upward mobility *and* immobility within the service class. This is not just an arithmetic quirk. The advantage enjoyed by being a member of the service class, and the disadvantage of being in the manual working class, affects different proportions of people. In 1972, the service class were 13.2 per cent (old schema) or 14.5 per cent (new schema) of the population's origins: by the early 1980s this had grown to somewhere between 15.8 per cent (Essex) and 17.9 per cent (BGES, new schema). In other words, a few more people in the country as a whole started off with that service-class advantage. Similarly, in 1972 the disadvantage of a manual class origin was experienced by between 54 and 57 per cent of the population: the later studies show this has fallen to between 47 and 51 per cent. While we need to be cautious about regarding respondents' origins as a direct indicator of population changes (Payne, 1987a: 97–100) this does pick up Saunders' argument about the 'moving column': more people are sharing in the mobility benefits of structural change.

Thus, in terms of absolute mobility rates, there is some evidence to support the New Right critique. Upward mobility has increased and working-class immobility has decreased, while the working class has contracted. Against this, downward mobility has not moved sharply in either direction, while service class immobility has risen a little, which counts against claims for greater openness.

A further piece of evidence comes from exploring the interaction of structural change with the mobility flows by means of relative mobility rates. These are shown in Table 11.3, calculated directly from Table 11.1 and therefore not directly comparable to the Goldthorpe and Marshall *et al.* version of relative mobility.

The first column shows that in 1972 men with service-class origins were 3.8 times more likely than those from manual origins to obtain a service-class destination. Second, the relative chances of a man born in the service class ending up in that class rather than in the manual

Table 11.3 Simple relative mobility rates in three recent English studies

	1972(old)	*1972(new)*	*1983(old)*	*1983(new)*	*1984(new)*
Disparity ratio: relative chances of men from service-class and manual-class origins obtaining service-class destination	3.8	3.6	3.0	2.6	3.0
Odds ratio: competition between men from service-class and manual-class origins to obtain service- or manual-class destinations	14.3	11.6	13.8	8.8	7.4

Sources: as Table 11.1.

class was 14.3 times greater than a man born in the manual class ending up in the manual class, rather than the service class.[5]

As with our earlier tables, we see that the intervening decade has improved the position of manual workers. The advantage of the service class has been reduced from 3.8 to 3.0, or from 3.6 to 2.6 or 3.0: at its most conservative, a reduction of 16 per cent in the original value of the ratio. The odds ratios drop by a greater percentage: on the new schema, this is from 11.6 to 8.8 or 7.4 – a drop of 24 to 36 per cent. This comparison of overall mobility is in contrast to Goldthorpe's conclusion (based on inter-cohort comparisons) that disparity ratios show there is 'increasing inequality in class mobility chances' (Goldthorpe *et al.*, 1987: 77). However when Goldthorpe compares 1972 and 1983 (Goldthorpe and Payne, 1986: 10–14) he says 'that a change has occurred, and that what has happened is that inequalities in chances of being in the service class have diminished somewhat'. Again, taking the full range of odds ratios (although these are not reported) he says that inter-cohort odds ratios show no clear sign of decreasing (1987: 80) and that they are 'unchanging' between 1972 and 1983, although here the meaning of his text is less clear. The results in Table 11.3 also contradict Marshall and Rose's claim, again based on inter-cohort log-linear modelling, that

> opportunities for the working class *have* increased since the war, but they have also increased in proportionate measure for the middle classes as well. (Saunders, 1989: 5)

In as far as we restrict ourselves to the service and manual classes, the evidence in Tables 11.1, 11.2 and 11.3 point towards a small but clear increase in mobility. The boundaries between the social divisions of the three classes have weakened. This change has taken place in about a dozen years. If one were to speculate about the pattern already forming in the early 1990s, the simplest model would be a repeat of the previous decade: i.e. the movement from the manual class might be up to 25 per cent, and the relative advantage compared with the sons of the service class could be down to 2 or 2.5 – still substantial, but well below the picture one might have taken from *Social Mobility and Class Structure in Modern Britain.* Even if we do not wish to adopt this simple model, we cannot dismiss Saunders' appeal to the empirical evidence. This is not to accept his entire explanation that Goldthorpe and Marshall *et al.* wilfully distort their perceptions of mobility but rather to accept that he is right when he says that there has been an increase in mobility, and that this higher level of movement has to some extent been under-recognised (Payne, 1990). The question with which we are left is whether Saunders is correct in his claims about the significance and causes of this mobility.

THE SIGNIFICANCE AND CAUSES OF SOCIAL MOBILITY

Why does Saunders believe that the empirical evidence shows England to be a relatively open society, whereas Goldthorpe and Marshall *et al.* describe it as relatively closed?

It was suggested earlier that the latters' position is largely explicable in terms of a dominant paradigm and the conventions of statistical analysis, rather than political bias. However, it must be recognised that an uncomfortable finding perturbs the theoretical framework underlying any research. To borrow Gluckman's observation about magic, there is an internal logic to belief systems, which normally contain subsidiary beliefs serving to explain away any apparent failures of the system to deliver (Gluckman, 1960). If Saunders is correct that Goldthorpe and Marshall *et al.* do make more of the constancy of log–linear modelled relative mobility rates than the increase in absolute mobility or simple relative mobility rates, because this helps them to sustain their basic position, then presumably the same process of selectivity is likely to operate in the work of other sociologists, not least Saunders himself.

As Saunders approaches social division from a neo-liberal standpoint, he starts with two underlying value positions. First, he accepts the desirability of structured inequality as a means of motivating the entrepreneur. Following Hayek (1960) he sees inequality as the price to be paid for a dynamic capitalism in which everybody benefits from the rising material standards created by the successful entrepreneur's efforts. However, in contrast to Hayek, he welcomes high rates of upward and downward mobility as an indication that England has become more meritocratic and therefore fairer: occupational outcomes reflect more accurately the abilities of the incumbents, so showing a decline of unnecessary and undesirable process inequalities (e.g. closure) and a purer form of competition between people from different backgrounds. On this second point he is not far from those whose political views he criticises.

However, if we turn to immobility we see a significant difference. For Saunders, not only is it necessary for some to be better off than others, but it can also be legitimate. Here he draws on the idea of social justice, raising doubts about the 'social democratic' position as exemplified by Rawls (1972). He criticises Rawls' 'difference principle' (that an unequal distribution of resources would only be tolerable if it were shown to benefit those with the least) on the grounds that it is not possible to put it into simple operation (Saunders, 1990a: 47–8). His second objection to Rawls is that raised by Nozick (1974), namely that the idea of a 'distribution' of resources implies that resources are somehow free from claims upon them, and available for transfer. In other words, justice or fairness is not about the way things are distributed *per se*, but rather about how the resources were obtained:

> The idea that people's possessions, legitimately acquired, can be taken away and given to someone else is not a realisation of social justice but a negation of it (Saunders, 1990a: 47).

To express this in terms of social mobility, a position obtained meritocratically is legitimated: the comparative advantage passed on to one's children is therefore also legitimate.

This lies at the heart of his objection to his version of the Goldthorpe position. People, in Saunders' view, can be entitled to their advantageous position, and this has nothing to with notions of rights to equal opportunity. He therefore rejects any argument which ultimately draws on the principle that society cannot be open 'until such time as destinations are randomly related to origins' (Saunders

1989: 4). The problem with this position, as he acknowledges in his discussion of Nozick, is that 'many people in a country like Britain seem to own things to which they are not entitled' (1990a: 50). Land-ownership has origins in conquest and patronage, not the free exchange of gifts and market transactions: this could not be rectified, because of its historical complexity and absence of information, without a change to public ownership of land (Saunders, 1990a: 51), an outcome which is unrealistic.

If we take land-ownership literally, the occupational group which shows up most clearly in mobility analysis is the farmers. In a study of Scotland by the present author 67 per cent of farmers were found to be the sons of farmers, presumably because they could inherit the land. Agricultural labourers also display distinctive patterns, with few men entering the occupation except from similar backgrounds, and a high 'export' of sons off the land and into non-agricultural jobs. This can be seen as the other side of the land-inheritance coin. Support for this explanation comes from the occupational group with the next highest self-recruitment (32 per cent) and high export of sons – the small businessmen, who also operate in a work field where property inheritance (of the family firm) is common.

Second, the place of the small businessman and the self-employed become a significant issue in the construction of occupational class hierarchies. These are the entrepreneurs, albeit on a small scale, who feature so largely in neo-liberal thinking, and interestingly receive particular attention in the construction of the Hope–Goldthorpe scale (where the 'self-employed' employment status moves many low-skilled occupations up the scale). Some of this is missed by concentrating on service class/manual class movements. Ironically it is precisely the sort of exercise which Marshall *et al.* attempted (and which Saunders criticises) that helps to clarify the nature of the hierarchy in which mobility takes place.

On the other hand, if we take land ownership as an indicator of non-legitimate ownership and advantage in general, then the door is opened to the argument put by Marshall and Rose that, so far from being a meritocracy,

> countless studies (from all political quarters) . . . show that, even controlling for educational achievement, children from middle class backgrounds have greater opportunities than do their working class counterparts for access to further education, highly-rewarded jobs, and generally privileged positions in the class structure. (Marshall and Rose, 1989: 5)

In terms of Saunders' argument, this would mean that the self-recruited service class has no moral right to its advantage, because its incumbents are not more able.

Behind the repost from Marshall and Rose is the idea that even when children have similar abilities there are inequalities of outcome. Saunders recognises inequalities of outcome, but proposes that these result from a range of differences in abilities. While he rejects the evidence from IQ testing, and says that it is not possible to tell whether social inequalities are produced by natural inequalities (1990a: 73), he reserves the right to claim that innate differences exist and are relevant:

> recent discoveries in biochemistry have shown far more features of personality and character are transmitted genetically from generation to generation than had previously been realised . . . a relative lack of movement across wide spans in the occupational hierarchy may be due as much to genetic inheritance as to social closure. After all, in a perfect meritocracy, the most talented people would occupy the top positions, and *if* talent is to a large extent transmitted through genetic inheritance, it would not be surprising to find that most of their offspring come to occupy these positions as well. (Saunders, 1990a: 73, original emphasis)

Or, to put it more polemically, in 'the idealised world of left sociologists' there is no room for

> nasty bourgeois notions about differences of individual effort, still less of individual ability. Everybody is the same; everybody is equally endowed, capitalism is to blame for making them unequal. (Saunders, 1989: 4)

A simple textual analysis of these quotations shows how ill-conceived they are. We are not told which biochemical findings Saunders means, nor which 'personality and character' are inherited, nor how these correlate with social mobility. It is then asserted that genetics as much as closure cause mobility patterns: we have already seen that Saunders accepts that closure in a general sense has a considerable effect. This then slips into 'most' of the service class being self-recruited, via two very large 'if' statements which propose meritocracy and genetic inheritance as largely explaining the distribution of talent necessary for meritocratic success. In fairness to Saunders, we are quoting a short introductory text, but until his arguments are more fully fleshed out, his position can only be one of conjecture.

This is not to say that genetics, talent or effort are irrelevant. The present author believes, *as do most Socialists*, that people are born equal only in the sense of their humanity and claim to human rights. Few socialists and fewer sociologists would claim that all people have identical abilities. If we wish to explain why one person is upwardly mobile and another from the same background is not, we probably need the idea of differential distribution of talent or effort, or at least blind chance, to produce an explanation.

The key difference is that *most* sociologists would logically then proceed to seek to discover what *social* processes enhance or retard a person's chances of having talent, or being defined as having talent. *Some* sociologists may assume that basic talent is randomly distributed in the population; others would accept that this cannot be 'known', and argue along with Marshall and Rose that there is good empirical evidence of talented people not achieving the careers for which their talents would otherwise equip them. And *few* sociologists would accept Saunders claim that all members of the middle classes are more able, and that inheritance of social advantage is due to inheritance of genetic advantage, at this stage of our empirical knowledge. On the contrary, as Marshall and Rose argue (1989: 5) the indirect evidence from many a sociological study points in the opposite direction.

Nonetheless, let us for the moment take Saunders' genetic model a step further. If we suppose that the service class does indeed have greater innate abilities, the Essex data (for example) shows that 60 out of 100 men born in the service class inherit the required factors to become members of that class as adults. By the same argument, 60 out of 300 men born into the manual class also inherited the required talents, because they made it to the service class. Thus the inheritance of talent rate lies somewhere between 6 in 10, and 2 in 10.

If we then move the model forward a generation, what would take place? First, we must allow for the fact that the size of the relevant classes would in any case have changed, following current structural trends, as Figure 11.1. shows.[6]

Here, the upper part of the figure is the current or 'now' generation, closely resembling the Essex data, and the lower part is the 'next' generation. The sons in the 'now' generation become the fathers in the 'next' generation: 200, 150 and 250. The distribution of their sons in the next generation has been projected, to allow realistically for continued occupational transition and class differentials in fertility effects (Payne, 1987a). For present purposes we can concentrate on the left-hand columns, showing the service class.

The 'next' generation can contain 120 service-class sons reproduced at a 6 in 10 rate from 200 service-class fathers, 60 service-class sons at a

Figure 11.1 Mobility under Saunders' genetic model

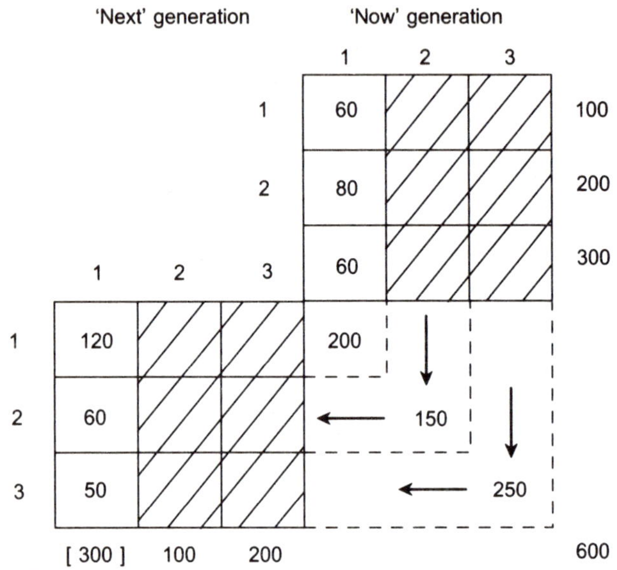

4 in 10 rate from 150 intermediate-class fathers, and 50 service-class sons from 250 manual-class fathers. This gives us a total of only 230, not the 300 needed to fill up the 'next' service class. Worse, we 'selected out' 60 of the most able sons of the manual class in the 'now' generation, into the service class, so they cannot bear sons in the manual class for the next generation. The inflow mobility rates worsen in the next generation, unless we can make up the 300 with untalented sons from the intermediate and manual class. *But if the talented are not there, then it is reasonable to suggest that it will be the untalented with the advantages of a higher-class origin who will succeed.* At the very least, there can be very few talented sons available to become mobile (Saunders' model allows for some blockage to the talented) or alternatively that talents reoccur in a complex way with fathers who lack talent reproducing sons who do 'inherit' it.

Neither of these options should be very comforting to Saunders. The first implies that mobility rates should historically be seen to decline, because of a shortage of genetic talent. However, Saunders also wishes us to believe, as we have seen, that mobility rates are *increasing*. The second option means one of two things: either we require a rather more sophisticated genetic model, which is not what Saunders suggests or what this chapter can attempt, or the necessary talent occurs in a way which is not neatly determined by inheritance. Neither would make a very straightforward message in order to legitimate natural rights to possession of a service-class position in two successive generations.

This argument from within Saunders' own premises is reinforcement for the kinds of indirect evidence of inequality of achievement from various sociological studies referred to above. It follows that it is insufficient for Saunders to show only that it is logically possible for 'natural inequalities' to occur. It is incumbent on Saunders to produce more evidence to support his claims for the talent of the service class.

Indeed, his own position is unclear: he cites Durkheim's view that social harmony is dependent upon social inequalities being congruent with natural ones (Saunders, 1990a: 72–3), but then asks whether we could actually know if this state had been reached, because measurement of talents is so difficult. And yet this is only a preface to his claims about natural differences and genetics already quoted, while elsewhere he argues for meritocracy.

Even if we were to concede that talent is not randomly distributed, this would be a far cry from accepting the bulk of Saunders' case. There is a considerable distance between agreeing that certain limiting conditions logically exist, and that major elements of a pattern can, in their present form, currently be explained by the same factors. For example, it is likely to be widely accepted that a proportion of people are for genetic reasons unlikely to carry out service class roles: those who inherit serious physical or mental disabilities are unable to compete. Others show such limited intellectual powers that basic skills such as literacy and numeracy are beyond them. If they are born into the manual class they will remain there. Thus not every one in the manual (or any other) class can join the service class – but the limiting proportion is probably *low*, perhaps 5 or 10 per cent, nor have we reached the point in the history of mobility where such a limiting condition comes into play. The figure of 5 or 10 per cent pales into insignificance against the proportion of people who cannot enter the service class because of another genetic inheritance barely mentioned by Saunders: namely, women. While 75 per cent of service class jobs are 'male' jobs, women are allocated to other classes by structural and, in this sense, genetic processes which owe little to ability, natural rights, or the success of capitalism.

This returns us to one other key inconsistency. Saunders would also wish us to accept that improving rates of mobility are due to the dynamics of capitalism. It is difficult to reconcile an argument based on biology with one based on economics, although as Figure 11.1 shows, a discussion of inheritance patterns has to be connected to patterns of structural change. There is an inherent tension between an argument based on genetics, which points to declining upward mobility or at least stability, and an argument about the merits of capitalism, which attributes increased mobility to the success of the system. The two could be reconciled, provided an increase in talented people was posited. Such a change over a decade (see Table 11.1) implies either some kind of hidden but powerful natural-selection process, or a dramatic human mutation otherwise not observed by worldwide physical science.

SOME CONCLUDING REMARKS

This leaves us seeking an explanation of increasing rates of mobility – a point well taken from Saunders – which is probably not going to be *primarily* genetic. While again there is strength in his 'moving column' observation about material mobility and how this fits uneasily with a simple class analysis, Saunders' full-scale claim for the dynamics of capitalism as the key causal factor remains to be established. To a degree, he recognises the significance of structural change in employment as one agent in this process, but he does not develop this fully. This is an opportunity missed.

It could therefore be argued that, via this occupational transition, capitalism has caused an increase in mobility. We must however be cautious: first, rather different types of capitalisms have generated broadly similar shifts, while non-capitalist nations such as Poland and Hungary also display occupational transition and increased mobility rates (as the various working papers of the Comparative Analysis of Social Mobility in Industrial Nations project show (Erikson and Goldthorpe, 1986)). The point here is that 'capitalism' is not a unitary system, and that non-capitalist economic and political systems also produce change. We therefore do not need Hayek's unfettered entrepreneurs or material inequalities to sustain mobility rates, but should seek to elucidate what elements integral to capitalism generate the observed structural changes.

However, in the light of events in Eastern Europe, it is possible to argue that some kinds of social arrangements 'do it better'. Thus the totalitarian regimes which were a historically unique outcome of global politics particularly after 1939, produced slower economic development, less occupational transition, and so lower rates of mobility than did the other countries in Europe. The precise relationship between structural change, mobility and polity is as yet unclear (see Payne, 1987a; and for a less structuralist approach see Kaelble, 1985 and Mach and Wesolowski, 1986): however, it is a problem that cannot be unravelled by using crude unitary concepts such as 'capitalism' and 'socialism', or by sweeping generalisations about 'bias'.

It is also necessary to keep a sense of proportion. Pawson graphically reminds us that mobility is only, after all, a by-product of greater events: in Marshall and Rose's article

> we make the massive journey from static relative mobility...[to] the entire failure of British social and educational policy...With Saunders, we travel effortlessly from high absolute mobility rates being the measures of social fluidity to them being the emblem of the wonders of capitalism (as if the captains of industry scanned the daily shifts in the mobility, as opposed to the share index). (Pawson, 1990: 230)

Until we have explored the jungle between mobility and these broad political and economic uplands, we would be as well to treat both our data and our present conceptualisation of social divisions with some circumspection.

Notes

1. See Goldthorpe *et al.* (1987: Chap. 1) and Payne (1987a: Chaps 3 and 4) for discussions of a variety of both ideological approaches and critiques. It is interesting that, as against Saunders' allegation of Left bias, Goldthorpe feels the need to defend mobility research from attacks *from* the Left that it is no more than a bourgeois apologia!
2. While the area of consumer rights is what is chiefly meant here, it is worth remembering that women were only fully enfranchised in 1929, and have still to win full access to the public domain of politics. It is not the writer's intention to claim a uniform level of affluence, or to ignore the growth of an underclass: Saunders himself subscribes to Dahrendorf's (1987) estimate of 5 per cent of the population as 'a reasonable figure to take...(for) a stratum of people who are generally poor, unqualified and irregularly or never employed' (Saunders, 1990a: 121).

3. Change in mobility rates is calculated by comparing mobility in an older cohort with a younger one. It has long been recognised that this is a poor substitute for having two, time-separated studies: men in the older cohort have had longer in which to achieve mobility, and have done so in historically unique conditions. Career progression, history and mobility rates confound each other, so giving a poor measure, even before we get to log–linear models (Payne, 1987b: 155–71).
4. The BGES study does include women, but there is so little gap between 1983 (BGES) and 1984 (Essex) that no time transition discussion is possible. The results of the two studies are, however, very close, and show patterns which on the indices used here are distinctly different from those of males (Payne and Abbott, 1991).
5. In a 3 × 3 mobility table (e.g. each panel of Table 11.1) the disparity ratio between outflow percentages is given by

$$\frac{f_{11}}{f_1} \div \frac{f_{31}}{f_3}$$

where f is the frequency in cell 1–1, f_1 is the row marginal, and we are interested in the first (service) and third (manual) classes. Similarly the odds ratio is given by

$$\frac{f_{11}}{f_{13}} \div \frac{f_{31}}{f_{33}}$$

The closer the values come to 1, the more 'equal' is the competition, or in statistical terms, the weaker is the association between origins and destinations. It should be remembered that we are addressing only service-class/manual-class moves: there are five other cells in a 3 × 3 table, and 'gains' in respect of one movement are not necessarily manifested elsewhere in a full mobility table.
6. There are two obvious limits to the utility of this model. First, can structural change continue at its present levels – presumably we cannot all be non-manual workers within the generation from 1984? Second, the model assumes all mobility processes are male only processes: hardly a sound assumption, given the state of our biological science.

Bibliography

ABERCROMBIE, N. and URRY, J. (1983) *Capital, Labour and the Middle Classes* London: Allen and Unwin.
ABERCROMBIE, N., HILL, S. and TURNER, B.S. (1980) *The Dominant Ideology Thesis* London: Allen and Unwin.
AGLIETTA, M. (1979) *A Theory of Capitalist Regulation: the US Experience* London: New Left Books.
ALLEN, J. and HAMNETT, C. (eds) (1990) *Housing and Labour Markets* London: Unwin Hyman.
ANDERSON, Sir Colin (1960) *Grants to Students*, HMSO: Cmnd 1051.
ARBER, S., DALE, A. and GILBERT, G.N. (1986) 'The limitations of existing social class classifications for women' in A. Jacoby (ed.) *The Measurement of Social Class* London: Social Research Association.
ASSOCIATION OF BRITISH INSURERS (1989) *Insurance Statistics 1985–1988* London: Association of British Insurers.
ASSOCIATION OF UNIVERSITY TEACHERS (1983) *University Student Numbers: a Response to DES Report 99 – Future Demand for Higher Education in Great Britain* AUT, September.
BARLOW, J. and SAVAGE, M. (1986) 'The politics of growth: conflict and cleavage in a Tory heartland' *Capital and Class*, No. 31.
BAUDRILLARD, J. (1988) *Selected Writings* Oxford: Polity.
BAUMAN, Z. (1988) *Freedom* Milton Keynes: Open University Press.
BELL, C. (1968) *Middle Class Families* London: Routledge and Kegan Paul.
BELL, D. (1974) *The Coming of Post-Industrial Society* London: Heinemann.
BELL, D. (1976) *The Cultural Contradictions of Capitalism* London: Heinemann.
BEST, G. (1987) *The Future of NHS General Management* Kings Fund College, Project Paper 75, London: Kings Fund.
BIBBY, J. (1975). 'Methods of measuring mobility' *Quality and Quantity*, 9, 2.
BLACKBURN, R.M., and MARSH, C. (1991) 'Education and social class: revisiting the 1944 Education Act with fixed marginals' *British Journal of Sociology*, 42, 3.
BLACKBURN, R.M., MARSH, C., PRANDY, K. and SILTANEN, J. (1990) 'A new approach to studying changing inequality' (British Sociological Association Conference 1990) *Working Paper 2* Cambridge: Sociological Research Group.
BLAU, P. and DUNCAN, O.D. (1967). *The American Occupational Structure* New York, Wiley.
BLAU, P. and SCOTT, W.R. (1963) *Formal Organizations* London: Routledge and Kegan Paul.
BODENHEIMER, T., CUMMINGS, S. and HARDING, E. (1977) 'Capitalizing on illness: the health insurance industry', in E. Navarro (ed.) *Health and Medical Care in the US* New York: Baywood.
BOSANQUET, N. (1983) *After the New Right* London: Heinemann.

BOSANQUET, N. (1988) 'An ailing state of national health' in R. Jowell, S. Witherspoon and L. Brook (eds) *British Social Attitudes: the 5th Report* Aldershot: Gower.

BOSWORTH-DAVIES, R.(1988) *Fraud in the City: Too Good To Be True* London: Penguin.

BOURDIEU, P. (1973) 'Cultural reproduction and social reproduction' in R. Brown (ed.) *Knowledge, Education and Cultural Change* London: Tavistock.

BOURDIEU, P. (1984) *Distinction: a Social Critique of the Judgment of Taste* London: Routledge and Kegan Paul.

BOWLES, S. and GINTIS, H. (1976) *Schooling in Capitalist America* London: Routledge and Kegan Paul.

BOWLING, A. and JACOBSON, B. (1989) 'Screening: the inadequacy of population registers' *British Medical Journal*, 298.

BRAVERMAN, H. (1974) *Labour and Monopoly Capital* New York: Monthly Review Press.

BROOKS, P. (1985) *The Melodramatic Imagination: Balzac, Henry James, Melodrama and the Mode of Excess* New York: Columbia University Press.

BROWN, R. and BRANNEN, P. (1970) 'Shipbuilders' (I and II), *Sociology*, 4, 1 and 2.

BURROWS, R. (ed.) (1991) *Deciphering the Enterprise Culture: Entrepreneurship, Petty Capitalism and the Restructuring of Britain* London: Routledge.

BURROWS, R. and BUTLER, T. (1989) 'Middle mass and the pit: a critical review of Peter Saunders's sociology of consumption' *Sociological Review*, 37, 2.

BUSFIELD, J. (1990) 'Sectoral divisions in consumption: the case of medical care' *Sociology* 24, 1.

CAIN, M. (1983) 'The general practice lawyer and the client: towards a radical reconceptualisation' in R. Dingwall and P. Lewis (eds) *The Sociology of the Professions* Basingstoke: Macmillan.

CALNAN, M. (1988a) 'Towards a conceptual model for lay evaluation of health care' *Social Science and Medicine*, 27, 9.

CALNAN, M. (1988b) 'Lay evaluation of modern medicine' *International Journal of Health Services*, 18.

CARR-SAUNDERS, A.M. and WILSON, P.A. (1933) *The Professions* London: Frank Cass.

CARSWELL, J. (1985) *Government and the Universities in Britain: Programme and Performance 1960–1980*, Cambridge: Cambridge University Press.

CASTELLS, M. (1977) *The Urban Question* London: Edward Arnold.

CHILD, J. (1986) 'New technology and the service class' in K. Purcell, S. Wood, A. Waton and S. Allen (eds) *The Changing Experience of Employment* Basingstoke: Macmillan.

CLARKE, J. (forthcoming) *New Times and Old Enemies* London: Unwin Hyman.

CLARKE, M. (1986) *Regulating the City* Milton Keynes: Open University Press.

CLEGG, S. and DUNKERLY, D. (1980) *Organization, Class and Control* London: Routledge and Kegan Paul.

COCHRANE, A.L. (1972) *Effectiveness and Efficiency* London: Nuffield Provincial Hospitals Trust.

CORMELL, M., ARBER, S. and SAVAGE, M. (1988) *Survey of Council Tenants for Guildford Borough Council* Dept of Sociology, University of Surrey.

COUSINS, C. (1987) *Controlling Social Welfare* Brighton: Wheatsheaf.

COX, C. B. and BOYSON, C.R. (eds) (1977) *Black Paper* London: Temple Smith.

CROMPTON, R. (1989) 'Class theory and gender' *British Journal of Sociology*, 40, 4.

CROMPTON, R. (1990) 'Professions in the current context' *Work, Employment and Society* (Special Issue, May).

CROMPTON, R. and JONES, G. (1984) *White-Collar Proletariat: Deskilling and Gender in the Clerical Labour Process* Basingstoke: Macmillan.

CROMPTON, R. and SANDERSON, K. (1990) *Gendered Jobs and Social Change* London: Unwin and Hyman.

CROSLAND, C. A. R. (1956) *The Future of Socialism* London: Jonathan Cape.

CROUCH, C. (1985) 'Exit and voice in the future of the welfare state' *Government and Opposition*, 20, 3.

CROUCH, C. (1986) 'Sharing public space: states and organized interests in Western Europe' in J. A. Hall (ed.) *States in History* Oxford: Blackwell.

CURTI, L. (1988) 'Genre and gender' *Cultural Studies*, 2, 2.

DAHRENDORF, R. (1987) 'The erosion of citizenship and its consequences for us all' *New Statesman*, 12 June.

DALE, A. (1991) 'Stratification over the life course' in G. Payne and P. Abbott (eds) *The Social Mobility of Women* London: Falmer Press.

DAVIDSON, N. (1987) *A Question of Care* London: Michael Joseph.

DAVIS, H. (1980) *Beyond Class Images*, London: Croom Helm.

DAWSON, G. (1981) 'Unfitting to teach' In A. Flew (ed.) *The Pied Pipers of Education* London: Institute of Economic Affairs.

DAY, P. and KLEIN, R. (1987) *Accountabilities* London: Tavistock.

DAY, P. and KLEIN, R. (1989) 'The politics of modernisation: Britain's NHS in the 1980s' *The Milbank Quarterly* 67, 1.

DENNIS, N., HENRIQUES, F. M. and SLAUGHTER, C. (1957) *Coal is Our Life*, London: Eyre and Spottiswood.

DEPARTMENT OF HEALTH (1989) *Working for Patients* CM555, and eight working papers, London: HMSO.

DOBBIE, P. (1989) 'Calling all *thirtysomethings*' *The Mail on Sunday* 27/8/1989.

DUGDALE, A. M. and STANTON, K. M. (1989) *Professional Negligence* (2nd ed.) London: Butterworth

DUKE, V. and EDGELL, S. (1987) 'The operationalisation of class in British sociology: theoretical and empirical considerations' *British Journal of Sociology*, 38.

DUNLEAVY, P. (1979) 'The urban basis of political alignment' *British Journal of Political Science* 9, 4.

DUNLEAVY, P. (1980) *Urban Political Analysis: the Politics of Collective Consumption* Basingstoke: Macmillan.

DUNLEAVY, P. and HUSBANDS, C. T. (1985) *British Democracy at the Crossroads* London: Allen and Unwin.

EASTERLIN, R. A. (1987) *Birth and Fortune: the Impact of Numbers on Personal Welfare* Chicago: University of Chicago Press.

EDGELL, S. (1980) *Middle-Class Couples* London: George Allen and Unwin.

EDGELL, S. and DUKE, V. (1986) 'Radicalism, radicalization and recession: Britain in the 1980s' *British Journal of Sociology*, 37, 4.

EHRENREICH, B. and EHRENREICH, J. (1979) 'The professional–managerial class' in P. Walker (ed.) *Between Labour and Capital* New York: Monthly Review Press.

ELSTER, J. (1989) *Nuts and Bolts for the Social Sciences* Cambridge: Cambridge University Press.

ERIKSON, R. (1984) 'Social class of men, women and families' *Sociology*, 18, 4.

ERIKSON, R. and GOLDTHORPE, J. H. (1986) *National variations in social fluidity* Mannheim, Working Paper No 9, CASMIN.

ETZIONI, A. (1964) *Modern Organizations* New Jersey: Prentice Hall.

FALLOWS, J. (1990) 'Wake up America!' *New York Review of Books*, 1390.

FEATHERSTONE, M. (1987) 'Lifestyle and consumer culture' *Theory, Culture and Society* 4.

FEATHERSTONE, M. (ed.) (1988) *Postmodernism* London: Sage.

FEATHERSTONE, M. (1990) 'Perspectives on consumer culture' *Sociology*, 24, 1.

FEATHERSTONE, M. (1991) *Consumer Culture and Postmodernism* London: Sage.

FERLIE, E. and McKEE, L. (1988) 'Planning for alternative futures in the NHS' *Health Services Management Research*, 1, 1.

FEUER, J. (1984) 'Melodrama, serial form and television today' *Screen* 25, 1.

FLEW, A. (1976) *Sociology, Equality and Education* Basingstoke: Macmillan.

FLEW, A. (1982) 'Educational fundamentals' in C.Cox and J. Marks (eds) *The Right to Learn* London: Centre for Policy Studies.

FLYNN, N. (1989) 'The "New Right" and social policy' *Policy and Politics*, 17, 2.

FLYNN, R. (1988) *Cutback Management in Health Services* Report to the Netherlands National Hospital Institute, University of Salford.

FORREST, R. and MURIE, A. (1986) 'Marginalisation and subsidised individualism' *International Journal of Urban and Regional Research*, 10.

FORREST, R. and MURIE, A. (1987) 'The affluent homeowner: labour market position and the shaping of housing histories' in N. Thrift and P. Williams (eds) *Class and Space*, London: Macmillan.

FOX, A. (1974) *Beyond Contract: Work, Power and Trust Relations* London: Faber and Faber.

FRIEDMAN, M. (1962) *Capitalism and Freedom* Chicago: University of Chicago Press.

FRIEDSON, E. (1970) *Profession of Medicine* New York: Dodd, Mead.

GALLIE, D. (1988) 'Employment, unemployment and social stratification' in D. Gallie (ed.) *Employment in Britain* Oxford: Blackwell.

GBC (1987) *Housing in Guildford* Guildford Borough Council.

GEDDES, M. (1988) 'The capitalist state and the local economy: restructuring for labour and beyond' *Capital and Class*, 35.

GERSHUNY, J. (1978) *After Industrial Society: the Emerging Self-service Economy* Basingstoke: Macmillan.

GERSHUNY, J. and MILES, I. (1983) *The New Service Economy: the Transformation of Employment in Industrial Societies* London: Frances Pinter.

GILBERT, G. N., BURROWS, R. and POLLERT, A. (eds) (1991) *Fordism and Flexibility: Division and Change* Basingstoke: Macmillan.

GINARLIS, J. (1988) *The Savings War* London: Banque Paribas.

GLASS, D. V. (1954) *Social Mobility in Britain* London: Routledge and Kegan Paul.

GLUCKMAN, M. (1960) 'The logic in witchcraft' in M. Gluckman *Custom and Conflict* Oxford: Basil Blackwell.

GOLDTHORPE, J. H. (1978) 'The current inflation: towards a sociological account' in F. Hirsch and J. H. Goldthorpe (eds) *The Political Economy of Inflation* London: Martin Robertson.

GOLDTHORPE, J. H. (1982) 'On the service class, its formation and future' in A. Giddens and G. Mackenzie (eds) *Social Class and the Division of Labour* Cambridge: Cambridge University Press.

GOLDTHORPE, J. H. (1983) 'Women and class analysis: in defence of the conventional view' *Sociology*, 17, 4.

GOLDTHORPE, J. H. and PAYNE, C. (1986) 'Trends in intergenerational class mobility in England and Wales'. *Sociology*, 20, 1.

GOLDTHORPE, J. H., with LLEWELLYN, C. and PAYNE, C. (1987) *Social Mobility and Class Structure in Modern Britain* (2nd ed.) Oxford: Clarendon Press.

GORZ, A. (1982) *Farewell to the Working Class* London: Pluto.

GORZ, A. (1985) *Paths to Paradise* London: Pluto.

GOSDEN, P. H. J. H. (1973) *Self-Help: Voluntary Associations in the 19th Century* London: Batsford.

GOULDNER, A. W. (1957) 'Cosmopolitans and locals; towards an analysis of latent social roles - I', *Administrative Science Quarterly*, 2.

GOULDNER, A. W. (1958) 'Cosmopolitans and locals; towards an analysis of latent social roles: II' *Administrative Science Quarterly*, 2.

GOULDNER, A. W. (1979) *The Future of Intellectuals and the Rise of the New Class* London: Macmillan.

GRAHAME, P. R. (1989) 'The construction of a sociological consumer' in J. F. Gubrium and D. Silverman (eds) *The Politics of Field Research* London: Sage.

GRANT, G. (1985) *Private Health Care in the UK* London: Economists Intelligence Unit.

GREEN, D. G. (1985) *Which Doctor?* London: Institute of Economic Affairs.

GREEN, D. G. (1988) *Everyone a Private Patient* London: Institute of Economic Affairs.

GRIFFITH, B. and RAYNER, G. (1985) *Commercial Medicine in London* London: Greater London Council.

GRIFFITH, B., ILLIFFE, S. and RAYNER, S. (1987) *Banking on Sickness: Commercial Medicine in Britain and the USA* London: Lawrence and Wishart.

GROSSBERG, L. (1987) 'The in-difference of television' *Screen*, Spring.

HABERMAS, J. (1976) *Legitimation Crisis* London: Heinemann.
HALMOS, P. (1970) *The Personal Service Society* London: Constable.
Halsbury's Laws of England vol. 30 (1980) 4th ed London: Butterworths.
HALSEY, A. H., HEATH, A. and RIDGE, J. M. (1980) *Origins and Destinations: Family, Class and Education in Modern Britain* Oxford: Clarendon Press.
HAM, C. (1986) *Managing Health Services* Study no. 3, Bristol: School for Advanced Urban Studies.
HAMNETT, C. (1984) 'Housing the two nations' *Urban Studies* 43, 389–405.
HAMNETT, C. (1989) 'Consumption and class in contemporary Britain' in C. Hamnett, L. McDowell and P. Sarre (eds) *The Changing Social Structure* London: Sage.
HARLOE, M., PICKVANCE, C. and URRY, J. (eds) (1990) *Place, Policy and Politics* London: Unwin Hyman.
HARRIS, R. and SELDON, A. (1977) *Not from Benevolence* London: Institute of Economic Affairs.
HARRIS, R. and SELDON, A. (1979) *Over-Ruled on Welfare* London: Institute of Economic Affairs.
HARRISON, S. (1988) *Managing the National Health Service* London: Chapman and Hall.
HARRISON, S., HUNTER, D., MARNOCH, G. and POLLITT, C. (1989) 'General management and medical autonomy in the National Health Service' *Health Services Management Research*, 2, 1.
HARVEY, D. (1989) *The Condition of Postmodernity* Oxford: Blackwell.
HAUSER, R., KOFFEL, J., TRAVIS, H., HARRY, P. and DICKINSON, P. (1975a) 'Temporal change in occupational mobility' *American Sociological Review*, 40.
HAUSER, R., KOFFEL, J., TRAVIS, H., HARRY, P. and DICKINSON, P. (1975b) 'Structural change in occupational mobility among men in the US' *American Sociological Review*, 40.
HAYEK, F. A. (1944) *The Road to Serfdom* London: Routledge.
HAYEK, F. A. (1960) *The Constitution of Liberty* London: Routledge and Kegan Paul.
HEATH, A. (1981) *Social Mobility* London: Fontana.
HEATH, A., JOWELL, R. and CURTICE, J. (1985) *How Britain Votes* London: Pergamon.
HERSCH, P. (1988) '*thirtysomething*therapy' *Psychology Today*, October.
HIGGINS, J. (1986) 'Comparative social policy' *Quarterly Journal of Social Affairs*, 2, 3.
HIGGINS, J. (1988) *The Business of Medicine* Basingstoke: Macmillan.
HILLGATE GROUP (1986) *Whose Schools?* London: Hillgate Group.
HINDESS, B. (1987a) *Freedom, Equality and the Market* London: Tavistock.
HINDESS, B. (1987b) *Politics and Class Analysis*, Oxford: Blackwell.
HIRSCH, F. (1977) *The Social Limits to Growth* London: Routledge and Kegan Paul.
HIRST, P. and ZEITLIN, J. (1991) 'Flexible specialisation versus post-Fordism: theory, evidence and policy implications', *Economy and Society*, 20, 1.

HIRSCHMAN, A. (1982) *Shifting Involvements: private interest and Public Action* Princeton, NJ: Princeton University Press.
HISKETT, M. (1988) *Choice in Rotten Apples* London: Centre for Policy Studies.
HOGGET, P. (1987) 'A Farewell to mass production?' in P. Hogget and R. Hambleton (eds) *Decentralisation and Democracy* Bristol: School of Advanced Urban Studies.
HORNE, D. (1986) *Public Policy Making and Private Medical Care in the UK Since 1948* PhD thesis, University of Bath.
HOUSTON, B. (1984) 'Viewing television: The metapsychology of endless consumption' *Quarterly Review of Film Studies*, 9, 3.
HUGHES, E.C. (1958) *Men and their Work* Glencoe, Illinois: Free Press.
HUMPHRIES, J. and RUBERY, J. (1984) 'The reconstitution of the supply side of the labour market: the relative autonomy of social reproduction' *Cambridge Journal of Economics*, 8.
ILLICH, I.(1977) *Limits to Medicine* Harmondsworth: Penguin.
INDEPENDENT HOSPITALS ASSOCIATION (1989) *IHA Acute Hospital Survey, 1989* London: Independent Hospitals Association.
INEICHEN, B. (1981) 'The housing decisions of young people', *British Journal of Sociology*, 32, 2.
INGLEHART, R. (1981) 'Post-materialism in an age of insecurity' *American Political Science Review*, 75, 4.
JOHNSON, T. (1972) *Professions and Power* London: Macmillan.
JOHNSON, T. (1980) 'Work and power' in G. Esland and G. Salaman (eds) *The Politics of Work and Occupations* Milton Keynes: Open University Press.
JONES, G. (1987) 'Leaving the parental home: an analysis of early housing careers' *Journal of Social Policy*, 16, 1.
JOWELL, R., WITHERSPOON, S. and BROOK, L. (eds) (1988) *British Social Attitudes: the 1988 Report*, Aldershot: Gowen.
JOYRICH, L. (1988) 'All that television allows: TV melodrama, postmodernism and consumer culture' *Camera Obscura*, 16.
KAELBLE, H. (1985) *Social Mobility in the 19th and 20th Centuries* Leamington Spa: Berg.
KEAT, R. and ABERCROMBIE, N. (eds) (1991) *Enterprise Culture* London: Routledge.
KELLY, A. (1991) 'The enterprise culture and the welfare state: restructuring the management of the health and personal social services', in R.Burrows (ed.) *Deciphering the Enterprise Culture*, London: Routledge.
KEMENY, J. (1987) 'Toward a theorised housing studies: a counter-critique of the provision thesis' *Housing Studies*, 2
KERR, C., DUNLOP, J.T. and MYERS, C.A. (1973) *Industrialism and Industrial Man* Harmondsworth: Penguin.
KING, D.S. (1987) *The New Right* Basingstoke: Macmillan.
KINGS FUND INSTITUTE (1989) *Managed Competition* London: Kings Fund Institute.
KLEIN, R. (1983) *The Politics of the National Health Service* London: Longman.

KNIGHTS, D. (1988) 'Risk, financial self-discipline and commodity relations' in M. Neimark (ed.) *Advances in Public Interest Accounting vol. 2* Greenwich, Conn.: JAI Press.

KNIGHTS, D. and MORGAN, G. (1990) 'Management control in sales: a case study from the labour process of life insurance' *Work, Employment and Society*, 4, 3.

KNIGHTS, D. and MORGAN, G. (1991) 'Selling oneself; subjectivity and the labour process in the sale of life insurance' in C. Smith, D. Knights and H. Willmott (eds) *White Collar Work: The Non-Manual Labour Process* London: Macmillan.

KNIGHTS, D. and VURDABAKIS, T. (1990) 'Technologies of risk' Mimeo: UMIST Working Paper.

KRECKEL, R. (1973) 'Towards a theoretical re-orientation of the sociological analysis of vertical mobility' in W. Muller and K. Mayer (eds) *Social Stratification and Career Mobility* The Hague: Moulton.

LAING, W. (1985) *Private Health Care* London: Office of Health Economics.

LANTOS, J. (1987) 'Talking 'bout my generation' *American Film* 13, 2.

LASCH, C. (1979) *The Culture of Narcissism* New York: Norton and Co.

LASH, S. and URRY, J. (1987) *The End of Organized Capitalism*, Cambridge: Polity.

LE GRAND, J. and ROBINSON, R. (1984) *The Economics of Social Problems* London: Macmillan.

LENSKI, G. (1958) 'Trends in inter-generational occupational mobility in the United States' *American Sociological Review*, 23.

LETWIN, O. and REDWOOD, J. (1988) *Britain's Biggest Enterprise: Ideas for Radical Reform of the NHS* London: Centre for Policy Studies.

LEVI, M.(1987) *Regulating Fraud: White Collar Crime and the Criminal Process* London: Tavistock.

LIPPMAN, J. (1989) 'The pain of yuppie love' *The Sunday Times* 26/2/1989.

LIPSET, S.M. and BENDIX, R. (1959) *Social Mobility in Industrial Society* Berkeley: University of California Press.

LOCKWOOD, D. (1966) 'Sources of variation in working class images of society' *Sociological Review*, 14, 3.

LOVERING, J. (1990) 'A perfunctory sort of post-Fordism: economic restructuring and labour market segmentation in Britain in the 1980s' *Work, Employment and Society* (Special Issue, May).

MACFARLANE, A. (1979) *The History of English Individualism*, Cambridge: Cambridge University Press.

MACH, B. and WESOLOWSKI, W. (1986) *Social Mobility and Social Structure* London: Routledge and Kegan Paul.

MACKENZIE, D. (1979) 'Eugenics and the rise of mathematical statistics in Britain' in J. Irvine, I. Miles and J. Evans (eds) *Demystifying Social Statistics* London: Pluto Press.

MACKENZIE, S. and ROSE, D. (1983) 'Industrial change, the domestic economy and home life', in J. Anderson, S. Duncan and R. Hudson (eds) *Redundant Spaces?: Studies in Industrial Decline and Social Change* London: Academic Press.

MAGNUSSON, M. (1983) *A Length of Days: The Scottish Mutual Assurance Society 1883–1983* London: Henry Melland.

MANN, M. (1970) 'The social cohesion of liberal democracy' *American Sociological Review*, 35.
MARKOSKY, C. (1989) 'Forget the quality, watch the ratings' *The Daily Telegraph* 8/3/1989.
MARSH, C. (1986) 'Occupationally-based measures of social class' in A. Jaccoby (ed.) *The Measurement of Social Class* London: Social Research Association.
MARSHALL, G. (1983) 'Some remarks on the study of working class consciousness', *Politics and Society*, 12, 3.
MARSHALL, G. (1990) *In Praise of Sociology* London: Unwin Hyman.
MARSHALL, G. and ROSE, D. (1989) 'Reply to Saunders' *Network*, 44 (May).
MARSHALL, G., NEWBY, H., ROSE, D. and VOGLER, C. (1988) *Social Class in Modern Britain* London: Hutchinson.
MARSHALL, T.H. (1939) 'The recent history of professionalism in relation to social structure and social policy' *Canadian Journal of Economics and Political Science*, 5.
MARSHALL, T.H. (1951) 'Citizenship and social class' in T.H. Marshall *Sociology at the Crossroads* London: Tavistock.
MARSLAND, D. (1987) *Bias Against Business* Harrow: Educational Research Trust.
MARSLAND, D. (1988) *Seeds of Bankruptcy: Sociological Bias Against Business and Freedom* London: Claridge Press.
MARXISM TODAY (1990) *New Times* London: Verso.
MASON, C. (1991) 'Spatial variations in enterprise: the geography of new firm formation' in R. Burrows (ed.) *Deciphering the Enterprise Culture* London: Routledge.
MAURICE, M., SELLIER, F. and SILVESTRE, J.J. (1986) *The Social Foundations of Industrial Power* (trans. A. Goldhammer) Cambridge, Mass: MIT Press.
MAYNARD, A. (1989a) *Whither the National Health Service*? York: Centre for Health Economics.
MAYNARD, A. (1989b) 'Incentive contracts', paper presented at the European Conference on Health Economics, Barcelona.
MAYNARD, A. and BOSANQUET, N. (1986) *Public Expenditure on the National Health Service* London: Institute of Health Service Management.
MCDOWELL, L. (1989) 'Gender divisions' in C. Hamnett, L. McDowell and P. Sarre (eds) *The Changing Social Structure* London: Sage.
MEDHURST, A. (1989) 'Life begins at thirty' *Marxism Today*, June.
MERTON, R.K. (1965) 'Patterns of influence: local and cosmopolitan influentials' in R.K. Merton *Social Theory and Social Structure* New York: Free Press.
MERTON, R.K. (1982) 'Institutionalised altruism: the case of the professions' in R.K. Merton *Social Research and the Practicing Professions* Cambridge, Mass.: Abt Books.
MINSKY, T. (1987) *Rolling Stone* 3/12/1987.
MONOPOLIES AND MERGERS COMMISSION (1990) *The British United Provident Association Ltd and HCA United Kingdom Ltd* London: HMSO.

MOONEY, G.H. (1986) *Economics, Medicine and Health Care* Hemel Hempstead: Harvester Wheatsheaf.
MOORHOUSE, H. (1983) 'American automobiles and workers' dreams' *Sociological Review*, 31.
MORAN, M. (1986) *The Politics of Banking* (2nd.ed.) London: Macmillan.
MORGAN, G. (1990) 'The management of sales forces' *Personnel Review*, 19, 3.
MORGAN, G. and KNIGHTS, D. (1989) *The Impact of the Financial Services Act on Life Insurance Companies* Manchester: Financial Services Research Centre, UMIST.
MORGAN, M., CALNAN, M. and MANNING, N. (1985) *Sociological Approaches to Health and Medicine* Beckenham: Croom Helm.
MOWER, S. (1989) '*thirtysomethings* rule, UK?' *The Independent* 20/2/1990.
MULVEY, L. (1987) 'Notes on Sirk and melodrama' in C. Gledhill (ed.) *Home is Where the Heart is: Studies in Melodrama and the Women's Film* London: BFI.
MUNRO, M. and MCLELLAN, D (1987) 'Intra-urban changes in house prices' *Housing Studies*, 2.
MURPHY, J. (1990) 'A most respectable prejudice: inequality in educational research and policy' *British Journal of Sociology*, 41, 1.
NAHA (1987) *NHS Economic Review 1987* Birmingham: National Association of Health Authorities.
NAHA (1988a) *NHS Economic Review 1988* Birmingham: National Association of Health Authorities.
NAHA (1988b) *Making Ends Meet* Birmingham: NAHA.
NAVARRO, V. (1986) *Crisis, Health and Medicine* London: Tavistock.
NEALE, S. (1986) 'Melodrama and tears' *Screen*, 27, 6.
NEWBY, H. (1977) *The Deferential Worker* London: Allen Lane.
NICHOLL, J.P., BEEBY, N.R. and WILLIAMS, B.T. (1989) 'Comparisons of the activity of short stay independent hospitals, 1981 and 1986' *British Medical Journal*, 198.
O'HIGGINS, M. (1987) 'Egalitarians, equalities and welfare evaluation' *Journal of Social Policy*, 16, 1.
OFFE, C. (1984) 'Some contradictions of the welfare state' in C.Offe *Contradictions of the Welfare State* London: Heinemann.
OFFE, C. (1985a) 'Work: the key sociological category?' in C.Offe *Disorganized Capitalism* Oxford: Polity.
OFFE, C. (1985b) *Disorganised Capitalism* Cambridge: Polity Press.
OFFICE OF POPULATIONS CENSUSES AND SURVEYS (1989) *General Household Survey, 1987* London: HMSO.
ORGANIZATION FOR ECONOMIC CO-OPERATION AND DEVELOPMENT (1987) *Consumers and Life Insurance* Paris: OECD.
OUCHI, W.G. (1980) 'Markets, bureaucracies and clans' *Administrative Science Quarterly*, 25.
PAHL, R. (1965) 'Class and community in English commuter villages' *Sociologica Ruralis*, 5, 1.
PAHL, R. (1984) *Divisions of Labour* Oxford: Blackwell.
PAHL, R. (1988) 'Some remarks on informal work, social polarization and the social structure' *International Journal of Urban and Regional Research*, 12, 2.

PAHL, R. and WALLACE, C. (1988) 'Neither angels in marble nor rebels in red' in D. Rose (ed.) *Social Stratification and Economic Change* London: Hutchinson.

PAPADAKIS, E. and TAYLOR-GOOBY, P. (1987a) *The Private Provision of Public Welfare* Brighton: Wheatsheaf.

PAPADAKIS, E. and TAYLOR-GOOBY, P. (1987b) 'Consumer attitudes and participation in state welfare' *Political Studies*, 35.

PARKIN, F. (1979) *Marxism and Class Theory: A Bourgeois Critique* London: Tavistock.

PAWSON, R. (1990) 'Half-truths about bias' *Sociology*, 24, 2.

PAYNE, G. (1987a) *Mobility and Change in Modern Society* Basingstoke: MacMillan.

PAYNE, G. (1987b) *Employment and Opportunity* Basingstoke: Macmillan.

PAYNE, G. (1989a) 'Social mobility' *British Journal of Sociology*, 40, 3.

PAYNE, G. (1989b) 'Social mobility' in R. Burgess (ed.) *Investigating Society*, London: Longmans.

PAYNE, G. (1990) 'Social mobility in Britain: a contrary view' in J. Clark, C. Modgil and S. Modgil (eds) *John H. Goldthorpe: Consensus and Controversy* London: Falmer Press.

PAYNE, G. and ABBOTT, P. (eds) (1991) *The Social Mobility of Women* London: Falmer Press.

PAYNE, G., DINGWALL, R., PAYNE, J. and CARTER, M. (1981) *Sociology and Social Research* London: Routledge and Kegan Paul.

PAYNE, J. and PAYNE, G. (1977) 'Housing pathways and stratification: a study of life chances in the housing market' *Journal of Social Policy*, 6.

PEARSON, R. (1990) 'Thrift or dissipation? The business of life assurance in the early nineteenth century' *Economic History Review*, 43, 2.

PERKIN, H. (1989) *The Rise of Professional Society* London: Routledge.

PICKVANCE, C. (1989) 'Beyond state v. market: towards a sociology of public service provision', paper presented at the Urban Change and Conflict Conference, SAUS, Bristol, September.

PIORE, M. (1986) 'Crisis, market and small business', in P.Julien, J.Chicha and A.Joyal (eds) *Les PME en Devenir dans un Monde en Mutation* Quebec: Les Presses de l'Université du Quebec.

PIORE, M. and SABEL, C. (1984) *The Second Industrial Divide: Prospects for Prosperity* New York: Basic Books.

POLLERT, A. (1981) *Girls, Wives, Factory Lives* London: Macmillan.

POLLERT, A. (ed.) (1991) *A Farewell to Flexibility?* Oxford: Blackwell.

POLLITT, C. (1988) 'Bringing consumers into performance measurement' *Policy and Politics*, 16, 2.

PRANDY, K. (1986) 'Similarities of life-style and occupations of women' in R. Crompton and M. Mann (eds) *Gender and Stratification* Cambridge: Polity Press.

PRANDY, K. (1990) 'The revised Cambridge Scale of occupations' *Sociology*, 24, 4.

Promoting Better Health (1987) London: HMSO.

PURCELL, K.G. (1986) *Gender and Experience at Work: an Ethnographic Study of Work and Social Interaction in a Manufacturing Workshop* PhD thesis, University of Manchester.

RAWLING, L. (1990). 'The Right Attack on Sociology' *Social Science Teacher*, 19, 3.

RENNER, K. (1978) 'The service class' in T. Bottomore and P. Goode (eds) *Austro-Marxism* London: Oxford University Press.

RICHMAN, J. (1987) *Medicine and Health* Harlow: Longman.

ROBBINS, Lord, Chairman (1963a) *Higher Education; Report of the Committee appointed by the Prime Minister under the Chairmanship of Lord Robbins 1961–63* HMSO, Cmnd 2154.

ROBBINS, Lord, Chairman (1963b) *Higher Education; Appendix One: The Demand for Places in Higher Education* HMSO: Cmnd 2154–I.

ROBINSON, R. (1988) *Efficiency and the NHS: a Case for Internal Markets* London: Institute of Economic Affairs.

ROBINSON, R. and JUDGE, K. (1987) *Public Expenditure and the NHS* London: Kings Fund Institute.

ROBSON, B.T. (1975) *Urban Areal Analysis* London: MacMillan.

ROOTES, C.A. (1990) 'Towards the dominance of the intelligensia? The expansion of higher education and the prospects for political participation' mimeo, University of Kent at Canterbury.

ROSE, N. (1991) 'Governing the enterprising self' in P. Heelas and P. Morris (eds) *The Values of the Enterprise Culture: the Moral Debate*, London: Harper Collins Academic.

RUDD, E. (1987) 'Students and social class' *Studies in Higher Education* 12, 1.

RUSTIN, M. (1989) 'The politics of post-Fordism; or the trouble with "New Time"' *New Left Review*, 175.

SABEL, C. (1982) *Work and Politics* Cambridge: Cambridge University Press.

SAUNDERS, P. (1984) 'Beyond housing classes: the sociological significance of private property rights in means of consumption' *International Journal of Urban and Regional Research*, 8, 2.

SAUNDERS, P. (1985) 'The New Right is half right' in A. Seldon (ed.) *The New Right Enlightenment* London: Economic and Literary Books.

SAUNDERS, P. (1986) *Social Theory and the Urban Question* (2nd ed.), London: Hutchinson.

SAUNDERS, P. (1988) 'The sociology of consumption: a new research agenda' in P. Otnes (ed.) *The Sociology of Consumption: an Anthology* New Jersey: Humanities Press.

SAUNDERS, P. (1989) 'Left Write in Sociology' *Network*, 44 (May).

SAUNDERS, P. (1990a) *Social Class and Stratification* London, Tavistock.

SAUNDERS, P. (1990b) *A Nation of Home Owners* London: Unwin Hyman.

SAUNDERS, P. and HARRIS, C. (1987) 'Biting the nipple? consumer preferences and state welfare' paper presented to the 6th Urban Change and Conflict Conference, Kent University.

SAUNDERS, P. and HARRIS, C. (1989) *Popular Attitudes to State Welfare Services* Research Report No. 11, London: The Social Affairs Unit.

SAUNDERS, P. and HARRIS, C. (1990) 'Privatisation and the consumer' *Sociology*, 24, 1.

SAUNDERS, P. and WILLIAMS, P. (1988) 'The constitution of the home: towards a research agenda' *Housing Studies* 3.

SAVAGE, M. (1988) 'The missing link? The relationship between spatial mobility and social mobility' *British Journal of Sociology*, 29, 4.

SAVAGE, M. (1991) 'Making sense of middle class politics: a secondary analysis of the 1987 British General Election Survey' *Sociological Review*, 39, 1.

SAVAGE, M., DICKENS, P. and FIELDING, T. (1988) 'Some social and political implications of the contemporary fragmentation of the "service class" in Britain' *International Journal of Urban and Regional Research*, 12, 3.

SAVAGE, M., WATT, P. and ARBER, S. (1990a) 'The consumption sector debate and housing mobility' *Sociology*, 24, 1.

SAVAGE, M., WATT, P. and ARBER, S. (1990b) 'Housing mobility and social stratification: an analysis of council tenants in Guildford', *Surrey Occasional Papers in Sociology and Social Policy*, no. 20.

SAVAGE, M., WATT, P. and ARBER, S. (1990c) 'Social class and housing mobility', paper presented to 1990 BSA Annual Conference, University of Surrey, April.

SAYER, A. (1989) 'Post-Fordism in question' *International Journal of Urban and Regional Research*, 13, 4.

SCITOVSKY, T. (1976) *The Joyless Economy: an Inquiry into Human Satisfaction and Consumer Dissatisfaction* New York: Oxford University Press.

SCOTT, J. (1986) *Capitalist Property and Financial Power* London: Wheatsheaf.

SIVANANDEN, A. (1990) 'The hokum of new times' *Race and Class*, 31, 3.

SMITH, N. (1979) 'Towards a theory of gentrification: a back to the city movement by capital not people' *American Planning Association Journal*, 45.

SMITH, N. (1987) 'Of yuppies and housing: gentrification, social restructuring and the urban dream' *Environment & Planning D: Society and Space*, 5.

SOCIAL SERVICES COMMITTEE (1988a) *Resourcing the NHS: short-term issues* CM264, House of Commons, London: HMSO.

SOCIAL SERVICES COMMITTTEE (1988b) *The Future of the NHS* CM613, House of Commons, London: HMSO.

STACEY, M. (1976) 'The health service consumer: a sociological misconception' in M. Stacey (ed.) *The Sociology of the National Health Service* University of Keele: Sociological Review Monograph 22.

STANWORTH, M. (1984) 'Women and class analysis: a reply to Goldthorpe' *Sociology*, 18, 2.

STARK, D. (1980) 'Class struggle and the labor process' *Theory and Society*, 9, 1.

STARR, P. (1982) *The Social Transformation of American Medicine* New York: Basic Books.

STEWART, A., PRANDY, K. and BLACKBURN, R.M. (1980) *Social Stratification and Occupation*, Basingstoke: Macmillan

STOKER, G. (1990a) 'Creating a local government for a post-Fordist society: the Thatcherite project?' in J. Stewart and G. Stoker (eds) *The Future of Local Government* Basingstoke: Macmillan.

STOKER, G. (1990b) 'Regulation theory, local government and the transition from Fordism' in D. King and J. Pierre (eds) *Challanges to Local Government* London: Sage/ECPR.

STRONG, P. and ROBINSON, J. (1988) *New Model Management* University of Warwick: Policy Studies Centre.

SULLIVAN, O. (1989) 'Housing tenure as a consumption sector divide: a critical perspective' *International Journal of Urban and Regional Research*, 13, 2.

SUPPLE, B. (1970) *The Royal Exchange Assurance: A History of British Insurance 1720–1970* Cambridge: Cambridge University Press.

SWINNY, S.H. (1919) 'Sociology: its successes and failures' *Sociological Review*, 11.

TAYLOR-GOOBY, P. (1985) 'The politics of welfare: public attitudes and behaviour' in R. Klein and M. O'Higgins (eds) *The Future of Welfare* Oxford: Basil Blackwell.

TAYLOR-GOOBY, P. (1986) 'Privatisation, power and the welfare state' *Sociology*, 20, 2.

TAYLOR-GOOBY, P. (1987) 'Welfare attitudes: cleavage, consensus and citizenship' *Quarterly Journal of Social Affairs*, 3, 3.

TAYLOR-GOOBY, P. (1989) 'Disquiet and state welfare' *International Journal of Urban and Regional Research*, 13, 2.

THOMPSON, E.P. (1968) *The Making of the English Working Class* Harmondsworth: Penguin.

THORNS, D. (1982) 'Industrial restructuring and change in the labour and property markets in Britain' *Environment and Planning A*, 14.

THRIFT, N. (1989) 'Images of Social Change' in C. Hamnett, L. McDowell and P.Sarre (eds) *The Changing Social Structure* London: Sage.

TORRES, S. (1989) 'Melodrama, masculinity and the family: *thirtysomething* as therapy' *Camera Obscura*, 19.

TOWNSEND, P., DAVIDSON, N. and WHITEHEAD, M. (1988) *Inequalities in Health* London: Penguin.

TREBILCOCK, C. (1985) *Phoenix Assurance and the Development of British Insurance, vol. 1: 1782–1870* Cambridge: Cambridge University Press.

TREBLE J.H. (1984) 'The record of the standard life assurance company in the life insurance market of the United Kingdom, 1850–1864', in O.M. Westall (ed.) *The Historian and the Business of Insurance* Manchester: Manchester University Press.

TURNER, B.S. (1987) *Medical Power and Social Knowledge* London: Sage.

TURNER, B.S. (1988) *Status* Milton Keynes: Open University Press.

URRY, J. (1981) 'Localities, regions and social class' *International Journal of Urban and Regional Research*, 5, 4.

URRY, J. (1989) 'Class, causal powers and the analysis of space', mimeo, University of Lancaster.

URRY, J. (1990a) *The Tourist Gaze*, London: Sage.

URRY, J. (1990b) 'The "consumption" of tourism' *Sociology* 24, 1.

UTTLEY, S. (1991) *Technology and the Welfare State*, London: Harper Collins Academic.

VEBLEN, T. (1925) *The Theory of the Leisure Class: an Economic Study of Institutions* London: George Allen and Unwin.

WARDE, A. (1988) 'Industrial restructuring, local politics and the reproduction of labour power: some theoretical considerations' *Environment and Planning D: Society and Space*, 6.

WARDE, A. (1990a) 'Production, consumption and social change: reservations regarding Peter Saunders' sociology of consumption' *International Journal of Urban and Regional Research*, 14, 2.

WARDE, A. (1990b) 'Introduction to the sociology of consumption' *Sociology*, 24, 1.

WATSON, W. (1964) 'Social mobility and social class in industrial communities' in M. Gluckmann and E. Devons (eds) *Closed Systems and Open Minds*, Edinburgh: Oliver and Boyd.

WEALE, A. (1986) 'Ideology and welfare' *Quarterly Journal of Social Affairs*, 2, 3.

WILKIN, D., HALLAM, L., LEAVEY, R. and METCALFE, D. (1987) *Anatomy of Urban General Practice* London: Tavistock.

WILLIAMS, A. (1989) *Creating a Health Care Market* York: Centre for Health Economics.

WILLIAMS, F. (1989) *Social Policy: A Critical Introduction*, Oxford: Polity Press.

WILLIS, P. (1977) *Learning to Labour* Farnborough: Saxon House.

WRIGHT, E. O. (1985) *Classes* London: Verso.

WRIGHT, E. O. (1989) 'Women in the class structure', *Politics and Society*, 17, 1.

YOUNG, M. and WILLMOTT, P. (1957) *Family and Kinship in East London* London: Routledge and Kegan Paul.

ZIMMECK, M. (1985) 'Gladstone holds his own: the origins of income tax relief for life insurance policies' *Bulletin of the Institute for Historical Research*, 58.

ZUKIN, S. (1990) 'Socio-spatial prototypes of a new organization of consumption: the role of real cultural capital' *Sociology*, 24, 1.

Author Index

Subject Index